Theatre(s) and Public Sphere in a Global and Digital Society

Volume 1

Studies in Critical Social Sciences

Series Editor
David Fasenfest (*Wayne State University*)

Editorial Board
Eduardo Bonilla-Silva (*Duke University*)
Chris Chase-Dunn (*University of California–Riverside*)
William Carroll (*University of Victoria*)
Raewyn Connell (*University of Sydney*)
Kimberlé W. Crenshaw (*University of California, Los Angeles/ Columbia University*)
Raju Das (*York University*)
Heidi Gottfried (*Wayne State University*)
Karin Gottschall (*University of Bremen*)
Alfredo Saad-Filho (*King's College London*)
Chizuko Ueno (*University of Tokyo*)
Sylvia Walby (*Lancaster University*)

VOLUME 235

The titles published in this series are listed at *brill.com/scss*

Theatre(s) and Public Sphere in a Global and Digital Society

Theoretical Explorations

Edited by

Ilaria Riccioni

BRILL

LEIDEN | BOSTON

Cover illustration: "Tango Macondo. Il venditore di metafore", dramaturgy and direction Giorgio Gallione. Courtesy of Teatro Stabile di Bolzano. Photo: Tommaso Le Pera.

The Library of Congress Cataloging-in-Publication Data is available online at https://catalog.loc.gov
LC record available at https://lccn.loc.gov/2022050720

Typeface for the Latin, Greek, and Cyrillic scripts: "Brill". See and download: brill.com/brill-typeface.

ISSN 1573-4234
ISBN 978-90-04-52654-9 (harback)
ISBN 978-90-04-52981-6 (e-book)

Copyright 2023 by Ilaria Riccioni. Published by Koninklijke Brill NV, Leiden, The Netherlands.
Koninklijke Brill NV incorporates the imprints Brill, Brill Nijhoff, Brill Hotei, Brill Schöningh, Brill Fink, Brill mentis, Vandenhoeck & Ruprecht, BöhlauBöhlau, V&R unipress and Wageningen Academic. Koninklijke Brill NV reserves the right to protect this publication against unauthorized use. Requests for re-use and/or translations must be addressed to Koninklijke Brill NV via brill.com or copyright.com.

This book is printed on acid-free paper and produced in a sustainable manner.

Contents

Preface VII
Acknowledgements XIV
List of Figures and Tables XV
Notes on Contributors XVII

1 Artistic Processes and Characteristics: Key Problems of the Sociology of the Theatre
  In Dialogue with Pierre Bourdieu 1
    Maria Shevtsova

2 The Social and Political Impact of the Theatre in Contemporary Society 16
    Ilaria Riccioni

3 Theatre at University as a Way to Increase the Sense 41
    Roberta Paltrinieri

4 Staged Passages between Art and Everyday Life 49
    Gerhard Glüher

5 Urban Environment, Places for Performance
  A Groundbreaking Experience: Renato Nicolini and Estate Romana *(1976–1985)* 64
    Raimondo Guarino

6 The Theatre as the Stage of an Elusive Further Society 71
    Mariselda Tessarolo

7 Paris and Popular Theatre in Robert Michels
  La foule *and the Audience in the Years of Classical Sociology* 84
    Raffaele Federici

8 The Undone Discipline
  A Historical and Critical-Theoretical Account of the Sociology of the Theatre 94
    Marco Serino

9   Theatre as Intersubjective Space for the Mediation of Collective Identity
    Outline of a Psychoanalytic Perspective   110
        Maria Grazia Turri

10 Historical Reenactment and Theatrical Performance
    On New Perspectives of Educational Methods   122
        Elena Olesina and Elena Polyudova

11 Political Theatre in the 20th Century
    Elements for Archaeology   139
        Marisol Facuse

12 Blast Theory between Public Space and Social Space   150
        Vincenzo Del Gaudio

13 Live/Life Sharing
    The Use of Social Media by Contemporary Theatre Companies in Italy   162
        Laura Gemini and Stefano Brilli

14 Theatre as a Means of "Interpreting" Lockdown
    The Case of Staged   177
        Jessica Camargo Molano

15 Cultural Welfare
    Theatre in the Limelight   186
        Annalisa Cicerchia and Simona Staffieri

16 Measuring Culture – How and Why?   197
        Giulia Cavrini

    Index   213

Preface

The *raison d'être* of this volume derives from the urgency to understand social dynamics in relation with the entirety of its deeper motives that, besides economic and normative needs, include the very human and social need for artistic and cultural forms which can consolidate cohabitation and make it meaningful, therefore contribute to the quality of life. With their fundamental contribution, artistic and cultural forms, as imaginative forms of collective social practices, weave the meaning of a territory, a context, and a people, but also of the generations who traverse these same cultures.

These forms of meaning dialogue with the social imagery, mediate marginalization, transform barriers into bridges, and are the indispensable tools for any social coexistence and its continuous rethinking in everyday life. Accordingly, this volume is the result of a dialogue: a multifaceted dialogue between different forms of observation and contact with the performative activity and its institutional dimension, between expressive forms as manifestations of collective needs, but also as expressions of thought, criticism, or social resistance. Or of the social avant-garde.

If art – in this case theatre and performance – has any social value, if it has a role in building the social fabric as a collective good, in this volume we wish to give voice to evidence of this role through the knowledge acquired and the reflections developed by both research and collective experience. The various scientific disciplinary approaches present here, with a certain predominance of sociology, refer to diverse epistemic fields, such as sociology (naturally), theatre studies, but also the sociology of cultural processes, psychology, the culture economy, and social statistics which share the object of observation, namely, theatre, in its significance as a social phenomenon.

So the object under the microscope here is theatre, in all of its accepted meanings, in its relationship with society, institutions, cultural and local norms, and the collective imagination which these reveal. A volume which has arisen from the typically sociological need to reconstruct the interconnection between the meanings of the various partial disciplines which, through their extraordinary specificity, acquire slivers of knowledge about the role of performance in digitized society, but which, unless recomposed in their interdependence, tend to lose sight of the social fabric they are a part of and in which they acquire and, at the same time, help to produce, meaning.

The volume consists of disciplinary reflections, social field research, experiences of performance and the transformative potential unleashed by theatres, in their forms as repertory theatres or even only in dramaturgy, which constitute fruitful moments for the cultural growth of territories, for the mobilization of citizenship, for the elaboration of the specific problems of the contexts with which they interact, according to their demographic, cultural and social composition, and the marginality or cultural and linguistic centrality that characterizes them.

Special attention has to be paid to the translation of the Italian denomination of "Teatro Stabile", which is often kept here in the original language. The reason for this anomaly resides in the impossibility of translating the concept of an Italian *Teatro Stabile* into an equivalent in English. The translation into "repertory theatre", which is mostly the only possibility for a translation in English, has a completely different meaning.

A repertory theatre in English means a theatre in which a resident company presents works from a specified repertoire. A *Teatro Stabile*, instead, does not always have a resident company (and this is partly what makes being an actor in Italy highly uncertain) and is characterized by an artistic project integrating production and formation, as well as promotion, hospitality, and service for theatrical innovation.

Therefore, as the translation of *Teatro Stabile* is not matched with that of *repertory theatre*, it has here been left in its original term of *Teatro Stabile*.

The meaning and any value of this volume reside in three points: the first one in presenting a plurality of voices and presences that confirm just how much theatre is still a form of social involvement and resistance, as well as a starting point for social reflection at different levels, both scientific and cultural; a second point which tends to revalue and rethink cultural institutions in their multiple social needs: both for the construction of the collective fabric and for the institutional role of mediation, listening and restitution in creative-cultural terms of the needs of the city fabric of which they are a manifestation; the third point concerns the need to valorize the many meritorious forms of research and perspectives of analysis which propose culture and art as forms of social resistance, civil organization and the construction of collective meanings, not in contrast with the contemporary forms of institutional and digital communication, but by returning to the overall picture of society its social practices from below and not only those institutionalized by the dominant media.

In other words, this volume has a place in that specific territory of social disciplines in which the attempt is to analyse the experience to build its profound meaning beyond the routine of everyday life, a process of construction revealing the relevance which culture has today in the social fabric, both in building it and in manifesting its urgencies and current forms with and through institutions. It can be said to be a volume of meta-research, since it is itself a material for analysis in understanding approaches, perspectives, convergences – but also divergences – in observing a cultural phenomenon in terms of its social impact and fundamental development process.

Delving into the detail of the composition of the volume: the first chapters have a more explicit critical-reflexive approach to the function or role of theatre and the practice of performance in society, to then progressively arrive at chapters which deal with specific case studies.

The first chapter by Maria Shevtsova is a testimony to dedication and, at the same time, a firm conviction of the necessary and decisive presence of art in society and therefore of art as a social phenomenon necessarily included in sociological reflection. Through a dialogue with Bourdieu, Duvignaud, and Gurvitch, but also with the acute and indefatigable observation of both sociological and theatrical university environments and contexts, Shevtsova reaffirms how fundamental, and at the same time not academically valued, is the scientific work which filters the profound evolution of social equilibrium through the lenses of art. Several issues make this path complex; on the one hand, the alleged social marginality of art, on the other the question of the text, context, and dramaturgy which theatre invokes with its specific collective artistic form: "in both Bogomolov's and Castorf's productions brings up a second key problem of the sociology of the theatre: dealing with sociocultural and political *context* in *aesthetic* terms and so beyond the assumption that the theatre is, before all else, a matter of content – story, plot, what it is about and whether it has a 'message'." (Shevtsova) In this sense, Shevtsova's essay opens up to all the problems that will be dealt with later, in a separate way and from different angles, in the two volumes. Art as a social phenomenon, art and theatre as expressive and narrative forms of social contexts, art as a profound expression of the internal movement of society and it cultural values, capable of anticipating future explosions, needs, urgencies, but also an expression of social resistance, participation, and civic commitment. Art as a manifestation of social relations, not merely an aesthetic form, but also and above all an ethical form of collective living, capable of indignation, compassion, and profound solidarity with the injustices and inadequacies of the social system.

The second chapter by the undersigned author contains the reflections which originated the development of this book. Personally engaged for years in field research and in theorizing the social role of culture and art, in all its forms, from the avant-garde as a form of anticipation, to cultural institutions as places for the organization of collective cultural needs and aggregation (see in this regard the vast production which starts off from the first works on Futurism up to the recent publications on the contemporary Russian avant-garde and the social turning point of museums, Riccioni, 2003; Riccioni, in Polyudova, 2020; Riccioni and Halley, 2021), the time had arrived to launch a dialogue between experts and scholars of these issues to create an exchange and generate a form of reflection and recognition of what has been done so far. How the sociological discipline observes social phenomena and their interdependencies and how it deals with the expressive nature of its vital forms. Is theatre still a vital form of expression in our society? There is no theatre without a society, consequently, a discipline which observes society cannot escape the expressive form which gives it its measure of profound vitality.

In the third chapter, Paltrinieri develops a reflection on the way social practices pass through performative forms of citizenship, of which theatre is an integral part and a fundamental tool. In this sense, the role of the University, as a complex organization with elevated social responsibility, writes Paltrinieri, has the aim of forming citizens who are, sooner than being professionals, capable of opinion and criticism, with the result that the use of theatrical practices at university can prove essential to integrate these cultural citizenship paths.

In the fourth chapter, Glüher, an art historian, develops a fundamental conceptual transition from theatre as a form of art, to the use of performance in contemporary art as a form of recovering uniqueness and the relationship between space and time. The ephemeral in art, its presence in the here and now is achieved through the use of the hybrid artistic form of the performance, which involves all sensorial activities and restores the vital and transformative form to art: in this sense the sources of 'extreme art' are cited and traversed, from Beuys to Laurie Anderson, from the Viennese Actionism of Günter Brus to the works of Gina Pane.

In the fifth chapter, Guarino focuses on the inseparability of the performative forms from the forms of life and "also assumptions and consequences on the environment, the general economy, and the local and global relationship between biology and techniques. Therefore, it is not possible to neglect the active role and the profound influence of performative practices on an encompassing notion of ecology and on a redefinition of both the common environment and the 'public sphere'."

In the sixth chapter, Tessarolo retraces some perspectives of reflection on theatre starting from the studies of Francastel, for whom: "the expression 'theatrical space' relates not only to the material container [...], but also to a mindset: the evocation or re-creation [...] which ultimately reaches the soul of the audience." Aware of the complexity of the artistic form which manifests in the theatre, Tessarolo uses both her studies on the sociology of art, and her role as a scholar of communication processes, to give shape to an essay which also yields the complexities of the dialogue between the subjects.

In Chapter 7, Federici outlines and contextualizes the observation of theatre in the scientific production of a classical sociologist, Roberto Michels, a

German naturalized Italian, who is well known for his studies in the field of the *elitists*, that is, together with Gaetano Mosca and Vilfredo Pareto, on politics and observation of the forms of democracy in society in the early twentieth century. Federici, in underlining that for Michels, sociology had not so much the task of elaborating systems, "but of increasing knowledge", through a description "of the structural form of social life" (Michels, 1966, pp. 7–8) notes how much he tried: "to identify a dividing line between the *Ancien Régime* theatre and popular theatre. A demarcation which determined the birth of a modern audience and such new ideal types as the bohemians to whom Renano dedicated a little-known work. (Michels, 1932, pp. 801–816)."

Chapter 8 by Serino focuses above all on the development, which has more or less already happened, of the sociology of theatre as a field of research. It offers a "historical overview of the projects, manifestos and programmes for the sociology of theatre proposed over time (Gurvitch 1956; Duvignaud 1965a; Shevtsova 1989; Pavis 1996)" substantially recognizing how much the dominant work and critical review of the various approaches to this discipline was widely addressed and even partially resolved, in its own terms, by Maria Shevtsova (1989; 1997; 2001; 2009) also in a dialogue with Bourdieu's work (Shevtsova, 2001, 2002).

In Chapter 9, Turri investigates, as a specific form of active participation between the spectator and a live performance, the centrality of the unconscious emotional dimensions which: "move through the psyche of actors and spectators" (Turri, 2016, p. 125). "As such, the self-reflexivity which is generated through the actor's interpretation of the character must lead, at least in part, to the construction of a collective identity." The evident fact also emerges from psychological research that performative activities, also by virtue of the unconscious forms they activate, become processes which build the social fabric and identity of a territory or people.

In Chapter 10, Elena Polyudova and Elena Olesina investigate the educational dimension of theatre as "Educational activities [which] personalize a historical socio-cultural landscape and incorporate it into school subjects in collaboration with cultural institutions." In this essay, Polyudova and Olesina develop "several points about historical re-enactment in Russian education as developed in the last decades. The first is the nature and definition of historical re-enactment in modern Russian education. The second is the current state of the method in schools, its structure, and the teacher's role in the process of applying school content to the interactive engagement. The third is a case study of a historic re-enactment which took place in a middle school, with a description of the stages of preparation and execution, with illustrations, and a description of the aftermath of the lesson for the students who participated in it." (Polyudova, Olesina).

In Chapter 11, Marisol Facuse investigates the relationship between art and politics in theatre. She tries to define an archaeology of the artistic practices in theatre mainly referring to artists from different historical periods who have recognized theatrical experiences implicated in the social struggles of their time. Meyerhold as agit-prop theatre in USSR, the politic theatre of Piscator in Germany that ended up in 1920 in the Proletarian Theatre, the intervention theatre after May 1968 in France and how it shaped different social and individual needs such as the dimension of affect and emotion that started to acquire new importance and thus shaped a different type of theatre as well.

In Chapter 12, Del Gaudio introduces the practice of Blast Theory, a British company, which since the late 1990s has produced performances: "which undermine the idea of a defined physical space and work on the boundaries between physical and digital spaces." Their work is mainly developed in urban spaces and on the one hand has the aim of elaborating spatial relations binding performance, media, and audience, in which the public space becomes the result of a "continuous negotiation between the actions of the performers, the actions of the audience, and the particular media involved".

In Chapter 13, by Brilli and Gemini, a different analysis opens, of a very specialized kind which, through in-depth interviews and an analysis of the Facebook profiles of artists and companies, aims to investigate the use of social media by contemporary theatre companies in Italy, or "how performance artists manage the boundaries between online and offline performativity, and between self-narration and artistic promotion."

Camargo Molano, in Chapter 14, takes up the theme of the use of digital technology in theatre companies contextualized in the first period of lockdown in the United Kingdom: "Among the activities closed during the lockdown in the United Kingdom (...) is *Staged*, a project produced by the BBC to respond to the need of British citizens to enjoy theatre even in the condition of closure of the physical places where theatre takes place" and has the look of a "video-call series". A kind of metatheatre which dons the appearance of an adaptation, highlighting the fact that: "there are hardly any differences between a live event and a mediated one" through "the mediatization of live events".

Following the reflection of a theatre which goes beyond the aesthetic dimension to rise to a participatory and transformative one, in Chapter 15 Cicerchia and Staffieri present the figures of culture and theatre. The dimensional picture of how much culture has an impact, but is also a part of, the daily life of citizens and cultural policies, and is in fact the premise for that immersive and transformative leap in the life of individuals. Here the transition from welfare to cultural welfare is brief, presenting in this case the data and results of research which highlights the path for achieving collective wellbeing through theatre. The presence of projects to "improve verbal communication in preschool children and children with verbal communication problems" up to projects for "contrasting cognitive decline in the elderly" and its form as a "powerful support for carers" shows, data in hand, how much the discourse on the social role of the participatory form of art is in fact a precious and little-valued tool in contemporary societies, but which is reversing its marginality in a pervasive centrality in the major museums, in research centres for welfare and in alternative wellbeing courses for citizens.

Cavrini's Chapter 16 explores, through statistical data, the relationship between culture and the level of wellbeing. Both education and training play a fundamental role in the widespread wellbeing of citizens since they open up greater opportunities and prospects for growth.

All that remains is to wish good luck to this multi-voiced project, which recovers the profound meaning of performativity as a conscious social interaction brimming with meanings.

Acknowledgements

A special thanks goes to all the staff and director of the Teatro Stabile of Bolzano for helping me tirelessly for the success of the conference "Theatre and public space" that took place in Bolzano on September 9–11th, 2021, of which this book is the result. The conference has been, indeed, the final phase of the research project "The role and social impact of theatre in a globalized society. The case of the Teatro Stabile di Bolzano" I carried out as Principal Investigator with the funds CRC granted by the Free University of Bolzano-Bozen.

Figures and Tables

Figures

2.1 The social dynamics of theatrical work   28
10.1 The members of the Reenactment club display details about the living history in Old Russia   132
10.2 After exploring the handmade replicas of the ammunition and life of the time, students are eager to take a picture with the club members and the objects   133
10.3 After the presentation lesson, it is the time for self-introspection and analysis. It goes also together with the club representative in a costume of the Old Russia   134
10.4 The grand finale: creating your own object based on the studied material with guidance and support of the teacher   135
10.5 The results of the survey   136
12.1 Extent of Presence Metaphor (EPM) dimension   153
13.1 Number of Facebook posts published in the year 2019 by the 38 profiles we examined (via CrowdTangle)   170
15.1 Percentage of people aged 6 and over who attended theatre performances at least once in the last 12 months by sex – 2010–2020   190
15.2 Percentage of people aged 6 and over who attended theatre performances at least once in the last 12 months by class age – 2020   191
15.3 Logistic model estimates of coefficients (a) in model with life satisfaction as dependent variable   194
16.1 Percentage of monthly household expenditure on recreational activities, entertainment and culture out of average monthly household expenditure by Region – Year 2019   203
16.2 Percentage composition of Italian household expenditure on culture – Year 2017   204
16.3 Percentage of regular readers in Europe, Eurostat survey conducted between 2008 and 2015   205
16.4 Percentage of Italians who have never read a book by region – Year 2019   206
16.5 Early exit from education and training by gender, geographical breakdown, citizenship, educational qualification and highest occupation of parents – Year 2019   207

Tables

13.1 Results of coding a Facebook post's function and mean number of interactions (like + shares + comments) per function   171
13.2 Coding of an object promoted in a Facebook post   171
13.3 Coding of the presence of references to artists or events in Facebook posts not directly related to the activity of the company/artist   171
16.1 ISTAT: Average monthly household expenditure and monthly household expenditure on recreational activities, entertainment and culture by Region – Year 2019 (Euros)   202

Notes on Contributors

Stefano Brilli
is a postdoctoral research fellow at the Department of Communication Sciences, Humanities and International Studies (DISCUI) of the University of Urbino "Carlo Bo". His research interests are centred on irreverence and celebrity in digital culture, performing arts audiences, and sociology of the arts.

Jessica Camargo Molano
is a PhD student at International Telematic University "UniNettuno". She is an art critic; her research focuses on the way in which the concepts of avant-garde and technological innovation are combined in artistic experimentation. At present, she is an assistant lecturer in Sociology of Electronic Arts and Sociology of Multimedia Entertainment at the University of Salerno (Italy).

Giulia Cavrini
is a Professor of Social Statistics at the Faculty of Education of the Free University of Bolzano. Over the years, her research has focused on health and ageing, longevity, health-related quality of life, and intergenerational relations, with particular attention to grandparents' social role and grandchildren's care.

Annalisa Cicerchia
an economist of culture, she works on the impact assessment of cultural policies, cultural indicators, and the relationship between culture, art and wellbeing, in Italy and Europe. She has been a member of the Scientific Committee of the ISTAT project for the measurement of Equitable and Sustainable Wellbeing, a member of the Board of Editors of the journal *Economia della Cultura*, and Vice-President of the Cultural Welfare Centre. She is the author of books, research reports, and scientific articles.

Vincenzo Del Gaudio
is research fellow at the University of Salerno where he teaches Theories and Techniques of Multimedia Performance. He teaches History of Theatre and Performing Arts at the University of Tuscia and History of Contemporary Theatre at the eCampus University. His studies focus on theatre as a social device and forms of remediation between theatre and digital media. His writings have a deep focus on issues related to the aesthetics of performance and on social mediation as a form of understanding the contemporary social

imaginary. Among his latest publications: *Theatron. Verso una mediologia del teatro e della performance* (Meltemi, 2020).

Marisol Facuse

has a PhD in Sociology of Art & Culture, a Master in Sociology of Art and the Imaginary (University of Grenoble), and a Master in Philosophy and Sociology (University of Concepción, Chile). She is an associate professor at the Department of Sociology, Faculty of Social Sciences, University of Chile and Coordinator of the Sociology of Art and Cultural Practices Study Group. She has coordinated the Latin American Sociology Association (ALAS) Sociology of Art and Culture Work Group and the Sociology of Art Work Group for the Chilean Sociology Congress; she is a member of the Sociology of Arts Research Committee of the International Sociological Association, ISA. Her research focuses on political theatre, popular culture, immigrant music, cultural hybridization, museums and museology.

Raffaele Federici

teaches Sociology of Cultural Process and Communication in the Graduate Programme at the Department of Civil and Environmental Engineering of the University of Perugia. He also teaches Sociology of Art at the Accademia di Belle Arti of Perugia. His research interests include the sociology of modernity, the history of social thought, and the sociology of arts. He is the author of: *Confini stravolti. Entropia e pandemia di un secolo incerto* (Intermedia, 2020); *Landscape and Hashtag. The ambivalent Dialogue with Genius Loci Through the Media* (Springer, 2021). Federici has also published articles and book chapters on digital media, and their respective involvement in everyday life.

Laura Gemini

is an associate professor of Sociology of Cultural and Communicative Processes at the Department of Communication Sciences, Humanities and International Studies (DISCUI) of the University of Urbino "Carlo Bo". Her research interests focus on the relationship between performance, media, and social imaginaries.

Gerhard Glüher

is a philosopher and art historian; since 2007 he has been a tenured professor of Philosophy and Art Theory in the Faculty of Design and Art at the Free University of Bolzano. Selected publications: *Die Fotografie am Bauhaus. Neues Sehen und Neue Sachlichkeit als Medienexperiment.* in: Moderne. Ikonografie. Fotografie. Band 1 Das Bauhaus und die Folgen 1919–2019, Magdeburg

(E. A. Seemann) 2019; *Images of Borders and Edges*, in: Burgio, Valeria (Ed.): *Europa Dreaming* (Bozen-Bolzano University Press) 2019.

Raimondo Guarino
is a full professor of Theatre and Performance Studies at the University of Rome "Tre". Regarding site-specific performance and public spaces, he edited the collective work *Teatri Luoghi Città* (Rome, Officina, 2008) and has published papers for the periodicals *Teatro e Storia* and *Storica*. He recently edited, with Lene Buhl Petersen, *Beyond Books and Plays. Cultures and Practices of Writing in Early Modern Theatre* (*Journal of Early Modern Studies*, 2019). His paper "Commedia dell'Arte and Dominant Culture" was included in the collective volume *Commedia dell'Arte in Context*, Cambridge University Press, 2018. Among his books: *Il teatro nella storia. Gli spazi, le culture, la memoria* (Rome-Bari, Laterza, 2005); *Shakespeare. La scrittura nel teatro* (Rome, Carocci, 2010).

Elena Olesina
works at the Institute of Art Education and Cultural Studies, Russian Academy of Education, and teaches specialists in the field of Art Pedagogy. She has many years of experience in managing the state programmes of applied art education and cultural studies research. Her academic interests include the study of perception of art by modern children, and the transformation of the museum and school interaction.

Roberta Paltrinieri
(PhD) is a Professor of Sociology of Culture at the Department of Arts, University of Bologna. She is the Director of DAMSLab and a member of the board of CRICC, Centre for Interaction with Creative and Cultural Enterprises, a research team of the University of Bologna. Her research interests concern social and cultural innovation, sharing social responsibility, audience development, and civic engagement.

Elena Polyudova
works at the Institute of Foreign Languages, Peoples' Friendship University of Russia (RUDN), where she leads Russian programmes and teaches Russian Cultural Studies to international students. Her academic interests are sociolinguistics, the aesthetic experience in art education, and the integration of the museum and school activities.

Ilaria Riccioni
is a tenured researcher and qualified associate professor of General Sociology at the Free University of Bolzano-Bozen. She holds a PhD in *Theory and Social Research* at the University of Rome "La Sapienza" on the Social impact of Avant-garde art. She has been a visiting researcher in France, Austria, the USA, and Australia inquiring into social theory, sociology of culture and the avant-garde and is currently President of the Research Committee *Sociology of the Arts* at the International Sociological Association, ISA. Among her recent publications: Riccioni I., *Teatro e società: il caso dello Stabile di Bolzano* (Carocci 2020); Riccioni I., *Futurism: Anticipating Postmodernism. A sociological Essay on Avant-garde Art and Society*, (Mimesis International 2019).

Marco Serino
(PhD in Sociology, Social Analysis and Public Policies) is currently a Research Fellow in Sociology at the University of Naples "Federico II", Italy. He has been Visiting Research Fellow at the School of Business and Management of Queen Mary University of London. His research interests range from the sociology of culture and the arts to social network analysis and the sociology of scientific knowledge. Among his recent scholarly publications: "Culture and Networks in Online Social Fields. Studying the Duality of Culture and Structure in Social Media through Bourdieu's Theory and Social Network Analysis", *Italian Sociological Review*, 11, 2021.

Maria Shevtsova
(Goldsmiths University of London) is author of *Sociology of Theatre and Performance* (2009) and *Rediscovering Stanislavsky* (2020), among other books and salient articles translated into fifteen languages. She is editor of *New Theatre Quarterly* and is on the editorial team of *Critical Stages* (International Association of Theatre Critics). Her public work includes lectures and interviews at major international theatre festivals.

Simona Staffieri
is a statistician at the Italian National Statistical Institute where she works on health and disability statistics. She obtained a PhD from "La Sapienza" in 2013, discussing a thesis on Youth Tourism. For the last five years she was adjunct professor of Statistics at the Faculty of Arts and Humanities at Sapienza University. Since 2012, she is an external member of the Research Group Sustainability in Hospitality and Tourism at the Academy of International Hospitality Research, at NHL Stenden University. In recent years she participated in various research projects on culture and well-being.

Mariselda Tessarolo
is a Senior Scholar at the Studium Patavinum. Her fields of interest concern communication interpreted from the point of view of Symbolic Interactionism. Her main publications in the field of artistic communication include: *L'espressione musicale e le sue funzioni* (1983, Giuffrè); *L'arte contemporanea e il suo pubblico* (2009, Angeli). On the topic of language, she has published *Minoranze linguistiche e imagine della lingua* (1990, FrancoAngeli) and *La comunicazione interpersonale* (2007/2013, Laterza).

Maria Grazia Turri
is a Senior Lecturer at Queen Mary University of London and the co-director of the MSc in Creative Arts and Mental Health. She is a psychiatrist, psychoanalytic psychotherapist and theatre scholar and practitioner. Her research focuses on understanding processes of identification in theatre through psychoanalytic theory and her current project is a study of the unconscious power dynamics underpinning laughter. She is the author of *Acting, Spectating and the Unconscious* (Routledge, 2016). Her theatre practice includes performing and writing for devised theatre projects with the Gaia Drama Group and directing children's community theatre projects.

CHAPTER 1

Artistic Processes and Characteristics: Key Problems of the Sociology of the Theatre

In Dialogue with Pierre Bourdieu

Maria Shevtsova

"Tout est social" declared Pierre Bourdieu in *Magazine Littéraire* (1992[a]) with something like dramatic flourish, as if he had discovered the wheel. This was at the time when *Les Règles de l'art: Genèse et structure du champ littéraire* (1992[b]) was being published. Of course, Bourdieu was driving a point home for non-sociologists, but he was also well aware that, while his announcement might be a platitude *for* sociologists, it still needed to be repeated among them with regard to the arts as fully worthy of serious study.

Step back to the mid 1980s, when I was introduced to Jean Duvignaud, sociologist, anthropologist, and author of the 1965 first book claiming the title of "sociology of the theatre", which he wrote more or less in tandem with his exploration of the sociology of the actor (1965[b]). Duvignaud observed with a touch of bitterness that he had got nowhere with this "stuff"; his significant research in this area had never been properly acknowledged and, fortunately, he had abandoned it long ago for something more in the mainstream of sociological concerns. Duvignaud was clearly pointing out the disinterest of the social sciences in the subject as a warning. The predecessor of his indubitably valuable first volume was sociologist of knowledge Georges Gurvitch's essay "Sociologie du theatre" (1956), published in *Lettres Nouvelles*, a pre-eminent literary journal with philosophical interests. Gurvitch leaned towards philosophy, Duvignaud, towards the sociology of professional groups, defined, in his case, as dramatists.

Step further back from my meeting with Duvignaud to the 1970s: I am face to face with my soon-to-be supervisor at the University of Paris. Nervously, I ventured to name the area of my proposed research, to which he exclaimed, spluttering Gauloise cigarette ash down from the corner of his mouth: "*La sociologie du théâtre?! Mais mademoiselle, qu'est-ce que c'est que ça*"? He was a noted Brechtian, presumably having read Brecht's great friend Walter Benjamin, and I had reasoned that, for such a scholar, Brecht's theatre was an integral part of the *tout* that was social, which sociology studied: thus what was specifically *of* the *theatre* was *of* a given society at the same time. The question, then, as I saw it, was not whether the aesthetic and the social were interconnected, but *how* this interconnection was to be identified, shown, analysed and explained.

My supervisor's mistrust of sociology's presence on theatre territory, to whose status he was deeply committed, had surprised me. Perhaps it was a defence of theatre studies, which had only recently been recognized as an academic discipline in France, basically with and just after *Mai'68*. Continued conversation revealed that, for him, sociology primarily involved measurements – statistics, graphs, charts – while theatre was concerned with the humanities and thus with issues defined by drama together with drama's literary aspects or "learned culture", as Mikhail Bakhtin (1984]) had called the culture of the word consistently throughout his writings. It is significant that Gurvitch had lodged his idea, essentially of theatre-as-word, in a journal marked *lettres* and that Duvignaud's *sociologie du theatre*, when it drew attention to theatre artefacts, was precisely this – a sociology of plays on the page.

These personal, anecdotal remarks are not a replacement for that dictum of British culture – always begin a speech with a joke. While lightly humorous, their purpose is to place the early history of the sociology of the theatre (Shevtsova, 2009[a]: 21–82) with which, since the very cusp of the 1970s, my own particular, and in many respects quite different, research trajectory coincides; and to place these historical steps in relation to this field's present situation in which my research continues, especially because the field cannot but be indebted incrementally to Bourdieu and his legacy. What *was* developed in the sociology of the theatre after its foundational years and as Bourdieu's great relevance to it gradually became apparent? This question is bound to prove its pertinence in the thick of Covid-driven social and, perforce, artistic change.

The immediately more important reason for my anecdotes is that they directly lead to the first key problem that had confronted the sociology of the theatre at its beginnings and which *still* confronts it to this today, leaving the field underdeveloped. The problem is a narrow, inadequate perception, conception, understanding and experience of what, in actual fact, *constitutes* the theatre, which is not 'theatre' unless it thoroughly embraces what is performed. The latter involves *performance*, which is intrinsic to the theatre; otherwise, 'theatre' remains dramatic text, while 'performance' is co-opted by extra-theatre discourses in which it serves as an analogue to social behaviours, or else as a metaphor for social structures and immediately apparent social influences. Such, for the latter, is Guy Debord's *La société du spectacle* (1967), ubiquitously co-opted, for decades, for all manner and kind of social organization and spin-off under the trope of 'performance', into which the French '*spectacle*' readily translates. In the meanwhile, *theatre* performance in itself, without metaphorical, or symbolic, or any other figurative sense, is lost to view.

Narrowness of perception is not confined to sociologists and other social scientists for it is widespread in university theatre departments whose members tend to reduce focus to their particular turf – their 'own' plot on far larger terrain. It would seem that a broad but profound education for enriching and illuminating a chosen field is simply not a priority today (despite much talk of interdisciplinary methodology), and this can only exacerbate the problem of myopia flagged up here.

The term 'theatre' in its various linguistic avatars is polysemic. Yes, it does refer to dramatic texts and, moreover, it includes those devised by actors and directors from novels – a grand tradition in Russia, for instance, since the Moscow Art Theatre's innovations at the turn of the twentieth century; young non-conformist directors today, notably Konstantin Bogomolov in Moscow, have taken it up enthusiastically. Bogomolov considers scripts devised from novels – *not* adaptations from novels (there is a big difference) – sufficiently ample for his fertile creativity as well as critical eye, wherever it falls. It fell sharply on Dostoevsky's knot of moral and social failings as a lens for delivering a thoughtful but scathing *The Karamazovs* in 2015, the noun 'brothers' removed from Dostoevsky's title because a woman plays one of them. Prompted, particularly by salacious episodes, club music, and other signs of the present, which accumulate rapidly towards its end, the production can be interpreted as an assessment of both controlling and contesting forces and the tensions between them in contemporary Russia.

Bogomolov followed up with *Dostoevsky's Demons,* whose themes of the ubiquity of people's capacity for wrongdoing the actors play with relative detachment, as if to confirm truisms. Premiered in November 2020, a witty reference at the end of the production to Covid-19 situates it precisely, temporally speaking, from within the production itself. The date of its premiere indicates that it was developed and rehearsed at various points during the lockdown. *Dostoevsky's Demons* ran for almost four hours, *The Karamazovs* closer to five, its exact duration depending on the pace of performance taken by the actors on different nights.

Devising long performances on a large scale has been the hallmark of Bogomolov's senior by twenty-five years, Frank Castorf, director of the Volksbühne from 1992 to 2017, when the government ignominiously sacked him, allegedly for commercial reasons. Monetary returns were hardly the mission of an institution anchored in the Free People's Theatre initiative in Germany at the end of the nineteenth century, as elsewhere in Europe. Castorf's let-it-rip productions, mixed explosive theatricality with big social punches that resounded locally in former East Berlin – in other words, in the time-and-place/space, the "chronotope" (Bakhtin, 1981[b]: 84–258) in which their speech accents, physical gestures, and visual imagery had germinated: an image recurs in Castorf's cornucopia of them that recalls the *wurst* (sausage) kiosk under the railway bridge of Friedrichstrasse station, a veritable icon not only of all-embracing German culture but quite precisely of acknowledged East Berlin culture.

My attention here to details that specify time and location in both Bogomolov's and Castorf's productions brings up a second key problem of the sociology of the theatre: dealing with sociocultural and political *context* in *aesthetic* terms and so beyond the assumption that the theatre is, before all else, a matter of content – story, plot, what it is about and whether it has a 'message'.

The issue of context is by not means straightforward. Note, nevertheless, that the extensive filming actors as they act in the presence of live audiences has well and truly become a signature of these two directors from the dawn of the twenty-first century. Filmed scenes (mostly of a documentary order) projected during theatre performances go back to the first decades of the last century and especially to Erwin Piscator and Vsevolod Meyerhold, both exponents of programmatic, agitprop political theatre. What is new more than a hundred years later is the actual filming, *in the here and now* of stage action, projected simultaneously on one, two, and more screens. (*Dostoevsky's Demons*, in one section, has five synchronized screens appearing together but showing different material.) Novel, too, is the visibility of the filmmakers who, while filming on the stage, become part and parcel of the stage's means of production. They are, as well, written into the production's scenography, thereby becoming aesthetics elements.

By the same token, the ongoing moviemaking, with cameramen walking about, operates as a composite sign of belonging to modern times. In other words, reference of this kind from within productions situates the chronotope outside them, although, for these particular cases, I have offered only a generalized and loose sense of actual time. Thomas Ostermeier of the Schaubühne in Berlin and the British director Katie Mitchell, who worked for a prolonged period at the Schaubühne and in many ways perfected its camera-shooting techniques, are epigones of this Castorf-inspired, cinema-live theatre style, contributing to a significant pre-Covid trend that should not to be confused with Covid-lockdown digital performances.

These remarks say that the theatre's constituent components are larger in number and range and have a broader remit and reach than 'text'. Theatre encompasses diverse theatre practitioners, spectators, productions, performances, companies, buildings, venues, public institutions, public funding, cultural and financial policies and the very institution of a practice that is distinct from other art practices but also from non-cognate practices like, say, medicine. And it is 'theatre', regardless of cross-arts interweave or even cross-arts fusion, when, for instance 'installation', 'performance art', or just plain 'performance' might be the terms that spring to mind rather than 'theatre'. Distinction of practice defines what is practised, but crucial for the sense and meaning of practice is *how* it is done. *Why* it is done inevitably accompanies the doing. My one or two clues above suggest the 'how' that is core to theatre aesthetics: cameras apart, there is the overall sardonic tone of Bogomolov's *The Karamazovs*; the accents of Castorf's actors among other indicators convey geographical and physical place but also the social place that his protagonists occupy on the social scale.

Bourdieu's concept of practice is valuably on call here (1977; 1980; Bourdieu and Sayad, 1964) for two reasons. Bourdieu tightly binds practice to *work* and the processes of working (which joins the theatre practitioner's understanding of doing – 'theatre practice'). On another but related strand of his argument, he binds practice to his concept of habitus. "Habitus" is essential for the sociology of the theatre and especially where theatre's artistic work is concerned (Shevtsova [a] 2009: 83–108). This is because the values, behaviours, attitudes, expectations and aspirations that structure habitus while habitus is structured by them (Bourdieu's repeated "structuring structures") can be identified in the 'what', 'how' and, crucially, also 'why' of a given artistic work.

The goal in evoking Bourdieu's theory regarding habitus for the theatre is not to prove its conceptual validity or efficacy, but to *use* it for understanding more clearly and in greater depth and finesse the richness of a chosen work or cluster of works, like the cluster brought together in this keynote presentation. The fact that habitus is fundamentally social, generated by and within a social class, class fraction or social group – a category that encompasses any number of identity groups – makes the concept a reasonably precise instrument for identifying the social markers embodied in artistic works. Think, again, of Castorf's popular (of the people) theatre universe, rather than that of another social group; and consider *why* these are the prevalent markers so that *this* universe rather than any other is present.

Another example, this time from Giorgio Strehler, a lyrical, poetic director by contrast with the hard-rock Castorf, sheds further light on the issue. Strehler's aim at the Piccolo Teatro di Milano to democratize the theatre entailed rescuing from oblivion both Goldoni's plays, the majority of them centred on the 'little people', and the *commedia dell'arte* performance mode, which Strehler aligned with popular culture. This task required assiduous archival research, research into masked playing, and training in quick and deft corporeal acting.

Strehler first staged *Arlecchino, servitore di due padroni* for the Piccolo's inaugural season in 1947 in which a scene – a constant of subsequent versions – shows Arlecchino spinning plates of food thrust at him at speed, alternately from left and right, by hands without bodies (curtains hide them). He spins without dropping one single plate while his hands and body increasingly bend closer to the floor. He talks ceaselessly through this virtuosic and incredibly funny performance, which, while being spectacular theatre, is a *tour de force* of social commentary without appearing to be this at all. The spinning plates encapsulate the merciless demands on Arlecchino not of one master but two – two by comic error – and the scene becomes an extrapolation of the social relations between servants and masters, the first obliged to obey and the second predisposed to command. Here, in a nutshell, is a case of the habitus of two social classes.

Strehler kept reviewing *Arlecchino* as his social perspective shifted. In the sixth, 1977 version, which I saw that very year, an exquisite vignette gives a glimpse of servant obedience in the form of a door, that is, two actors play a door by standing perfectly still at door width from each other, holding lit candelabras in their hands at the height where the candelabras could have been fixed to the wall. There is nothing else on the stage other than the door. The actors, totally upright, are costumed in elegant liveries, and become a replica of the same door in an identical space for the second master, who walks in to signal the change of scene. The utterly beautiful, poetically evocative, and humorous quality of this vignette in a soft palette of golden and pinkish tints, with lights softly dimmed right across the stage, images a master's sense of himself and his standing in the world. One master exactly reproduces another, implying by this cloning a collective master rather than a unique instance. (Design and costumes were by the celebrated Ezio Frigerio.)

Elegance counteracts the suggestion that these servants have been reified into things. But, the contradiction between appearance and reality is 'resolved' as the production moves towards its conclusion and the once wily, resourceful, and buoyant Arlecchino of thirty years before cedes to an ineffable sadness emanating from the stage. Does this indicate a stalemate for Arlecchino? Defeat? Probably. It is often hard to judge precisely because the theatre works on emotions and the subliminal levels of the unconscious and there is only so much the unconscious of a spectator can tell the reasoning mind during a performance. This having been said, how the social markers of habitus traverse a piece of theatre should not be reduced to a matter of dry sociological classification for they vehicle the subtleties of feeling and expression and the nuances of meaning of that piece.

Theatre practice generates multiple genres, forms, shapes, structures and compositional elements, like the visual disposition and colour of *Arlecchino, servitore di due padroni*. It produces stylistic devices, stylistic characteristics, stylistic specificities, and stylistic idiosyncrasies. All primarily concern aesthetics and are integral to theatre aesthetics. They are neither solely nor primarily the defining items of the position required for the position-taking (*prise de position*) that operates, Bourdieu insists, in any field of art. Bourdieu's field in *Les Règles de l'art* is the French literary field of the late nineteenth-century, constituted by 'movements' ('naturalism', 'symbolism') that compete for their position by virtue of the individuality that they claim and which, in addition, is attributed to them. Given Bourdieu's perspective, their claimed characteristics could be called the gambling chips of their position-taking against each other for prominence and prestige – chips that they exchange, so to speak, for their winnings.

Meanwhile, a small-scale avant-garde somewhere in Bourdieu's designated field is *hors jeu*, having deliberately fashioned its relative autonomy from the rules of the game. Most unfortunately, these pages are Bourdieu at his crudest, demonstrating his recourse to conventional, schematic, and outmoded literary textbooks (a movement follows a movement follows a movement), together with his formulaic packaging of ideas and his assignment to the margins the task of searching for a language of aesthetics fit for sociological inquiry. Where are the compositional elements of those genres that Bourdieu cites ("naturalism", "symbolism", "avant- garde") in order to make sense of them before there can be any talk of "movements" and why, indeed, they move? Bourdieu was well aware of his disadvantages when it came to art (the exception being photography), but a glitch of this kind within his considerable achievements shows that to write about art entails really *knowing* about art; and his momentary slip of authority can only be taken as reassurance that our research always requires initiative, imagination, and rigour.

The question posed above regarding seriously informed method segues into a third, double-edged problem for the sociology of the theatre. On one side of the same edge is the matter of aptitude and a 'feel' for the theatre *from within* the theatre. The idea of 'within' implies, from my vantage point, garnering maximum experience of the theatre from every possible angle, starting with seeing as much of it as possible in every possible variety, and storing it in body memory in whichever shape it comes. Bourdieu, in a personal, generously supportive conversation about my research near the end of the 1990s, described my "within'" as "insider access", which he saw as a definite advantage.

Access, however, does not come all by itself, let alone randomly. It is not an inherited privilege – a kind of capital passed by habitus. Nor is it freely given – a Biblical "ask and ye shall receive". It has to be worked for, frequently against refusal and obstacle. Some barriers, like these, are erected by artists' mistrust of 'intellectualizing'. Others arise from scholarly over-confidence in book-learning and 'bookish' views of materials not fashioned with scholarly tools in scholarly environments. And then, in any case, every researcher must grapple with objective limits and personal limitations. But the best that can be said is that the more researchers draw close to the theatre and experience it, thus also getting a 'feel' for it, the better for the sociology of the theatre.

The obverse side of the problem's double edge concerns limited awareness of the advantages sociology offers for understanding the theatre. The method of the double-edge is that of approaching the theatre from two angles simultaneously in an interactive, dialogical manner rather than passing from one box into another, sociology in one, theatre in the other, and more boxes lined up in a row in case they contain something useful. In actual fact, a dialogical method, layered into a dialectical method, throws into relief a fourth problem, which is that of accurately ascertaining why the numerous activities involved in the theatre are actually done. Why theatre? And why does it matter? An accompanying question is for whom does it matter? The next questions asks where does it matter and when?

All the aesthetic features cited identify *the* theatre but differentiate between the kinds of theatre that produce a plurality of *theatres*, a number of which are made to be performed outside dedicated theatre spaces (to start with – site-specific, promenade, immersive, and variants of community theatre, among which appear immigrant theatres and other theatres of exclusion). These features, call them also stylistic features, can be anything from breath-taking to brutal or non-descript, or just plainly inept. But all are invented, imaginatively conjured up by actors, directors, dancers, musicians, scenographers, light designers, and other theatre makers – sometimes they are spectator-participants – all of whom work *in* and *on* a *collaborative* process aiming for something performed.

Collaborative action makes theatre social by this very fact. Its social character holds whether collaboration occurs within a permanent ensemble company like the Théâtre du Soleil in Paris, in its fifty-seventh year in 2021, or in a team that comes together for a chosen project and then dissolves, like Robert Wilson's, where some team players return for subsequent projects, while others are replaced. Collaboration changes enormously according to the artists involved; and it changes according to the kind of involvement required of them individually. It changes with the exigencies of changing social conditions and political and economic circumstances (just look at the digital domination of these Covid years). But the effort and energy of the work that theatre practitioners do is concretized in that work, embodied in its structure, compositional details, atmospheres, perspectives, views, and, when it happens, an emergent worldview.

Wilson's pathbreaking 1976 *Einstein on the Beach*, which everyone will have heard of if not seen, is a case worth inspecting. (New spectators had their chance during its reprise on world tour, with a change of cast, during 2012 to 2014.) Philip Glass wrote his musical score independently of Wilson – on a 'separate track', as Wilson puts it (Shevtsova, 2019[b]: 99–102). Wilson worked on his architectural structure, as he likes to call his arrangement of space, and its scenographic components. Salient ones are: a column of iridescent white light rising alone, extremely slowly, in black space from the stage floor to a vertical position, taking twenty mesmerising, even mystical, minutes to straighten up; a wall the full height of the stage in rows of large orange circles of light that whirr out of sync with the belted-out cacophonous music; a small spaceship speeds across the length of the stage, denoting, as became clear on analysis after the event, the exterior view of the spaceship whose interior had been denoted by the panel of blazing lights a few seconds earlier.

Lucinda Childs crafted her choreography independently of both men's work on their individual tracks, and she danced her solo of repetitive steps, walking backwards and forwards with a light bounce. Her group choreography in circular motion of leaping dancers was similarly independently conceived and constructed. Performance analysis afterwards revealed that her abstract group dance was a metaphor for the spaceship travelling across space.

However, these three team members –Wilson was later to have five, six and more of them as his productions became more complex – coordinated and adjusted their respective compositions when they came together for discussion, fashioning by their idiosyncratic team work an avant-garde piece, also thus named by its creators because they had broken all existent dramatic and performance conventions: no story, no narrative sequence going from a to z, no dialogue (only disconnected monologues), no apparent connection between parts, no protagonists, no characters, no character interaction, no conflict, no psychology, no direct connection between music and stage action, no connection between music and dance movement, no obvious content or context, and no apparent meaning. It was about nothing but itself in the moment of performance.

The creators of *Einstein on the Beach* unanimously claimed it had no meaning, although they probably needed to have said it had no *semantic* meaning for it *meant* on other levels of apprehension like feeling, imagining, fanaticizing and dreaming. Wilson, when pushed, said it was about space and time. Yet, if the word 'about' is the desired word, then it was also about light. Space, time and light hint as to why "Einstein" appears in the work's seemingly random title. Childs somewhere calls out "1905", the date of the theory of relativity. It can easily be missed as it flies by. Before then, when Childs steps rhythmically backwards and forwards, an anonymous performer rapidly, repeatedly and almost indiscernibly writes Einstein's famous equation E=mc2 into thin air. That too can easily be missed! In another piece invented by other practitioners, the date "1905", when framed by appropriate allusions, could have evoked the first Russian revolution.

While the semiotic processes (semioses) of *Einstein on the Beach* do not reveal, in an explanatory fashion, the social context in which they were incubated and grew, they point to its unencumbered, liberated, spirit. The production's loose structure, disconnections, innuendos, associations, and ellipses allow it to escape the references of a semantically organized universe to the material universe of referents, and just *be* – although not entirely about nothing but itself. In this, *Einstein on the Beach* shares the convictions of Wilson's contemporaries – Merce Cunningham, Lucinda Childs, Jerome Robbins (dance), John Cage (music), Jasper Johns, Robert Rauschenberg, Donald Judd (painting) and Susan Sontag (their theorist), who were concentrated in a small part of Lower Manhattan and worked and lived like an interconnected, yet personally free, New York coterie.

To my mind, it is in this overall area of coterie habitus that the most fruitful sociological research can be undertaken on this group's art, singly or collectively. So close were their artistic interests and so unfettered their creative means that the performing artists among them broke down the fences that had previously divided the arts to create the 'hybrid' 'intermedial', 'interdisciplinary' and 'multidisciplinary' forms (a few weeks ago I found myself writing 'cross-arts hybrid modes'!!) that characterize *Einstein*, and, indeed, all of Wilson's works thereafter right to the present day – video portraits, furniture, and other non-staged pieces, included. It is worth noting that Wilson popularised 'hybrid' in the 1980s, while 'interdisciplinary' gained currency in the late 1990s and the early 2000s, interspersed with 'cross-arts' and 'multidisciplinary', which appear to have been the preferred usages of the 2010s, while 'interdisciplinary' has regained traction for the 2020s. These variations on the theme of assailed borders indicate just how potent the legacy of the habitus of the 1960s breakers has been.

Paradoxically, the works of this same coterie have had widespread world following, while connecting most intimately with groups of spectators closest in outlook to them. Spectator engagement and interaction with theatre performances, wherever they are, are inseparable from the social of the theatre. Performances rely on recognition, resonance, and acknowledgement on the part of sociologically identifiable spectators, who resonate differently within fluctuating social conditions. Their energy is crucial for the dynamics between those who perform, as it is for their interchange – the electric charge – with spectators. Spectators are by no means an indiscriminate mass, and their respective, differentiated, habitus is activated during spectatorship. There are spectators who, when encountering infringements on their habitus, resist the transgressions of their beliefs and attitudes and disengage – not uncommonly aggressively.

Resonance has to do with shared emotional responsiveness in which the reverberation of our senses, plus a sixth, which is intuition, play their part. Otherwise, interchange could not occur. In the theatre, the locus of that interchange is the work performed in all its complexity of interconnected semiotic processes: my term 'processes', when discussing semiotics, indicates that multiple sign-making is made from someone to someone intelligibly in anticipation of an intelligible, interactional, response. Signs thus understood escape the thingness that typologies of signs confer upon them in theoretical discourse that stresses the function of systems without 'interference' from social agents. This kind of systems semiotics ran like wild fire through theatre scholarship in the later 1970s and throughout the 1980s, burning those embarking on the sociology of the theatre.

In the practice of the theatre, sign-making signs are meaningful because people makes them in socialised contexts in the social world. They do not function within a self-enclosed and self-explanatory system abstracted from the social world (the focus of systemic theories). Signs are carriers of the socially saturated meanings inscribed in social action, and they carry over into the imagined, fictional worlds of theatres. Reconfigured, they nevertheless make sense, have impact, affect emotions, and stimulate the imagination and thought. This is precisely how the 'outside' world comes into the 'inside' of theatre worlds. It is precisely how and why social contexts, although specified differently in different theatre performances, are always inside those performance and discernible in them, as my performance examples earlier were able to show.

Since social contexts are embodied within artistic processes, claims that they are merely backgrounds, *exterior* to the art forms at issue, seriously need to be questioned, first and foremost in theatre scholarship, where old dualistic habits die hard – aleatory 'background' contra real-deal theatre in the foreground. Even so, the issue is not one of seeking and finding exact replicas of corresponding social contexts in the semioses of theatre works.

A fifth key problem emerges from this false dichotomy between the inside and the outside of theatre works. It concerns the acute care to be taken in observing how sign processes support and sustain works rather than force them to say what you want them to say. The semiotic configuration of some theatre compositions eludes the question "Why is this so"? (*Einstein* is a case in point). The semioses of other compositions allow general deductions but do not necessarily yield specific sociocultural meanings. Still others complicate the issue of social and cultural specificity through intercultural and cross-cultural theatre where several cultural specificities are in play simultaneously. How are cultural specificities to be dealt with in a melange of disparate provenances purporting to be a cohesive unit? The interculturalists of the later 1980s (Yukio Ninagawa, Peter Brook, Ariane Mnouchkine, Eugenio Barba) sought to show cultural similarities and/or traits of 'common humanity', irrespective of culturally differentiated sign making. Those accentuating cultural differences often used two and more languages to strengthen their view. Quebecois Robert Lepage's productions are prime examples, with Japanese or Chinese dialogue intersecting French and English.

Ideologies of globalization problematize the notion of sociocultural specificity exponentially. This, taking a short cut, is the McWorld (Barber, 1995), the mcdonaldization syndrome. Yet, the pressures of uniformity imposed by avaricious commercialism open up opportunities, as occurs in theatre in China. The main trend today in non-traditional Chinese theatre (excluding the country's mania for North American and British musicals) is cross-cultural in the sense that it freely explores European theatre genres, expressions and devices, appropriating them in performance mixtures so as to fashion new theatre idioms for an advanced modern China. In other words, cross-cultural practices are used to forge a new-national kind of cultural specificity behind which figure political ambitions. The presence of classical Chinese theatre (known as 'Chinese opera') within the interweave is a means of updating traditional Chinese ways of performing and making them palatable for newly formed and, especially, young, upbeat audiences while endorsing the new-national perspective.

Take Tang Xianzu's sixteenth- century *The Peony Pavilion,* the most canonical and revered of all Chinese opera, used for the 2016 opera *Coriolanus and Du Liniang* directed by Guo Xiaonan. Shen Lin, a noted Shakespeare scholar teaching in Beijing, rewrote *Coriolanus* to facilitate the active and attractive, movie-like rather than staid, 'old-fashioned' tenor of the production's merger of these quite different plays, the one written to be spoken and the other to be sung. Both are modernized, while the director and the actress, who plays Coriolanus as well as Liu Mengmei, the heroine of *The Peony Pavilion,* romanticize Shakespeare's warrior, down to his uniform and dashing soft cap rather than helmet. But modernization for appeal to targeted audiences is far more than a marketing ploy in that it shapes taste and thus shapes habitus and, for this very reason, it requires closer sociological study.

Critiques of globalization, but especially of its neoliberalism, undermine so-called 'western' hegemony and the East-West axis of power to focus on the North-South axis. This is the mission of Swiss director Milo Rau and his team, who, in several Central African countries (The Democratic Republic of the Congo, Rwanda, and Burundi), have created theatre largely with non-actors and/or some aspiring actors. Such salient examples as *Hate Radio* (2011) and *The Congo Tribunal* (2015), followed by the latter's film version in 2017, are representative of Rau's Central African focus, which concentrates and then diffuses his sociopolitical drive, embracing like-driven aspirant performers as well as spectators to make theatre that is social through and through. This theatre, which is steeped in current affairs and daily language, and relies on verbatim-theatre, documentary, reportage, court-room examination and other legal-procedural techniques as it probes social realities, could, indeed, be describe as sociological theatre. And this suggests that theatre, when it is like Rau's, is another way of doing sociology.

The Rau-group theatre is an agitprop theatre with unambiguous, fully explicit signing through which the distinctions between theatre and life are erased, as is the very idea of theatre as make-believe. The theatre-act enacts and incarnates social justice – hence the idea of the tribunal, the *means* by which the first steps to justice can be secured; and enactment, incarnation, and tribunal endorsement, as well as moral confirmation, promote the necessity of social justice *in* reality, *not* in fiction. What of cultural specificity? No, here it is not at issue, and comes from another debate. For, here, life itself, understood as exploitation and corruption, is the theatre of requisite radical transformation, and this life is nothing if not public and political through and through.

We do not yet know what the theatre will be after the Covid-19 pandemic, a truly global phenomenon which, to boot, is accompanied by global warming's alarming evidence, day after day, of global calamity. One production among the Zoom inventions made for computer screens stands out for the glimpse it offers of a theatre constructed out of 'social distancing' – the tragic mantra of Covid-19 – which is, in effect, *physical* distancing and *antisocial*. And this production demonstrates how technology, when exceptionally skilfully manipulated, is not just a resource that *must* be used for theatre's survival, but becomes the very stuff, the fabric and texture, from which theatre artefacts are conceived and made. These artefacts are necessarily *of* a hybridized theatre that is de-socialized, but not devoid of meaning. 'De-socialized', in this discussion contrasts with 'socialization' in the customary terms of reference that embrace the idea of interactive togetherness in physically, personally shared, space.

The prominent screen-theatre work referred to is *'this body is so impermanent ...'* premiered online in March 2021. Three artists across three continents made their respective solo, never even to meet virtually within the piece: Ganavya Doraiswamy, a devotional singer living in the United States; Wang Dongling a master calligrapher in China, who, with his outsize brush, more the size of a broom than a fine-art utensil, has transformed the ancient art of calligraphy into highly calibrated writing-movement; Michael Schumacher, a 'contemporary' (non-ballet) dancer, working in Vienna. The chanted passages are from the second chapter of the *Vimalakirti Sutra* (1976), a first-century Buddhist text. Peter Sellars, the director-coordinator of these three different forms, each artist working exclusively by him/herself but simultaneously in real time, describes the whole as "simultaneous meditation" and a "multidisciplinary performance film" (Sellars, 2021). Each artist is filmed on home territory. Sellars' directorial hand is digital, and it is in the montage – in the cuts, shifts, juxtapositions and occasional shadow-like visual overlap of the three parts that make a three-solo entity a whole.

This whole contemplates the impermanence of the physical body and the body's transcendence – the spiritual posture is, after all, Buddhist – and it opens up space for healing, or rather, for the *sensation* of felt sharing, which precipitates healing. Its presage of healing stimulates hope for the social, or so it seems in these turbulent, deeply uncertain times when the very life-blood of the social appears to be draining away. Sellars' work offers the possibility of hope, as conveyed through his new aesthetic and its multi-layered sign processes. It remains to be seen what, exactly, the sociology of the theatre can do with singular works like this one, let alone with the, fundamentally mechanical, humdrum fare turning up on Zoom and other online platforms; and whether it will have to start afresh, although not from zero.

Bibliography

Bakhtin, M. (1984) *Rabelais and His World.* Translated by Iswolsky, H. Bloomington and Indianapolis: Indiana University Press.

Bakhtin, M. (1981) *The Dialogic Imagination.* M. Holquist (ed.). Translated by Emerson, C. and Holquist M. Austin: University of Texas Press.

Barber, B. (1995) *Jihad vs McWorld: How Globalism and Tribalism are Re-shaping the World*, New York: Times Books.

Bourdieu, P. (1977) *Algérie 60: Structures économiques et structures temporelles.* Paris: Minuit.

Bourdieu, P. (1980) *Le Sens pratique.* Paris: Minuit.

Bourdieu, P. (1992a) in interview with Pierre-Marc de Biasi. *Magazine Littéraire* 303 (October): 12.

Bourdieu, P. (1992b) *Les Règles de l'art: Genèse et structure du champ littéraire.* Paris: Le Seul.

Bourdieu, B and Sayad, A. (1964). *Le Déracinement: La Crise de l'agriculture traditionnelle en Algérie*, Paris: Minuit.

Debord, G. (1967) *La Société du spectacle*. Paris: Buchet-Chastel.

Duvignaud, J. (1965[a]) *Les Ombres collectifs: sociologie du théâtre*. Paris: Presses Universitaires de France.

Duvignaud, J. (1965[b]) *L'Acteur. Esquisse d'une sociologie du comédien*. Paris: Gallimard.

Gurvitch, G. (1956) "Sociologie du théâtre". *Lettres Nouvelles* 3: 196–210.

Sellars, P. (2021) Available (consulted July 4 2021) at: https://www.broadwayworld.com/los-angeles/article/Peter-Sellars-Multi-Disciplinary-Performance-Film-THIS-BODY-IS-SO-IMPERMANENT-Gets-World-Premiere-20210305.

Shevtsova, M. (2009) *Sociology of Theatre and Performance*. Verona: QuiEdit.

Shevtsova, M. (2019) *Robert Wilson*. Updated second edition. London: Routledge.

Vimalakriti, *Nirdesa Sutra* (1976) Translated by Thurman, R. Pennsylvania: Pennsylvania State University. Available (consulted January 17 2021) at: https://www.istb.univie.ac.at/wtmp/lva/vimalakirti/Thurman.pdf.

CHAPTER 2

The Social and Political Impact of the Theatre in Contemporary Society

Ilaria Riccioni

2.1 Introduction

What is society?
Sociology has several ways of defining what a society is. It can define it in terms of an empirical determination, or as a limiting idea of a significant group of members, ideally subjects with equal rights and duties geared to the good of all. Another way of defining society is to start from its observable elements: hence a world in which the significant interconnections that build socially shared values and forms of collective belief are consolidated.

2.1.1 What Holds Contemporary Society Together?

In the third millennium, certainly, no longer blood ties (typical of ancient tribal societies), no longer collective beliefs or rites (religion); no longer the elitist knowledge of a few, forms of elitist dominance typical of nineteenth-century societies with gory remnants of the twentieth-century's world wars. Contemporary society is less and less definable in terms of a group of members, and more recognizable in an exchange of relations based on an economic logic. Contrary to the artistic process in modernity until its denouement, or in contemporaneity, collective action has been portrayed in favour of individualized mass action; the steady disappearance of the collective phenomenon, initially in favour of a private reality, has gradually been transformed and transferred to the mass media, even appending the reduction of experience to the lack of a shared reality. As the new social networks are conceived and regulated by digital platforms through social networks, part of the social significance, which previously resided in a collective custom consolidated by collective practices in combination with the corporeality of society itself and its members, has now shifted to a situation of interconnection that involves not only human subjects, but also their technical and technological "extensions" – as McLuhan called them.

From public to private, nowadays, the social world appears to be segmented much more among interconnections with 'objects' and virtual platforms, not so much out of a collective will, but thanks to a progressive shift in the very geopolitics of power. The 'public space' referred to in this book appears to be an endangered species which will most likely never enjoy the protection generally reserved for rare species. The public space, in the sense of a place for meetings and the construction of opinions not linked to direct economic interests, appears to be a dimension obliterated by its very substance which indissolubly binds it to the creation of content, thinking, and potentially critical individualities. A situation, that of both content and critical capacity, which is simply not geared to the system of networks and private interests which manage them, and is therefore naturally obliterated by civil society itself which has replaced (arguably uncritically) the typically economic-productive functional assumptions with those of sharing and coexistence necessary for any democratic social coexistence. In this sense, it would appear that the public space is inevitably being sacrificed in favour of interests which consolidate the network society. And in turn, transforming the aspiration to non-utilitarian relationships into a new utopia.

From a sociological perspective, we must ask ourselves: what are the realities and social groups that potentially elude or do not enter the logic of this market dominated by formal rationality?

1) The sacred as opposed to the profane, in itself elusive;
2) All artistic forms;
3) The excluded, since they are not framed within the rational organization of production forces;
4) Both young and old in precarious positions, therefore not represented by specific rights;
5) Women as a gender endlessly at risk of discrimination;
6) Immigrants, always at risk of invisibility;
7) All those groups of citizens who belong to a sphere of non-power, of non-recognition.

Under what conditions can they present themselves as social forces or an antagonistic power?

Interconnection has been affirmed as a social form which 'connects' individuals, but it does not offer the possibility of sharing, nor does it require it. The contemporary citizen is increasingly a customer/user rather than a person belonging to the institutions.

This essay aims to develop a path through three points of reflection on the relationship between forms of artistic expression and society:
1) The social role of art and its potential impact in collective practices;
2) The peculiarity of theatre as a dynamic art along with its social relevance as a public space in the contemporary era;
3) An introduction to the theoretical foundations of empirical research carried out as a case study on the Teatro Stabile of Bolzano as an institution.

2.1.2 *Art and Society*

Why should art forms be studied from a sociological point of view? Because it can offer us insights into significant irregularities in terms of understanding society and its complex development dynamics.

Art is a manifestation of society, not separate from the human activities, collective values and imagery that these tenets nurture within a community. This places it fully within the context of the phenomena which contribute to its constitution and, as scholars focused on understanding society, forcing us to take into account in what way different art forms question contemporaneity. The relationship between art and society is dialectical and non-programmatic; a relationship of mutual conditioning, in which meanings, values, and forms are continuously elaborated and updated in a process that continually offers new insights into and perspectives of reality.

Art and society are therefore one inside the other, combined in a complex, ambiguous, and problematic relationship.

We could start from the question which Simmel asked himself when observing the social dynamic: what is it that holds society together? And in this sense, the dominant figure of society in the contemporary era is communication, and all those digital forms of communication which, however, we could say, 'vaporize' the materiality of society and its character of commonality. Communicating, or sharing, has today espoused a concept of dematerialized commonality, which virtually no longer needs the body and the place, thereby ultimately renouncing experience too. A society satisfied with imaginary, ephemeral connections loses the sense of itself and spawns increasingly refined processes of alienation. Some of the suggestive theories in this sense are those of Baudrillard according to whom hyperreality is the dominant figure of social contemporaneity: with relational practices built in interaction with simulacra of reality; thus, unable to give life through these relationships to an authentic self, such as that which is instead nourished in the experience of the relationship with the other. The body becomes the battle of reality, it represents the unavoidable form of accepting the human limit while regaining the sense of reality in a society which, according to Baudrillard, has instead lost exactly this sense given that it ignores the body experience. It is a society that puts abstraction, matrices, and operations separated from the imagination and the body before it, in other words, it puts the 'production of reality' before reality itself: "The real no longer has to be rational, since it is no longer measured against some ideal or negative instance. It is nothing more than operational." (Baudrillard, 1981: 11)

Art is in turn communicative, but goes beyond mere verbal communication and incorporates social processes in a synopsis which reveals, through the adventure of experimentation towards knowledge, the complex reality of experience and gives it form. Art is experience communicated through the talent of form. Each art is generated by the culture of a society. Out of both approval and rejection. It is a relationship with reality data to transform them into combinations and potentials which open up new perspectives. In turn, culture is equivalent to a series of social practices, more or less widespread, which underlie a conception of life and humankind, and which therefore generate a kind of ethics, a way of life, a civil and individual conduct, often identifiable with a particular context.

In contemporary society, contrary to the artistic process, collective action has been retracted in favour of individualized mass action.

In communication, a term which defines not only the means of mass communication, but also the forms of communication, the artistic form too re-emerges as an expression of society.

Art in all its possible manifestations: from the avant-garde of the beginning of the last century to the forms of contemporary 'performance art'. Thus, the gradual disappearance of the collective phenomenon, initially in favour of a private reality, was subsequently transformed and, we could say, transferred to the media. The new social and collective networks are conceived and regulated by digital platforms through social networks. The reticular relationality, the Web, favours the formation of communities, on platforms characterized by virtual reality, absent the body. In contrast, the new reality exactly recalls a renewed social interest in theatres as place for socializing, edification, and discussion, but also for 'education' in relationships. A place of 'discovery', for the very youngest generations, of the logic of presence, of relational intelligence and of the rules that must be made explicit from tacit expressions given that they belong to collective practices in transformation.

Like museums, theatres take on an unprecedented functionality in this social landscape: the functions of the institution are rediscovered as a place for interception, response and organization of collective needs (see also Riccioni, 2003; 2017; 2021).

With the end of the time of cultural institutions as elite places, these particular institutions have taken a radical relational and pedagogical change of direction.

Theatres also seem to respond to this need for institutions to open up to all kinds of audience, bringing the pedagogical energies and strategies of other structures into play.

In addition, the theatre is a place of aggregation for adult generations who have also been formed through reflection and the social commitment of theatre, a place of social resistance and celebration from the 1960s onwards, in a radically different reality from that which it represented throughout the entire previous century (see also Wirth, 1985).

Purely as an example: how can artistic processes mediate the socio-political transformations taking place? In the contemporary planetary world, where more and more individual actions are collectively disjointed but united by the same imagery (we could say 'affectively oriented' and oscillating between politics and society, relying increasingly on imaginary communities defined by social platforms), it is essential to grasp the link which holds together (if it does actually hold them together), the value dimensions and the affective-emotional load they carry, in relation to socio-political and cultural institutions.

In this respect, institutions are the 'places' of the social organization of collective needs, and as such they have the fundamental function of acting as an intermediate term between the reality of individuals and the structures of the organization of collective living and the economic-political power of a society (see Lynch, 2020).

What does it mean when, to give a very topical example, parts of civil society literally refuse to act for the common good, in the case, for example of the minor but existing opposition to using a mask and getting vaccinated for the common good. Beyond any consideration of whether this is right or not, whether it is legitimate or not to rebel against these collective measures, the question which arises is another one: how does this rejection fit within the universe of values to which it belongs? Can it be a demonstration of the erosion of the very concept of the collective good? Is it not attributable to a social action that Weber would have defined as 'affectively-oriented' even though it is a question that calls into question values, belonging, empathy and a sense of the other?

In this case, the privatization of society by neoliberal capitalism works by progressively eroding the values of a shared social sphere in favour of immoderate individuality. The idea of the public, understood as everyone's reality, a shared, common good, in the imagination of these grievances no longer exists, and clearly indicates from which side the collective imagination is expiring with its emotional, irrational, and difficult to justify charge which, however, modifies the balance of a society given that it is already configured as a transformation of collective values.

In this sense, a second meaning of art comes forward, that is, an art understood as socially engaged, not necessarily in terms of political art, but in the sense of an art whose widespread practices undeniably transform the way of perceiving the social fabric, identity differences and social inequality sanctioned by neoliberal social structures, placing reflection on the individual as a summary of a much larger reality of which it is a part. An art that becomes social criticism, capable of overcoming purely local barriers, be they cultural, political or economic, to explore the planetary meanings which surpass cultural differences to focus on collective social problems: damaged human rights, strident and nefarious inequalities, the world of necessities and places of resistance. Theatre today can hardly provide that metaphysical consolation of which Nietzsche spoke in the birth of the tragedy – I am thinking of Beckett's work, which by the first half of the last century was already staging the inability of communication between individuals, the individual closure even of intertwined experiences. A communication which distances the individuals while allowing them to dialogue, I am also thinking of Eugène Ionesco's *The Bald Soprano*, staged at the same time as Beckett's texts, and which emulates a meaningless, empty everyday language that communicates the alienation and distance between the subjects, incapable of perceiving themselves in the profound relationship that transforms those taking part in it.

For Nietzsche, it was no coincidence that Western theatre, Greek tragedy, was born from the spirit of music: at the origin of the theatre is an emotional language which loves a representation of what society often does not dare to reveal about itself, but in the Dionysian theatre, myths found their birth, which tended to unite the collective imagination but also "To recognize how everything that is born must die, we are forced to face the horrors of individual existence and yet not be petrified: a metaphysical consolation instantaneously delivers us from the bustle of the world of change. We are really in a brief instant the Primeval Being itself, feeling its raging desire for existence and pleasure of existence." (Nietzsche, 1977: 111)

In a tragedy, a people can recognize themselves and reflect on their own condition: the importance of classical tragedy lies in its ability to let a society understand the bounds of reason (Nietzsche, 1977) but also to discover its condition of unity and collective destiny.

2.2 Importance of Theatre to the Social Fabric

Moving on to the second point of reflection, theatre and social space, we can anticipate that the term *theory* from the Greek θεωρέω *theoréo* 'I look, I observe', is also the root of *theatre* – θέατρον (*théatron*, 'show'), from the verb θεάομαι (*theàomai*, namely, 'I see').

Therefore, the same root of the concept of theory, which implies a distant but specific look at a historically determined reality from which one tries to draw generalized considerations on a phenomenon, fact, or reality, is also the root of 'theatre', which is both the place, and the action of staging a spectacle of reality, a form of reality which 'is split' to be watched, and takes shape thanks to the spectator's gaze. Therefore, it has in itself the concept of a relationship, of an external gaze and a reflection of reality. Without a spectator there is no theatre. But on top of that, a spectator who shares with the actor the space, the atmosphere, and the moment of the staging. So both *theatre* and *theory* lean towards an objectification of reality, one through generalization, the other through the sharing of experience.

The doubt which arises today is whether theatre can still, in the era of digitalization, and possibly more than before, retain the social function of building collective meanings and consolidating the identity of a community that is no longer perceived solely in local terms, but also in global or planetary terms?

The relationship which founded this partnership lies first of all in the very principles of representation and, secondly, in the search for an authenticity which both modern and contemporary societies tend to deny the individual by virtue of increasingly complex superstructures.

The more complex and rationalized society becomes (Weber, 1969; Pareto, 1968–1916; Schutz, 1979; Ferrarotti, 2020; Merleau-Ponty, 1945; Bourdieu, 1968), the more the forms of relationship between individuals and institutions are structured in bureaucratic forms which are distant from the concept of community as traditionally understood.

Both theatre and the community are nourished in a symbiotic and dialectical relationship at the same time, according to historical periods and conditions: ever since the earliest conception, theatres have been places where the individual, both civil and cultural, became aware of the other through their presence, but also through reciprocity; gazing at the other and the spectator's gaze at a stage set are the main relationship which builds the relationship with otherness, not in subjective but in collective terms.

The theatre as the founding reality of the dynamic arts is the heart of ancient education, which finds its most "mature and complete incarnation" in the tragic chorus (Sini, 2003, p. 28): the role of the chorus in ancient theatre "embodies the rite of constitution of the human, the rite of initiation and formation [...]. The stage set was originally a projection of the chorus, its "vision" or hallucination and its "myth", of which the "tragic place" or Dionysian feast presents the founding sacrifice of the meal with God, or the constitutive act of the community" (Sini, 2003: 28–30). This constitutive act, therefore, is not conventional, but a participatory experience. An experience from which the original duality between worldly and divine things is realized through ritual, myth, and sacrifice or celebration. The feast expresses "communication with the divine, in other words, mediation" (Sini, 2003: 29) between these worlds through language, but also the threshold between one world and another, where one learns the eternal nature of the divine and the mortal nature of the human. Therefore, as a place of experience it is also a place for learning the limits of experience.

As a significant human aggregate, the community possesses characteristics which differentiate it from society seen as a structured reality of life in common. According to Norbert Elias, some common properties of communities, in the traditional sense of the latter term, can be defined. A community can be said to be a set of domestic groups settled in the same location and linked to one another by closer functional interdependencies than other groups or people within the wider social field to which the community belongs. Consequently, unlike a society, a community is a field of social interdependence between individuals where their survival is linked to the fate of the group, in both economic and relational terms. And it is for this reason that theatre as an art of movement, presence (and therefore of relationship) has the potential to enter into a relationship with the sense of the group and of belonging, with the path of formation and disintegration of the identities of a people, with the ability to create self-awareness, self-observation, motivation, and solidarity.

At the same time, however, the theatrical text and its staging cross the different societies through the foundation of the myth. The theatre of Aeschylus, with Antigone, Medea, and Oedipus, features figures who still question our social system, our contemporary social relations; for this reason, the construction of a myth rooted in the collective imagination is not simply the inheritance of a people but of a civilization.

2.2.1   *Theoretical Premises*

É. Durkheim (1912) in *The Elementary Forms of Religious Life*, refers to collective effervescence as a force for social transformation. A collective unifying experience.

According to Durkheim, the soul of society resides in religious thought, its ability to organize collective living in tacit and explicit norms according to a system of actions to which a positive or sanctioning value is attributed, and which contribute to the collective construction of the social structure and shared meanings.

Compliance with these norms occurs by virtue of the clear distinction between worldly and otherworldly facts, which in fact inhibits their transgression given that they are perceived as rules defined by a higher order.

At the same time, wrote Durkheim, these same rules can be overcome by the collective force released during rites; a collective effervescence which transforms individuals by virtue of an energy reached in moments of extraordinary affectivity or collective irrationality, again attributable to higher forces.

Durkheim referred to religious festivals, processions, and rites (Durkheim, 1912), but also the energy, which Duvignaud defined as *unifying*, of the theatrical representations of *creation* which express an emotional consonance achieved through a collective experience (Duvignaud, 1965).

In 1956, Georges Gurvitch published a pamphlet entitled *Sociologie du Théâtre* in which, for the first time, the study of theatre as sociological research in the field was postulated.

Gurvitch presented the sociological problem of the gap between sociological theory and practice in the field of social research as potentially surmountable by theatrical "technique": in other words "it is necessary to introduce consciously calculated 'theatricality' ubiquitously: as much in an investigation, as in an interview, the theatrical element can find its place without encountering too many obstacles" (Gurvitch, 2011: 41).

The most relevant and still valid observation of Gurvitch's intuition is the reflection which concerns the need for research as well as the theatre's need to look at society; a reciprocal gaze understood as a dialectical exchange between worlds which refer to collectively constructed meanings.

With the work of J. Duvignaud, a sociological trend on the study of the theatre became consolidated. In 1965, he published *Sociologie du théâtre. Essai sur les ombres collectives,* in which the anthropological perspective of the theatre as a ceremonial act is dominant, capable as it is of awakening desire and a sense of community.

With his prolific production alone, Duvignaud was an acolyte of Gurvitch; his sociological study is enriched with careful and considerable studies on theatre and on actors, always from a perspective which restores to the theatre its condition as an expressive form spread among the complex relationships of a given society: "le théâtre dans la société, la société dans le théâtre. [...] Création multiple, elle résulte de la volonté d'un dramaturge, du style d'un metteur en scène, du jeu des comédiens et de la participation du public. Mais, avant tout, est une cérémonie." (Duvignaud, 1965: 7). A ceremony which takes place in a precise location, has a select profane audience, and a group of actors isolated in an estranged world, with rigorous and refined costumes, gestures and movements, a poetic language which distinguishes itself radically from that of everyday life. A ceremony to be found in similar forms in everyday relationships. The ceremony, Duvignaud continued, is a collective act in which each individual plays a role within a dense network of interdependent relations from a script, and as such they are not editable by the social roles themselves which everyone embodies, individually but unanimously. It is the existence of participation in collective acts that brings society to theatre, not social life as an existential path of individual destinies. The existence of collective acts refers, in addition to the idea of a ceremonial, to awareness of a society's continuity of action, thus revealing a 'communion', among the meanings of the actions of the individual and the significance of collective actions. The ceremony is a collective action through which a communion is created between individuals; the theatrical performance re-proposes this moment of communion through the ceremonial of the everyday rendered in its fundamental archetypal aspects.

Instead, Erving Goffman, who published *The Presentation of Self in Everyday Life* in 1969, was responsible for the effective use of the theatrical metaphor as a form of social research. Goffman's ethnomethodological research is known above all for its study of microsocial dynamics which led to micro-sociological theories of social action in order to explain and describe interaction in groups: intra- and inter-group relations, to be precise. Erving Goffman developed a dramaturgic model for this purpose, or rather, used theatre as a metaphor to describe the dynamics of interaction: people behaving like actors on a stage consisting of a limelight area and a background. In the limelight area the roles are formalized, in the background the actors prepare informally for the formalized interaction that will take place under the limelight. According to this model, the actors try to influence the opinion that others have of them.

The relationship to *deception*, Goffman wrote, is exactly the process of awareness that is activated by an individual in society: "An individual may be taken in by his own act or be cynical about it. These extremes are [...] a little more than the ends of a continuum. Each provides the individual with a position which has its own particular securities and defences, so that there will be a tendency for those who have travelled close to one of these poles to complete the voyage." (Goffman, 1969: 31).

Taking up the concept of 'person', or mask, Goffman quoted Park (1950) "We enter the world as individuals, we acquire a character and we become people" (masks) (Park in Goffman, 1969: 31), and in this sense, theatre is the "putting on" of social masks repeated most in the routine of daily life; masks which, for every society, embody vices, virtues, and widespread human types in diverse ways.

Subsequently to these first scholars of the theatre from a sociological point of view, came the dense systematic research of Maria Shevtsova, who dedicated her life to the sociology of the theatre with the result of further consolidating the sector, guiding it, and repeatedly giving it continuous vigour beyond any fashions of the moment, while showing its sociological richness by deepening the various implications that theatre has, as an artistic discipline, an institution, a form of community work, but also as a politically assertive performance (Shevtsova 2018). In other words, Maria Shevtsova's endeavour goes beyond the initial stage of theatre as a research tool in her works, to investigate how theatre is in itself already a sociological form of observing society, its implications as a working world, its implications as an imaginary world organized around a social institution, passing via Bakhtin's semiotic analysis, Turner's anthropology (Turner, 1979), and applying Bourdieu's concepts of habitus and field to theatrical production (see also Levya 2019). Thus was a new page of the sociology of theatre written, aware that any definitions

> require sociological explanation: how each kind of theatre emerges, when, where and why, and what its impact or lack thereof says about its function and contribution, actual and projected, in the social structure where it appears.
> Since theatre and society are reciprocally explicative, what these theatres say about their societies, taken globally or partially according to the sectors, is equally important for a sociological account of them.
> SHEVTSOVA, 2009: 25

2.2.2 Theatre and Community Values

Sociological reflections around the theatre have enjoyed success since the 1960s, a period of cultural ferment that would lead to the cultural revolutions of 1968 in Europe and to Woodstock in 1969, both emblems of a renewed awareness of collective living.

In that period, the analysis of theatre as performance, as a collective manifestation, seems to have marked a crucial passage for the understanding of the new generations, who embodied the needs or aspirations of the society to come.

The production of sociological analyses of the dynamic arts, and especially the theatre, has been based on studies substantially rooted in post-1968 experiences, therefore fully involved in the collective processes of formation of culture and social practices that preluded a change in mentality and collective values (see also Becker, 1974 on music); according to Duvignaud, the theatrical discourse is deeply embedded in life and its difficulties, not only on a psychological level, which is reduced to relationships between individuals, but in the infinitely larger and more complex field of social groups manifesting in attitudes believed to be authentic and which are instead "rigged"; kinds of behaviour that involve actions different from our motivations, real obstacles which are the result of the crystallization of aspirations that were once free and have become institutionalized or hardened, of values venerated without knowing what they represent and without recognizing the evil they can do (Duvignaud, Lagoutte, 1974: 9).

In the 1990s, and throughout the first decade of the 2000s, hence for around thirty years, theatre was the subject of very few sociological studies.

To deal with the behaviour of the new generations, studies of a drug or drugs, of groups of youth culture and subculture and habits of distinction were preferred.

Theatre, and the arts in general, no longer seemed to inspire great interest in sociological studies, due to a social transformation in the sense of a progressive individualization of acting.

These began to be considered separate practices, enjoying a partial autonomy with respect to social practices in a sociologically observable sense, since they interrogated the sphere of creativity, still investigated above all in psychological terms.

One exception was the sociology of literature studies, rooted in the Marxist social studies developed first by the Frankfurt school, especially with Löwenthal (1977), Benjamin (1980), then further developed with the studies of G. Lukács (1967) and L. Goldmann (1971).

For Nietzsche, Western theatre, Greek tragedy, was born from the spirit of music: "at the origin of theatre was an emotional language which loved representing what society often did not dare reveal about itself".

In a tragedy, a people can recognize themselves and reflect on their own condition: the importance of classical tragedy lies in the ability to let a society understand the bounds of reason. (Nietzsche, 1977).

Theatre is a powerful and radical manifestation of the relationship between the creative deed and society (Simmel, 1998).

However, it also represents institutionalization.

In analysing theatre as an artistic form rooted in a relationship, it is necessary to distinguish between the two fundamental dimensions which make it up: on the one hand, theatre as a dramatic art, and on the other, theatre as an institution.

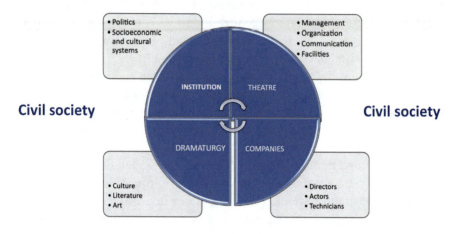

FIGURE 2.1 The social dynamics of theatrical work
Note: The peculiar circle of cultural exchange triggered by theatrical work impacts and involve the different areas of civil society. This shows clearly how culture and its institutions are crucial parts for a sustainable society in terms of creating work, diffusing culture, values and ethics, fostering economy, binding apparently unbound dynamics.

2.3   Theatre as a Social Institution

Theatre in the sense of a 'dramaturgic production' becomes part of the process of social change by interpreting it through forms suited to new expressive needs.

Dramaturgic production is not theatre until it is realized on stage. In this process, theatre as an 'institutional organization' comes into play.

The role of the theatre as an institutional organization is as crucial as the dramaturgic production since it constitutes the institution for the realization of dramaturgy, but also has a hinge function between the 'subjective' dimension of the author's production and the collective dimension of realizing the work: it is the detonator of meaning and the place of consecration of a work which, from dramaturgy, becomes theatre, scenography, direction, body, and word.

What does the concept of institution imply? An institution is the organization of a collective need in the form of "social regulations", "instances which mediate the social production of meaning and which allow stylizations of evaluation and norms to become binding" (Lepsius, 2006: 74).

The institutionalization process carries out "a mediation between ideas and the structuring of behaviour, creating an 'order' with a series of dimensions which delimit its 'property space' and are important in analysing institutions since they determine the content and effects of institutions on social processes" (Lepsius, 2006: 74–75).

R. M. The dimensions defined by Lepsius as the "property space" of institutions are:

1) *The development of rationality criteria* which an institution responds to: "In the process of institutionalizing a conception of value, ideas become maxims of action with claims of validity towards completely different men, with their own interests and motivations. [...] these maxims of action are rationality criteria. Their pursuit in a given situation of action is valid as a 'rationale' for the realization of a legitimate guiding idea [...] In the context of their institutionalization, the concepts of values and guiding ideas are concretized by means of the formation of rationality criteria which, in certain situations, make them relevant to the action." (Lepsius, 2006: 75) In this sense, rationality criteria are a part of the institution, but are related to the dominant idea of rationalization; consequently, in the contemporary neoliberal society the dominant rationality criteria correspond to criteria of economic rationality. So, in this sense, for theatre as an institution the concept of action will be linked to the choices of the billboard, to the sale of productions but also to the consolidation, from a dramaturgic point of view, of an idea of theatre (*of consumption or creation*).

2) *The differentiation of the validity contexts of institutions*: "The rationality criteria to which the action must be oriented do not apply in the abstract, but always and only within a limited action context. The effectiveness of a rationality criterion is therefore linked to the corresponding structuring of an action situation. The process of institutionalization includes not only the concretization of a guiding idea, but also always the determination of its validity context" (Lepsius, 2006: 76). As regards theatre as an institution, this second dimension translates into the various political, social and economic conditions within which the institution itself is located. Suffice to think of the different conditions of theatres in countries at war, or in a state of dictatorship, which legitimize the position of theatre within the context of conflict or social commitment.

3) *The institution's power to sanction* is the figure of the regulation of behaviour based on the institution itself, to validate its purported legitimacy. That is, in the case of theatre as an institution, the ability to operate as a legitimizing institution of performances, or rather of the 'narrative'

choices which each theatrical proposal makes in terms of direction, languages, and therefore relationship with the on the audience. "The type and power of sanctions – wrote Lepsius – are an element of the institutionalization process and in the case of theatre as an institution they concern the degree of 'subversiveness' which a theatre agrees to stage. This 'subversiveness' can be the result of the languages used in relation to the dominant culture of a social and political context, but also an economic one."

4) *The externalization of contingencies*, that is, the expectation of relevance which the institution can 'expect' in guiding behaviour. "Actions which refer to a guiding idea are therefore oriented towards valid rationality criteria and, based on these, they elaborate the problems which arise in the action context. [...] An institutionalized guiding idea is all the more effective the more it succeeds in successfully externalizing the contingencies connected to its validity and immunizing itself against the opposition that derives from it." (Lepsius, 2006: 78). For example, in the theatre as an institution, the externalization of contingencies takes place in the degree of regulation of expressive behaviour which corresponds to the more or less democratic dimension of a particular political-cultural system. The degree of conflict accepted in the staging becomes the threshold of the acceptable. We can think of the many cases of censorship, the various levels of conflict embodied by theatres, think of the distinction between permanent theatres and off-theatres, but also of the forms of collective theatre, social theatres, and the specific role which all of these diverse types of theatre play within the cultural system. The distinct types of audience they address, and the socio-political-cultural coordinates with which they are also intertwined in terms of support.

5) *The structuring of the potential for conflict between institutions* is generally high given that each institution generates rationality criteria within it which are usually in conflict with one another, while the areas of validity in which they try to impose themselves intersect. Concepts of value and guiding ideas are generally incompatible, otherwise they would not be differentiated. [...] This differentiation of competence and delegation of action dramatizes the guiding ideas, increases their validity and structures the potential for conflict between opposing institutions. (Lepsius, 2006: 78). In theatre, this can occur between the various types: repertory theatres, popular theatres, social theatres, research theatres, theatres of diversity, therapy theatres. Theatrical forms of expression which respond to often different logics, and that can generate conflict processes, especially if located in neighbouring territories or spaces.

A repertory theatre, or *teatro stabile* to use the Italian term, is an institutionalization of the balance between the various expressive forms, a laboratory which acts as a crossroads between the production, creation, consolidation and celebration of expressive forms in both mature and auroral forms, and is able to to position itself in a dialectic with the needs, national trends and international comparisons, and sanctioning the institutionalization of a certain theatrical expression.

2.4 The Political Force of Performance

The theatre today is potentially a place for the reconstruction of sociability and civic sense, of belonging and collective celebration.

In this sense, it has also regained a sociological meaning which, however, needs to be rediscovered and valorized.

Theatrical action is also collective for two different types of issue: on the one hand, in the concrete terms of putting together and realizing a show, the result of work shared between set designer, costume designer, director, technicians, actors, organization and marketing, press releases, up to box offices and masks, and so on and so forth; on the other hand, it means belonging to a group, with knowledge of it and the ability to read and interpret a cultural, political, value cross-section.

Theatres understood as a public space have an implicit relationship with politics understood as the art of organizing public reality. The very condition of realization of both consists in a public practice. These two ways of operating within the social fabric are distinct but also historically intertwined, just think of the early twentieth century and the 'deadly embraces' that the arts, both plastic and dynamic, exchanged with politics. Suffice to think of the avant-garde schools of the twentieth century. What theatre and politics have in common is a sociologically significant type of relationship that is rooted in human experience and in the qualities that can arise from that experience. According to Isaiah Berlin:

> In the field of political action there are practically no laws at all: skills are everything. What a statesman's success does, [...] is that he doesn't think in general terms: [...] His or her ability consists in grasping the unique combination of characteristics which constitute this particular situation – this one and no other. We are talking about the possession of a good political eye, or nose, or ear, or of a political sense which love, or ambition or hatred can mobilize, of a sense that crises and danger can sharpen

(or, alternatively, dull), for which experience is crucial, of a special gift, perhaps not entirely unlike that of creative artists or writers. We don't mean anything occult or metaphysical; we are not thinking of a magic eye capable of penetrating something which the ordinary mind is unable to grasp; we mean something perfectly ordinary, empirical, and, in the way it works, almost aesthetic.

BERLIN, 1996: 92–93

Politics, therefore, is nourished by experience, it captures the fundamental moments for action. Thus a visionary capacity is realized, typical of the political statesman, which is oriented towards the qualitative and not quantitative sense of looking at reality. Qualities which Berlin defined as "natural wisdom, imaginative understanding, or intuition", markedly found in statesmen and great novelists or playwrights, the only ones able to grasp that intertwining between "collective" and "psychological" of human characters in relation to the social conditions of the present moment.

According to Badiou's philosophical approach, theatre is "a State affair". A State affair which at the same time reveals the state of society, of its significant intertwining but also the continual changes of meanings and social priorities. For Badiou, the process of exemplifying the theory that theatre is a State affair, passes through those specific practices which unite theatre to political practice. The elements in common between politics and theatre are public practices, the relationship with spectators or an audience, practice understood as action, in acting terms for theatre, in legislative and executive terms when it comes to politics.

Politics is realized face-to-face, like theatre, writes Badiou, and this specific fact makes the realization of both a process to be completed, a process which is unfinished.

Badiou distinguishes between *Theatre* and *theatre*, that is, the possible forms of theatre that have different potentials: Theatre with a capital T is capable of entering the life of citizens, upsetting their certainties through performance of an Artaudian cruelty of realities silenced by convention; while 'theatre' with a small t is, in the language of Badiou, entertainment theatre, which does not speak *to* society, but *about* society. It arouses no discomfiture, it questions no social conventions, it awakens no one from their daily sleepwalking, but cradles them and protects them from waking up (Badiou, 2015).

2.4.1 *Theatre and the Public Sphere*

In Habermas' theorization, the public sphere is the place where public opinion is formed, not as a sum of private opinions, but as a result of confrontation and informed discussions, and as such it is crucial for the functioning of a democratic society. Habermas defines it as "a social network for communicating information, points of view, positions, in short, opinions. In this process, the filtered and synthesized communication flows convey into public opinions" (Habermas, 2013: 404).

2.4.2 Theatres as a Public Space

Like museums, theatres, take on an unprecedented functionality in this social landscape: the functions of the institution are rediscovered as a place for interception, response and organization of collective needs.

With the end of the time of cultural institutions as elite places, these particular institutions have made a radical relational and pedagogical change of direction.

Theatres also seem to respond to this need for institutions to open up to all kinds of audience, bringing the pedagogical energies and strategies of other structures into play.

Theatres understood as a public space have an implicit relationship with politics understood as the art of organizing public reality.

- "The public sphere has to do with all the conditions that help us form a reasoned opinion together with others on problems of general interest". We therefore find it, at least potentially, in all the places where we meet to reflect on something 'of general interest'. The physical location is important, but it can vary. A subway car, for example, despite being a public place, is not in itself a public sphere, but becomes one when the conversation takes on certain characteristics (Walter Privitera, 2001: XI).
- In short, the public sphere is the site of discursive forms of action based on the need to legitimize one's own positions through adequate arguments, whose claim to validity is itself offered to discussion. It is therefore the space in which public opinion is formed, not as a sum of private opinions, but as a result of confrontation and informed discussions, and as such it is crucial for the functioning of a democratic society (Jedlowski, 2011).

2.4.3 Theatre and Action between Social Construction and Deconstruction

There are three main perspectives according to which I develop here a reflection about the sociology of the theatre: a first one according to the revolution on stage brought about by Antonin Artaud, according to whom the Theatre can recover its new meaning in contemporary society through theTheatre of the Absolute as "pure experience"; Artaud's *absolute* recalls an individual's state of total freedom from social constraints, in order to recreate new collective values from the absolute (Artaud, 1938).

A second perspective is the one suggested by Jerzi Grotowsky, according to whom "In a civilized reality, theatre does not simply reflect society, but produces it" (Meldolesi, 1986: 143).

And a third perspective is given by the work of Claudio Meldolesi according to which "A theatrical performance encounters a social foundation: since it is the action that comes from the mind but with a collective rather than individualizing mode, controllable instead of dominating, immersive rather than introverted, bearers of artistic enrichment rather than compulsions to repeat. Although restricted to the framework of expressive communion, theatrical practice causes a reaction to the mechanisms of dissociation that corrode behaviour, then the personality, then the psyche and the principle of a person's solidarity, which is a fundamental means of defence in the life of the humble" (Meldolesi, 1994: 43).

2.5 Final Remarks

The language of Western cultures, seen as technically advanced, has become less and less inclined towards the languid nuances of poetry since it has tended to lose, or overlook, the metaphysical dimension. But a theatre lacking in poetry represents a 'technical' society, which is identified in the measurement of itself without leaving room for what exists, although neither visible nor measurable. Bringing "metaphysics", or magic, into the theatre means presenting the poetic meaning of life, which is not visible, but without which there would be no sense of living. How can we escape from this impasse? Theatre can have a *subversive* function, a process which, with the contemporaneity of its performance, attempts to reproduce the tension in life, the exceptional everyday life of a relationship. But while this type of function is progressively weakened by the habit of speed among communication tools, which make people unreflective, its metaphysical function, in contrast, enchants, restores meanings of forgotten plots through the momentary abandonment of social conventions.

The human being in society is forced, given that "society is unfair", writes Artaud in *The Theatre and Its Double*, and theatre can be a form of resistance if it accepts its ancient role, not staging types or characters, but returning to the roots of the cathartic representation, as Greek tragedy was already aware of, in that delicate and powerful function which places society face to face with itself. Artaud's reflections on theatre reveal the torments of the change in function of theatre in modern times, of its identity in transformation in relation to a society which does not always succeed in revealing its double, that unknowable or unacceptable side of collective living which brings completeness to reality. The complexity of Antonin Artaud's theatre will be the subject of a dedicated work, and cannot be dealt with here; however, it is necessary to draw on some insights offered by his work. For Artaud, the Theatre of Cruelty recovers the sense of the necessity of theatre while trying to update it to the contemporary world, offering it to the renewed needs of contemporary people, bewildered by the change of references and in constant danger of social and cultural unawareness. It implements non-daily action, symbolic actions as ones which refer to a higher truth and go beyond everyday practices, investing them with renewed meanings. In this sense, Artaud would introduce a distinction between "true theatre" and, simply, theatre. One arising as a gesture that remains beyond the everyday, which draws on the spiritual cords of the body and its gestural symbolism: ritual accompanied by poetic language. A theatre which ascends to the role of a revealer of ultimate truths, of symbolic gestures that draw from the roots of the Absolute, unlike that "theatre" which limits itself to a representation of, or a relationship with, daily life. But the spiritual potential in which Artaud saw the deep meaning of theatrical activity as a potential space of life in the Absolute, another space, for the alchemical transformation of everyday life. This brings it closer to Duvignaud's interpretation of theatre as a ceremonial act consisting of ritual functions which accompany it and mark the process of collective transformation and relationship to the other. However, there is a further way of observing the theatre-society relationship, on the part of theatre scholars, one which is oriented towards an exploration of the function of theatre in the community, and it is that indicated by Jerzy Grotowski, Barba's teacher, and wholly in line with the most significant theatrical forms of post-dramatic theatre. With the theatre of Grotowski, a different awareness emerged of the relationship between theatre and society since theatre itself seemed to need, in part, to take a distance from itself, in order to avoid falling into the trap of 'spectacularism', and actively reflect on the performance and the meaning of the action itself, within the network of social roles (see also Schechner 1988, 2002).

> Grotowski's 'post-theatre', inverting the order of comparison between theatre and society according to Gurvitch and Goffman, has identified a submerged consonance between theatre and life, meaningful and pressing to discover. He did not simply say, as Fersen did: theatre is not 'convention' but visionary space, ritual and trance. Instead, he understood that the 'failure' of theatre, in inverted commas, put an impotence as much as an archetype on the agenda; and that the prevalence of one or the other depended on our ability to experiment. [...] Grotowski's 'divided man' is not a fragment, a face of social behaviour, like Goffman's subject.

> Instead, it is a direct structure of the social framework, a microcosm of humanity, whose identification Grotowski reached through subsequent deletions of theatrical superfluity.
> MELDOLESI, 1986: 136

However, the process of reflection of Grotowski (1933–1999), in addition to inaugurating an anthropological approach to theatre that places it as a precondition for future performance studies, is also situated in a very 'hot' period from a social and political viewpoint, where the beginnings of the communication society were already widely subject to political criticism. His contemporary Guy Debord (1931–1994) wrote and published *La Société du Spectacle* in 1967, exactly on the eve of the student revolutions of 1968. Debord defined spectacle as a *Weltanschauung* which has become effective and has been transposed into material reality, at the same time the result and the project of the mode of production of modern capitalism which represents the heart of the unreality of real contemporary society. A spectacle is not a set of images, Debord continued, but a social relationship between individuals, mediated by the image. Basically, according to Debord, life in societies dominated by modern conditions of production announces itself as an "accumulation of spectacles" and everything that has been directly experienced is lost in the representation.

> The spectacle presents itself simultaneously as all of society, as part of society, and as an instrument of unification. As a part of society it is specifically the sector which concentrates all gazing and all consciousness. [...] Due to the very fact that this sector is separate, it is the common ground of the deceived gaze and of false consciousness.
> DEBORD, 1992: 16

According to Debord, the deception of modern society lies in the use of the gaze as a means of unification between individuals, which however turns out to be a partial gaze which embodies dominant interests and whose means is, in reality, also an end. By showing itself, this society requires a passive spectator, wrote Debord, and the spectacle "is the sun that never sets on the empire of modern passivity" (Debord, 1992: 21). In this sense, the theatre as a non-mediated form, in this period with the theorizations of Grotowski, of Barba, with the previous work of Artaud, and the subsequent one of Peter Brook, to name but a few, produces a reflection which establishes its own autonomy from the dominant tendencies of the society of the spectacle (Brook, 1968), in the terms used by Debord, or from the "semi-culture" of industrialized society, according to the terminology of Adorno (1981). In the process of emptying the stage, stripping away its costumes, in bringing attention back to the body as a means of expression, part of a complex dramaturgy made up of gestures and words, the poetic form of the theatre recovers and consolidates its function of social resistance.

The process of knowing theatre becomes an instrument of human knowledge if and when it adopts the liturgy of spoliation; a path which refers to the spirituality which gradually frees itself of earthly trappings to reach a deep interior truth not influenced by social conventions. An experimental theatre in Grotowski's sense embarks upon the road of the sacred, of the action that creates and does not merely reproduce: "Theatre nourished by civilization does not merely reflect society; rather, it produces society, it adds to it."(Meldolesi, 1986) and it is therefore this perspective that can prove of interest to a sociological process of understanding and identifying the function of theatre in society, an expressive means which uses its techniques to maintain its functionality in change, to resist the tendencies of standardization of modern societies. The idea that theatre can relate to society in specific ways which restore its profound figure even in contemporary society, combining the motivation of rational social action with the emotional one, bringing it to the stage through modern stories. A relationship between society and theatre, much more complex and articulated than has so far been hypothesized, a relationship that delves into the depths of both the deterministic sociological reading and theatre understood as a representation of social scenarios constituted by default roles. A space of experimentation for social science that involves the construction of new categories, novel approaches, new openings to the complexity of the social realm and the wealth of relational interweavings. A theatre as a generator of cultural meanings, hence bearers of a specific code, becomes a detonator of the sense of the collective imagination of modern society, in all its forms, from the most pop to the most committed ones. Through Duvignaud, Gurvitch, Goffman and Debord we have explored how sociology has observed theatre, and how it recognizes its social foundations; through the work of Artaud, Grotowski (1970), Meldolesi (1986, 1994), and Mango (1978), we have probed the profound vocation of theatre rooted in social life, in the imagination and in the transformation of reality using its own instruments. Theatre is at the centre of a complex relationship, not confined to an association with the cultural taste of the spectators, it has deep roots in the symbolic meaning of the culture in which it emerges; it evokes images, letting the emotions and the social constraints that affect destinies resound. And it is for this reason that it has the potential to enter into a relationship with the sense of the group and belonging, with the path of formation and disintegration of a people's identity, with the consequential capacity to create self-awareness, self-observation, motivation, and solidarity. In this sense, theatre can be a privileged observation post for the social realm and its deeper dynamics, through theoretical analyses of a sweeping sociological and cultural range, but also empirical analyses sociologically focused on the action of theatre and its potential impact on its surroundings.

These preliminary theoretical observations have guided the problematic reflection from which the elaboration of the research hypotheses on the Teatro Stabile of Bolzano as an institution began – to be discussed in the relevant chapter.

Bibliography

Adorno T. W. (1981) Prisms, trans. S. Weber, Cambridge, Massachusetts: MIT Press.

Artaud, A. (1938) Le Théâtre et son Double, in *Œuvres completes,* Tome IV. Paris: Gallimard.

Badiou, A. (2015) *Rapsodia per il teatro. Arte, politica, evento*. Cosenza: Luigi Pellegrini Editore. Formato digitale.

Barba, E. (1985) *Aldilà delle isole galleggianti*. Milan: Ubulibri.

Barba, E. (2017) "Il teatro è politica fatta con altri mezzi" Intervista a Eugenio Barba del 22.11.2017. Available at: https://www.ilsalto.net/teatro-politica-intervista-eugenio-barba/.

Baudrillard, J. (1981) *Simulacres et simulation*. Paris: Éditions Galilée.

Baumol, W.J. and Bowen, W.G. (1966) *Performing Arts–The Economic Dilemma*. New York: The Twenty Century Fund.

Becker, H.S. (1974) Art as collective action, *American Sociological Review*, Vol. 39, No. 6. (Dec., 1974): 767–776.

Benjamin W. (1980) *Il dramma barocco tedesco*. Milan: Einaudi.

Berlin, I. (1996). *Il senso della realtà*. Studi sulle idee e la loro storia. Milan: Adelphi.

Bourdieu P., (1968) Éléments d'une théorie sociologique de la perception artistique, *Revue Internationale Des Sciences Sociales*, XX, 4 : 640–664.

Brook, P. (1968) *The Empty Space*. London: MacGibbon; trad. it. 1998, *Lo spazio vuoto*. Rome: Bulzoni.

Debord, G. (1992) *La société du spectacle*. Paris: Gallimard.

Durkheim, É. (1912) *Les formes élémentaires de la vie religieuse*. Paris: F. Alcan.

Duvignaud, J. (1965) *Sociologie du théâtre. Essai sur les ombres collectives*. Paris: Presses Universitaires De France.

Duvignaud, J. and Lagoutte, J. (1974) *Le théâtre contemporain. Culture et contreculture*. Paris: Librairie Larousse.

Ferrarotti, F. (2020) *La socialità fredda*. Chieti: Solfanelli.

Goffman, E. (1969) *La Vita Quotidiana come Rappresentazione*. Bologna: Il Mulino.
Goffman, E. (2001), *Frame Analysis. L'organizzazione dell'esperienza*. Rome: Armando.
Goldmann, L. (1971), *La Création Culturelle Dans La Société Moderne*. Paris: Denoël.
Grotowski, J. (1970) *Per Un Teatro Povero*. Rome: Bulzoni.
Gurvitch, G. (2011) *Sociologia Del Teatro*. Calimera (Le): Ed. Kurumuny.
Habermas, J. (1987) *Il discorso Filosofico Della Modernità*. Bari: Laterza.
Habermas, J. (2013) *Fatti e Norme*. Bari: Laterza.
Horkheimer, M. and Adorno, T.W. (2010) *Dialettica dell'illuminismo*. Torino: Einaudi.
Jedlowski, P. (2011) "Socievolezza e Sfera Pubblica", in Review *Sociologia della comunicazione*. Vol. 41–42. Pp.15–29.
Lepsius, M. R. (2006). *Il significato delle istituzioni*. Bologna: il Mulino.
Leyva, R. (2019) Towards a cognitive-sociological theory of subjectivity and habitus formation in neoliberal societies, In review *European Journal of Social Theory*, 22 (2): 250–271. ISSN 1368-4310.
Löwenthal, L. (1977) *Letteratura, cultura popolare e società*. Napoli: Liguori.
Lukács, G. (1967) *Il dramma moderno*. Milan: Sugarco.
Lynch, K. (2020) Affective Equality and Social Justice, In Celentano, D. and Caranti, L. (Eds), *Paradigms of Justice: Redistribution, recognition, and Beyond*. New York and London: Routledge.
Mango, A. (1978) *Verso una sociologia del teatro*. Palermo: Celebes Ed.
Meldolesi, C. (1986) Ai confini del teatro e della sociologia, In Rivista *Teatro E Storia*, Vol.1, Annale 1986: 77–151.
Meldolesi, C. (1994) Immaginazione contro emarginazione, In Rivista *Teatro E Storia*, Vol.16, Annale 1994: 41–68.
Merleau-Ponty, M. (1945) *Phénoménologie de la perception*. Paris: Gallimard.
Nietzsche, F. (1977) *La nascita della tragedia*. Milan: Adelphi.
Pareto, V. (1968–1916) *Traité de Sociologie Générale. Oeuvres Complètes*. T. XII. Genève: Droz.
Park, R. E. (1950) *Race and Culture*, III. Glencoe: Free Press.
Privitera, W. (2001) *Sfera Pubblica e Democratizzazione*. Bari: Laterza.
Riccioni, I. (2017) I fondamenti relazionali e sociologici del teatro. In *Rivista Metis*, Vol. XXIV, n.1/2017. Padova: Cluep, 177–200.
Riccioni, I. (2003–2019), *Futurism: anticipating postmodernism. An Essay on Avant-garde Art and Society*. Milan: Mimesis International.
Riccioni, I. (2021) "The Social Turn of Institutions. Contemporary Museums towards Space, Community and Social Discourse". In Polyudova E. (ed.) *Art Museums in Modern Society*. Cambridge: Cambridge Scholars Publisher, 34–55.
Schechner, R. (1988) *Performance Theory*. New York: Routledge.
Schechner, R. (2002) *Performance Studies. An Introduction*. New York: Routledge.
Schutz, A. (1979) Sulle realtà multiple, in *Saggi sociologici*. Torino: Utet.

Shevtsova, M. (2018) *Il teatro politico in Europa. Da Est a Ovest, 2007–2014. Mimesis Journal Scritture Della Performance*, 7,1: 5–23. Available at: https://Journals.Openedition.Org/Mimesis/1255.

Shevtsova, M. (2009) *Sociology of Theatre And Performance*. Verona: Quiedit.

Simmel, G. (1998) *Filosofia dell'attore*. Pisa: ETS.

Sini, C. (2003) *Le arti dinamiche. Filosofia e pedagogia.* Milano: CUEM.

Szondi, P. (1962-2000) *Teoria del dramma moderno. 1880–1950.* Torino: Einaudi.

Tessarolo, M. (a cura di) (2009) *L'arte contemporanea e il suo pubblico. Teorie e ricerche.* Milano: Franco Angeli.

Turner, V. (1979) The Anthropology of Performance. In *Process, Performance and Pilgrimage*. New Delhi: Concept Publishing Company.

Weber, M. (1969) *The Rational and Social Foundations of Music*. Carbondale: Southern Illinois University Press.

Wirth, A. (1985) The Real and the Intented Theatre Audience. In CH. Thomsen (a cura di), *Studien zur Aesthetik des Gegenwartstheater*. Heidelberg: Winter.

CHAPTER 3

Theatre at University as a Way to Increase the Sense

Roberta Paltrinieri

3.1   Introduction[1]

The following reflections have a place within a wider debate on the role of culture and cultural policies in the development of communities. I would like to specifically deal with the role of cultural practices, as an expression of several arts, in social cohesion and the construction of a belonging identity.

In this essay, I would particularly like to consider the role of artistic practices in the process of building a community's social imagination, which translates as the construction of a possible future originating from institutional and political planning, as well as from irrational and linearly sequential practices, which could become both the starting point and purpose behind the action of the collective, politics, and the community in general.

Indeed, this perspective allows us to overcome the juxtaposition between the valorization of cultural heritage in economic terms and its valorization in aesthetic terms, in favour of a method which attributes 'social responsibility to culture' and its protagonists, both from the point of view of the offer, i.e., the cultural production, and the demand, i.e. the fruition of culture, and also of the planning and programming carried out by public administrations.

This essay was specifically inspired by the concrete experience I have gained over the past few years. A journey which began in 2018 and has had to cope with the Covid-19 pandemic, something which has undoubtedly been an accelerator of both processes and practices.

The subject I wish to develop regards the role of the University, which has increased the awareness – through what has been defined as the 'third mission' – of possessing a social responsibility towards the related community.

Reporting its own activities and making the outcomes of research explicit is a fundamental moment for the self-reflexive paths of such complex

---

1   Roberta Paltrinieri (PhD) is Full Professor at the Department of Arts, University of Bologna.

organizations as Universities, but in my opinion, this is just one of the possible strategic goals to be pursued.

Additionally, such complex organizations involve, and are involved in, a constant dialogue with their surrounding community, in a process known as 'public engagement'.

In this perspective, in order to reach a collaborative paradigm, the University itself could be more aware of its role as a stakeholder and of the fact that its actions take place within an innovative ecosystem in which all the possible synergies are increasingly horizontal and have consequences and impacts which require urgent evaluation.

The aim of the Theatre at University as promoted by the Department of Arts which I belong to, and specifically by the experimental laboratory known as DAMSLab does not exclusively study art per se, but reasons on the social function of the arts and, starting from this, seeks to become an activator of practices.

DAMSLab is a laboratory aimed at promoting culture at an urban level. Devised and managed by the Department of Arts of the University of Bologna, DAMSLab's goal is to valorize projects and foster synergies which find the key factor for territorial growth in cultural and artistic production and participation, as well as being a focal point for contemporary and future citizenship. The lab is open to the territory and brings various areas of knowledge into the dialogue. DAMSLab activates and facilitates synergies and collaborations with other departments and with the city, along with its cultural institutions, foundations, businesses, museums and associations, favouring social outcomes in terms of awareness-raising, participation, and cultural mobilization of the urban fabric.

DAMSLab employs a collaborative and participatory method, based on networking and co-planning, in order to develop original ideas and projects which can enhance the whole variety of languages and cultural and artistic forms of production. Both the direct connection with the teaching, research and planning activities of the Department of Arts and its inter-disciplinary character are important pillars of DAMSLab. The main objective is a constant dialogue with the University, the city, public institutions, other players in the artistic field, cultural and creative industries, and various bodies and associations of civil society.

In short, this means that its intrinsic value should not be the only aspect considered, but also, and above all, its investigation of the institutional and social values of culture.

3.2 Artistic Practices and Imagination Processes

In this essay, I have chosen to use the category of practices (Warde, 2005), since this conceptual category attenuates the over-determinism of the structures in favour of a renewed humanism, legitimating creativity, aesthetics, authentic enjoyment and the pursuit of pleasure, not only from a merely hedonistic perspective, but within a broader concept of far-sighted self-interest, or the Aristotelian "good living", in which happiness (Paltrinieri, 2012) is linked not only to a realization of one's own potential growth, but also to the possession of shared values.

Therefore, a *practice* is a space in which a radical form of tension and questioning endures, a space of connection, in which we can escape from immobilism and the isolation of people and things.

Obviously, to understand how artistic practices can form part of an imagination process, we should not forget what it means to invest in culture, in a way that not only examines the economic consequences, but also the social value of culture itself.

For me, investing in culture means getting to know the 'cultural abilities' of people and communities, in the sense of knowledgeability. If we look at Amartya Sen's idea of capability (Sen, 2004) from an anthropological and theoretical point of view, we see that it is the basis for developing a "capacity to aspire" as defined by Arjun Appadurai (2013). This capacity concerns the dimension of the needs, preferences, choices, and even the desires of individuals. This capacity to aspire is not simply a path of empowerment for individuals, but has a social implication, since aspirations belong to communities as a whole.

In summary, aspirations are a real cultural project, a horizon of meaning, a collective aspiration to a better and happier life, interpreted as social wellbeing, which has a precise timing: namely, the future which nourishes the longings of a community.

Imagining the future of a community means placing ourselves between a macro dimension of political and administrative planning and a micro dimension of creativity and pleasure, one summed up in *practices*, more specifically, artistic practices. Cultural welfare, which is a variation of community welfare, and an expression of a welfare society, must be interpreted in this sense. By synergically promoting artistic practices we must also promote co-planning and, in particular, the production of knowledgeability. In this way, the processes of redistribution aspire to increase an awareness of which model of society we wish to belong to.

That aside, by promoting culture in territories, and implementing cultural policies which promote places, spaces, and the cultural offer through potential partnerships between the public and private sectors, via processes of urban regeneration and a circular subsidiarity which does not simply decentralize but also acknowledges legitimacy and delegates widespread power, it is possible to inform real policies of happiness, in other words, social wellbeing throughout a territory.

The production and use of culture is a BES indicator (Fair and Sustainable Welfare) (Sen, Stiglitz and Fitoussi, 2010), a measure of the growth of territories, and today a fundamental element to promote paths of growth of individual and collective skills, supporting social cohesion and participation, trust and social capital, through co-design paths which appear as genuine shared collective actions, through the bridges built between generations and different cultures and religions, at the same time promoting a sustainable model of territorial and community development.

3.3 Perspectives of Cultural Welfare

Consequently, all those who participate in the wellbeing of communities– including universities– also participate in cultural welfare, that is, a community welfare based on two dimensions: the first concerning developments in connecting people, families and territory through the creation of relationships involving generative paths of accountability and a return to the community of the benefits obtained; the second concerning the development of governance models which are also open to unconventional subjects and citizens, to encourage a wider participation and allow a deeper understanding of needs, in order to comprehend even the most intangible fragilities of people.

Cultural Welfare appears to be a possible road towards innovative forms of response to both individual and collective needs.

In particular, we need to acknowledge the importance that cultural, artistic and creative activities and practices have in relation to: paths to promote individual wellbeing and life satisfaction, as well as health, to combat social inequalities and encourage social inclusion, thanks to the capacity that these practices have to foster relations and empowerment processes.

Reasoning in terms of Cultural Welfare means reasoning on the social value of culture while focusing on the impact that culture and the arts have, not only as an intrinsic value strictly linked to the artistic content, but also as an institutional value, one which represents the way cultural organizations behave when they create relationships with different stakeholders and asset holders, thereby strengthening the growth and resilience of local communities.

In cultural welfare, culture and social issues are not separate but coexist in governance processes involving administration of the city, in which such social and cultural spaces as libraries, neighbourhood and health centres as well as local markets express innovative responses to both old and new needs.

Cultural Welfare promotes a new idea of the city, a city which is the result of connections between 'project communities' based on proximity. 'Project communities' are ones created around themes which act as catalysts and become enablers of civil spirit, i.e. a civic sense and participation. This is certainly an innovative way of looking at such artistic practices as the theatre which are extremely important for this urban ecosystem (Manzini, 2021).

The development of knowledgeability opens up the possibility for people to become protagonists of change, to be able to bring new and different meanings to *action*. Given that knowledgeability is not equally distributed, but follows social, economic and cognitive inequalities, a redistribution is necessary. In this vision, it is necessary to rethink cultural consumption not as entertainment, but as a way of increasing a sense of citizenship and civil spirit.

Hence, a model of Cultural Welfare (Fancourt and Finn, 2019) whose salient characteristic is that it is neither 'reparative' nor standardized, but one capable of producing flexible, personalized, and multidimensional responses, a welfare which, by promoting forms of mutuality and sociality, is in itself universalistic.

In summary, Cultural Welfare must promote a truly inclusive and non-exclusive cultural citizenship, in which it is possible to assert the principle that there is no total untranslatability between the different worlds and forms of social life in the panorama of global society.

I do not believe it is easy to remove the many translation difficulties between identity languages and diverse cultures; however, it is the global society itself which these languages and pure cultures inhabit that produces such a complexity that it may even be possible to undertake dialogic relationships.

3.4 Cultural Welfare and Participation

Consequently, what Cultural Welfare needs to aim at is a process to increase and foster cultural participation. Here, the notion of participation refers to a 'maximalist definition of participation'. As Nico Carpentier (2017) has stated, there is a 'minimalist' model of participation linked to delegation, and a maximalist model where participation is bound up with decentralized and multidirectional spaces and decision-making processes. According to Carpentier, the maximalist version of participation is useful to analyse various emerging participatory practices, developed in different social fields, including the symbolic/cultural dimension, the sphere of the media, consumption and cultural enjoyment, as well as other fields of social action. This implies that, from the point of view of the cultural offer, businesses and cultural institutions must be aware that creating an audience – *audience engagement* – is not a decision dictated exclusively by economic return but, as stated in the Symbola report of 2018, "with the intention of producing value by creating more attentive and aware communities". As a result, artistic practices as forms in which cultural production is expressed are phenomenologies of a much deeper and more firmly rooted process than merely the creation of a system designed to stimulate community processes. And this second level of value makes it possible to activate territorial networks and alliances with the aim of encouraging the birth of a real cultural system of communities that can make the impact of the actions promoted sustainable over time.

Participation has been the recurring term in recent years, but it is not simply a question of adopting inclusive attitudes and listening skills with respect to the models of self-sufficiency which have dominated and restricted the work of cultural institutions for some time. Participation derives from the Latin *partem capere*, which means taking charge, taking care of a part of the world.

If this paradigmatic perspective is accepted, then it becomes important to think about some dimensions from which to derive non-economic indicators useful in the evaluation of cultural policies (Matarasso, 1997).

The first dimension concerns the impact on the community of cultural policies aimed at cultural integration. The players involved in cultural welfare processes – from institutions to civil society, to enterprises, including creative and cultural varieties – who act locally through co-planning, partnerships and the implementation of good practices, give life to new meanings of the concept of community. Indeed, they contribute to the creation of an identity of places, spaces, and territories, which must be continually updated because it itself is the result of horizons or panoramas that are constantly changing, producing the updating of a collective memory at a local level which is the result of continuous re-appropriation processes.

The second dimension concerns the 'production of social capital'. In fact, the social innovation which produces cultural welfare is such because it strengthens the social bond, i.e., *relational goods*.

Through partnerships and networks between players who together produce shared value, not only are exchanges between different knowledge and skills achieved, but also the culture of social responsibility is nurtured, and new forms of participation are activated, from which a sense of trust can arise that revitalizes respect for both a territory and its institutions.

The third dimension concerns *sustainability*, a concept to be understood in a far-reaching meaning which takes in the environment, society, and culture itself. Cultural integration is achieved through sustainable actions which redesign spaces and places. Reuse, reutilization and regeneration are all good sustainable practices which are at the centre of projects aiming to produce cultural integration, combined in turn with the ability to field forces which are also heterogeneous and to valorize a territory rather than exploiting it.

The fourth dimension concerns the creation of new audiences and the engagement of different communities, from the perspectives of *audience engagement* and *audience development*. Through cultural integration and the forms this embodies, new audiences and the engagement of new communities are generated, in an awareness that producing new audiences translates as cultural citizenship, or better, capacities and empowerment, by offering opportunities for participation and sharing, and therefore exchange and confrontation, while seeking to avoid conflict and opposition.

Accordingly, cultural participation calls into play an idea of cultural citizenship that is at the same time responsible citizenship, in which an individual who develops the capacity to act cannot call him- or herself a citizen unless he or she in turn feels involved in a collective dynamic which includes an intersubjective dimension in citizenship itself.

Observed in this way, culture becomes an enabling tool for social responsibility and, at the same time, the privileged object of current social responsibility policies, to be understood as everyone's individual responsibility being geared to achieving the common good. In short, cultural welfare must therefore aim to promote a culture of social responsibility.

In point of fact, it can induce modernization and institutional change through political reform or through a redefinition of cultures and organizational practices, given that it produces cultural innovation, favouring the diffusion of models of behaviour and social relations in daily life and in the market.

It feeds the proactivity of the subjects, which implies a willingness on the part of individual citizens to recreate the conditions of their own coexistence. It allows the practice of democracy to become deeply rooted through subsidiarity processes while pluralizing the centres of power, enabling an effective dispersion of such power, which is a guarantee against all forms of totalitarian degeneration.

Clearly, all of this represents a challenge; it entails creating paths of self-reflection for far-sighted administrations, a private sector which adopts the value of responsibility and reaches beyond the dimension of philanthropy, a civil society which ventures beyond self-referentiality to open up to networks and for all those who produce culture, who need to interrogate themselves on the social value of culture, and for the observers of the phenomenon themselves, who in all probability will need interdisciplinary paradigms to interpret the real outcome.

Bibliography

Appadurai, A. (2013) The future as cultural fact: Essays on the global condition. *Rassegna Italiana di Sociologia* 14(4): 649–650.

Carpentier, N. (2017) The Concept of participation: if they have access and interact, do they really participate?. In Musarò, P. and Iannelli, L. (eds) *Performative Citizenship. Public art, urban design, and political participation.* Udine: Mimesis International, 25–49.

Fancourt, D. and Finn, D. (2019) What is the evidence on the role of the arts in improving health and well-being? A scoping review. *WHO Health Evidence Network Synthesis Report.*

Manzini, E. (2021) *Abitare la prossimità: Idee per la città dei 15 minuti.* Milano: Egea.

Manzoli, G. and Paltrinieri, R. (eds) (2022) *Welfare culturale. La dimensione della cultura nei processi di Welfare di Comunità.* Milano: FrancoAngeli.

Matarasso, F. (1997) *Use or Ornament? The social impact of participation in the arts.* Stroud: Comedia.

Paltrinieri, R. (2012) *Felicità responsabile. Il consumo oltre la società dei consumi.* Milano: FrancoAngeli.

Sen, A. (2004) Capability and well-being. In Nussbaum, M. and Sen, A. (eds) *The quality of life.* New York: Routledge, 30–53.

Sen, A., Stiglitz, J. and Fitoussi, J. (2010) *Mismeasuring our lives: why GDP doesn't add up: the report.* New York: New Press: Distributed by Perseus Distribution.

Warde, A. (2005) Consumption and Theories of Practice. *Journal of Consumer Culture* 5(2): 131–153.

CHAPTER 4

Staged Passages between Art and Everyday Life

Gerhard Glüher

4.1   Introduction

Participating in a discussion on contemporary theatre as an art historian and philosopher has the disadvantage of not being an expert on the theory of theatre, but the advantage of being able to add new aspects to the discourses with a differently trained eye.

The following facts have been extensively discussed by art-historical and art-philosophical research and will not be explored further in this paper (Atkins, 2013; Battcock, 1984; Carlson, 1986; Carr, 1993; Dreher, 2001; Fischer-Lichte, 2004; Goldberg, 1998; Schimmel, 1998)

1)   Artists invented the form of 'performance' as a revolt against traditional mechanisms of art institutions and a too rigid concept of art. This is especially true of the 'happenings' and Fluxus actions of the 1960s, but even the Dadaist actions were performed as criticism and provocation.
2)   The majority of performances have the political claim of exposing social grievances.
3)   Performance is seen as a medium of feminist criticism of the male-dominated art system. There are significantly more female artists than male artists in this genre, and the themes of the works are more often gender-related. (Nochlin, 1971; Hess, 1971; Parker, 1987; Pollock, 1996; Battersby, 1989; Butler, 2007; Gabrielle, 2007; Isaak, 1996).

In this text, a distinction is made between the term 'staging', which is assigned to the context of theatre, and 'artistic performance' – hereafter only referred to as performance. This is a form of expression, or a means of expression, that artists use to create works which they realize in space in a temporally defined way through the use of their own and/or other people. Performances may – but do not necessarily – follow a concept or plan. Most of the time there is a participating audience, however, there are performances which are given only for the camera or the textual/written report. As an artwork, each performance is unique, regardless of whether it is repeated in the same or a different location.

In its pure form, the artwork performance is ephemeral and immaterial. The idea or concept lies in the extraction of a particular time-space. In its pure form, the piece survives only in the individual memory of those people who were present. Films, videos, photo series and descriptive texts produced by the performers themselves or by third parties commissioned by them serve as archiving and as aids against forgetting – they can never replace the psychophysical experience of presence.

A methodological note should be made at this point: in many documentations of performances, a wide variety of images gradually appear in publications or on the internet, and it is extremely difficult for art scholars to decide which ones depict actual events and which do not.

4.2 Artistic Performance as a Hybrid Medium

Performance is a hybrid art form which can be more representational or more object-like depending on the concept and type of action. With the inclusion of sound and body movements, it forms a synthesis of visual, sculptural and performing means, thus expanding the expressive possibilities of art. All performers are always also painters, filmmakers, musicians, composers, lyricists, sculptors, etc. who, depending on their intention, use actions to expand and adapt their repertoire of possibilities. Performance is thus also a testing ground for artists, used to open up media boundaries in order to create innovative forms of presentation. The affinity to theatre is already evident in the precursors of performance, the Dada actions which took place on vaudeville stages. The proximity to the concert becomes clear if one only reads the title of the first Fluxus action: "FLUXUS: Internationale Festspiele neuester Musik", and the international Fluxus tour organized by George Maciunas in 1963 was called "Festum Fluxorum Fluxus", with the subtitle "Das Instrumentale Theater" (Sahn, 1970)

Performance was rebellion, but never 'anti-art'. Historically, this process involving curators, institutions, critics and the media opened up the concept of art more and more until it then became an amalgam by the 1980s, at the latest, which to this day takes on many forms which are not immediately recognizable as artistic acts.

One could ask whether, historically, performance developed as a countercurrent or as a physical form of expression of minimal art. For conceptual art, this is a proven fact, because the common logic of the aesthetic concepts was the reduction of forms or their dematerialization, to extend Lucy Lippard's well-known term to ideas, concepts and structures (Lippard, 1997). One could argue that the emptiness of the 'white cube' of the gallery and museum space corresponds to the emptiness of the time period, which is raised to consciousness by the setting of an action. The loud and rebellious Fluxus actions and happenings were certainly a counter-movement to the quiet condensation of conceptual art, but performances in which almost nothing happened are, from a perceptual point of view, on a par with Robert Ryman's white canvases, Donald Judd's aluminium boxes, and Carl André's floor sculptures. *Pars pro toto* for a minimalist action is the "Composition 1960 #7" by the American musician and composer La Monte Young. This work consists of two intoned notes, which is already a tremendous reduction of form, but the interpretation instruction is even more significant. It is: "to be held for a long time". As a realization, this meant, for example, that the artist performed for over five hours in his most famous composition entitled *The Well-Tuned Piano*. One might argue that this example is not a performance, but La Monte Young has been working with his wife, the artist Marian Zazeela, creating light installations for these sound performances. This makes the musical action an environment of time, acting body, and light.

What actually happens in *The Well-Tuned Piano* is the opposite of a spectacle: a man can be seen sitting at the piano and playing extremely long loops, minimal chords, continuous repetitions, slow tempos and everything in a medium pitch for five hours. The performance space is bathed in an indirect magenta or blue light, there are no spotlights, no light movements, no colour value modulations. Duration, or stretched time to be precise, is the real theme of La Monte Young's performances. It is difficult to imagine that participants actually stayed in the rooms for more than five hours. This is attested by reports only for the three-hour performances the artist gave at documenta 5 in Kassel in 1972. Here, the section in which these daily actions were carried out from 3 p.m. to 6 p.m. bore the telling title: *Individual Mythologies: Self-Representation Performances Activities*.[1]

A performance *lasts*, this seems to be a banal statement, but the aspect of time was only a marginally investigated area until the 1980s, mainly because paintings, sculptures, and architecture had no duration that could be measured with an instrument. It was only after the 1985 exhibition entitled *Time – The Fourth Dimension in Art* and the subsequent investigations that this changed. (Baudson, 1985). Time is a constituting factor of performance, because there is no activity without time passing during it. The 'time used' influences the form, the effect, the intensity and the reception of the action to a considerable degree. The traditional genres of the visual arts consist of pictorial or verbal strings and designate surfaces, whereas a performance designates time itself: in other words, it designates a 'piece of time' as an object in infinity, which means

---

1 cf. Exhibition catalogue documenta 5.

that the performance is significant time. Of course, it is also significant for the recipient since he/she goes to the place where it will take place and stays there. This happens for as long as the action lasts, and the recipient understands neither content nor structure if he/she is not present for the entire duration. This is an imperative condition, because he/she cannot come back to look again at an exhibited artefact. Performed time is always *now*, the present, the presence of which can be remembered as fragments, but never the experience as a whole; it is understood spontaneously or reconstructed over time.

Daniel Charles uses the metaphor of the balancing act without a net to describe the uncertain situation of reception:

> Performances and happenings have in common that they evoke alogical situations rather than logical or illogical ones and use 'concrete' objects and materials that are bound to the everyday rather than to abstract symbolizations based on the imaginary. If there is any meaning, one does not know what it is: no associations, no clear configuration of details will dispel the indeterminacy of execution; no network of clues will banish the threat of ambiguity. One works without a net. Nor will one burden the effects achieved by the performers with the causal omnipotence of the author.[2]

There can be no such thing as a 'typical' recipient of performances because one must always assume individual experiences. The variables are too great to be able to establish something like a typology of reception. The interpretations of what reception of a performance is range from collective integration to witnessing, i.e. from detached emotional emphasis to narrative reporting. Nevertheless, when questioning even the analytical witness – should he/she exist purely hypothetically – we must take into account that the testimony is always an individually filtered perception.

The artists' bodies can be joined by objects, spoken or written texts, and any kind of visual or sound medium. All or a single one of these objects can remain as relics at the site of the action after the performance has ended. The function of such objects has been compared in art and media studies with those of cultic and ritual acts, but this is not strictly true, since the context of the performance is not cult but art. It would be just as wrong to treat the objects as props, because the latter cannot be charged symbolically as strongly as has happened with certain performance objects. Possible further fields of association could

---

[2] cf. Charles: 53. Original in German, translation by author.

be explored as well, such as the fetish, the fragment, the witness, the circumstantial, but this text cannot do that. Taking all these possible interpretations into account, it quickly becomes clear that one cannot give universal meanings and terminology to objects of performance, but rather that their function must be interpreted on a case-by-case basis within the respective context of the action and narration. Occasionally, performers do reuse their objects, photographs and video recordings. Such reactivation happens, for example, by using them in other works, or they may even become independent installations in new exhibitions.

In 1970, one of the founders of American conceptual art, Douglas Huebler, wrote a famous statement, dedicated to this art form, but which we could apply to performance art as well: "The world is full of objects, more or less interesting. I do not wish to add any more. I prefer, simply, to state the existence of things in terms of time and/or place." (Lippard, 1997: 74). But how did he reach or realize this conceptual idea? For example, the work with the title *Duration piece No.7* made in 1969, consists of 15 black and white photographs taken at one-minute intervals of "11 geese and an occasional pigeon" milling about a bench in Central Park New York, along with one of his characteristic written statements which explains his activity. (Van Leeuw and Pontégnie, 1997: 123ff).

Another example of quite marginal objects is an exhibition display-case entitled *Ausfegen* (Sweep-out), whose author is Joseph Beuys. The contents of this object originate in an action performed by Beuys on the 1st of May 1972. On this day, a political demonstration took place in Berlin for the 1st of May (Labour Day). Beuys and his students El Loko and Hiroshi Hirose used bright red brooms and a shovel to sweep up all the rubbish in Karl-Marx-Platz immediately after the demonstration.

This rubbish was collected by the students in several plastic carrier bags printed with the phrase "Organisation der Nichtwähler für Freie Volksabstimmung" (Organisation of Non-voters for a Free Popular Vote) and driven in a waiting VW bus to the René Block Gallery. There, Beuys poured the contents of the bags against a wall and arranged individual sheets of paper and the crumpled bags into a pile. He initially placed one of the brooms diagonally on top of the pile, but finally leaned it against the wall next to it. There is a colour film – lasting 26 minutes and 7 seconds – documenting the entire action. The original is in the archives of the Centre Pompidou, New Media Department, with the information that the author is Jürgen Böttcher, since the material was remounted and published in 1988 using Betacam SP and PAL format. El Loko later said in an interview about this action: "The thought material of others was not simply swept off the table, but kept in order to be able to have an ongoing dialogue with it." Beuys himself said in an interview with Keto von Waberer that his intention had been to act against an ideological fixation and a theorization of politics.: "This pure head culture has isolated itself in its intellectualism. Thus, we constantly experience how the head and the heart, and the formation of the will are isolated from each other, the whole human being does not come about."[3]

A fierce legal battle has been going on for two years over this display case of rubbish, because Beuys' widow, who is also his executor, forbids the owner of the work (the Neues Museum in Nuremberg) to exhibit it. The reason is difficult to understand, because the executor of the estate claims that it was not Beuys himself who put the rubbish in the display case or authorized it to be put there, but the gallery owner René Block who did so independently. Thus, the difficult question now arises as to what the actual work is: the display case with rubbish and broom, or just the rubbish without the container – or does it not matter at all for our context because only the performance and the film have any meaning anyway? Beuys often installed the objects of his actions in display cases and the rubbish from *Ausfegen* was also exhibited in exactly this container for years without the objection of the widow – its value, by the way, is €200,000.

Performing artists are not actors and they do not interpret or stage textual models, but always remain themselves, even if they refer to other 'figures' in their actions. One could call this a habitus which holistically conditions being – there are no times of day when the performer is a private person and others when he/she is practising his/her profession as an artist. Therefore, the spectator always sees the performer, not an acted role. In playing respective roles, an actor is practising his/her profession, that is, behaving in such a way that the achievement of the act attains the best possible result within the framework of social conventions and norms, because although his/her work is rewarded with recognition and respect through applause and positive reviews in the daily press and professional journals, it is always also a monetary matter which secures the actor's daily life. When the artist acts as a performer, he/she usually receives a fee for it from the institution where the performance is given, but I do not know any artist who could survive on this work. Performers do not create material 'goods' which can be sold through whatever markets and earn a material income, which is why things are often created out of or related to the performance and then sold on. Similar strategies are pursued with the exploitation and marketing of films, videos, pictures, and texts which are created in or during the performance. With such materials, acceptable

---

3   Richter: 185; (Interview was conducted in 1979).

prices can be achieved, especially if the editions are limited or are unique – the various forms of the so-called 'multiple' are examples of this, but also institutions and archives which lend out videos and films at frighteningly high daily rates – not to mention copyright levies. Despite such procedures for securing an income, one can nevertheless argue that performance cannot be considered professional work since it is not created to order or as a commission with clear specifications, but arises from an artistic 'self-commission', to use a term of Bazon Brock. Its cause is a necessity, an intellectual or emotional drive, the result of which is the action. There is no 'template', i.e. no referential other which already exists and then has to be transferred, implemented, realized, etc.; purely and simply, the artist has the idea for the concept of the performance, he/she is its author. The entirety of the performance lies solely in his/her hands and responsibility, which of course exposes the artist to a high level of psychological and physical strain, but on the other hand also leaves him/her all the freedom of decision. In the person of the artist, the professions of the creator, the author, the director, the curator and the choreographer are united, and in the end he/she himself is the 'object' which is exhibited. How long and how profound the conceptual preparation is or how well the action is performed do not necessarily depend on the duration or frequency of the 'exercise' with which the action is studied and learned, but on the moment in which it takes place. The artist often has to adapt to given situations under great time pressure, given that the spaces in which he/she acts are neither familiar nor provide meaning-bearing aids which can be used to tell the story.

This leads us to the place of performance. The place of performance is not a theatre and the space in which the artist works is not a stage.

Only if the performance is interpreted as a 'staging' can one say that the performer must make every space and every situation his/her stage, but if one assumes that the performer does not act nor play anything, then this construct is invalid. The thesis that the performer 'occupies' a place seems more appropriate. With his/her presence, he/she marks it as a special place where something new is constructed that enables him/her and the participants to gain new insights, at least for the duration of the performance. In a similar way to the selection of objects, the possibilities here are endless, because the living world provides the places – but the artists are also at its mercy. As vulnerable as a place makes the artist, it also stabilizes his/her actions, for it becomes the *platform*, the only foundation he/she has that can bring security and safety should the action get out of control. However, the physical entities which surround him/her are not stage sets, not images at all, but a built or natural space. A performance does not have pre-semanticized spatial constructions as in a theatre to help the audience build the imagery and illusions which the imagination needs to transform a place into a narrative. In contrast to theatre, it is often a hindrance when something is imagined in a performance space. To resist this temptation, artists have used everyday urban places that are open to meaning, such as empty factory floors, barren natural spaces, restaurants, department stores, escalators. Preference is given to places of passage, work, and consumption.

The simultaneous presence of daily life is a method and statement for integrating art into daily life, and even more so for declaring daily life as art.

This was particularly evident in the 1971 action *Organisation für Direkte Demokratie durch Referendum*, a forum for discussion and experimentation that worked towards the realization of a true democracy. This organization was not a theory, Beuys rented a shop in Düsseldorf's city centre, which was occupied daily. The following year he helped to establish the Free International University, which aimed to foster creativity beyond the walls of traditional academia. By then, his political activities and his work as an artist were closely intertwined. He formulated a theory of 'social sculpture', exploring ways in which the creative impulse which shaped a work of art could also influence the world in which we live. He believed that everyone should be involved in this process because we all possess a latent creativity, hence his motto "Everyone is an artist".[4]

The next year, 1972, Beuys moved this office to documenta 5 as his artistic contribution, and discussed social and political issues with visitors on a daily basis during the 100 days of the exhibition, concerning his programme on 'direct democracy'. In comparison with the contributions *Honigpumpe am Arbeitsplatz* (Honey Pump at the Workplace) at documenta 6 and *7000 Eichen* (7000 Oaks) at documenta 8, both of which made explicit sociopolitical and environmental statements, the *Office* was the action which was the most 'non-artistic' and immaterial, because its material was language in daily dialogue. Together with his expanded concept of art and the idea of a 'social sculpture', it becomes clear that Beuys understood all his artistic actions as shaping, shaping people, and the result would be an ideal social European State under guidelines of publicity, freedom, and public utility.

Such actions do not dissolve art, because ever since the 'readymades' of Marcel Duchamp we know that the authorization of the artist is sufficient to make a thing a work of art. It is merely evidence of an expansion of the term 'art'. The title of the famous exhibition "When Attitudes Become Form",

---

4 cf. Tate Modern Gallery London: Joseph Beuys: Actions, Vitrines, Environments; www.tate.org.uk.

curated by Harald Szeemann in 1969 at the Kunsthalle Bern, was a programme for the fact that even such an 'exhibition spectacle' was not a game, but wanted to show publicly that art is a state of mind.[5] With regard to performance, it is remarkable that especially the American artists who had their roots in conceptual art created almost all their works *in situ* two or three days before the opening. Some sent only photos or texts, like Richard Long, who performed his action alone in the mountains. Such a radically new form of exhibition was itself a performative act. It was the staging of a collective performance by artists who had not previously exhibited together. When Germano Celant re-installed this exhibition in Venice in 2013, he was still able to show existing material artefacts, however, the energy of the constructive work in manifold dialogues with a curator, colleagues and museum spaces can no longer be generated with a new staging.[6] *Hic et nunc*, this is an important constituent force of performance and the 'now' cannot be repeated. Every performance is therefore also the result of a rehearsal, whether a particular attitude works or not, because the execution is not a staging.

The question of whether and how an actor has managed to embody the character of a literary model is pointless, because nothing is played in the performance, instead it is a vivid excerpt of the artists' lives lived in this way and not otherwise. However, one might well ask what degree of artificiality this 'shown lifetime' has. The spectrum ranges from happenings in which one is allowed to watch the artists perform everyday actions to highly stylized physical arrangements such as those seen in Gilbert & George. This artist couple transform into a living sculpture when they stand motionless on pedestals for an hour.

This leads us to Laurie Anderson's curious question, "Am I really here or is it art?" This is not an ironic question but a philosophical one, since the author claims that firstly, for an artist, the living world is separate from the art world, and secondly, that the reality of art might irritate self-perception. This fictitious "other art reality" has long been discussed in art theory and aesthetics, but it has been considered outdated since the 1970s at the latest by two currents: first, to detach art from classical institutions; second, to merge participatory artistic processes with the everyday world. But if Anderson meant to say that the self-perception of artists in performance can be different from that in everyday life, then she may well be correct.

---

5 cf. exhibition catalogue *When attitudes become form*, Szeemann, H.
6 cf. exhibition catalogue, Celant, G.

Something will happen: this is the expectation with which a performance is attended. The visitors cannot plan the event, but the probability that something unpredictable will happen is high and this often results in the motivation to expose oneself to a performance.

The performance artist attaches more importance to the "event" of his/her action than does the theatre director or actor. This concentration is justified because when the audience rarely knows what they are going to participate in and the plot is intense, the performer must summon great physical and mental energy to heighten the experience. He achieves this less through the use of violent dramaturgical means – every theatre director does this today (an outstanding example of such a personality being Christoph Schlingensief) – but through immediacy, and the presence of the artists as authentic persons. Gestures, facial expressions, language and movement are also means of expression for the performers, but the consternation of the audience – that is, the emotional depth or the psychological shock – is much more pronounced due to the lack of protection of the fourth wall.

It is in the nature of things when a form of artistic expression that sees itself as a means of agitation takes on emotionally intense forms. The artists are always themselves and an analysis of the following more drastic examples shows that the "border raids" were attacks on morals, ethics, and/or social taboos because they were actually carried out. Masochism, suffering, pain, and disgust are deliberately used to shock an audience.

Günter Brus, a member of the 'Viennese Actionism' movement declared: "All products that man excretes, including excrement, urine and tears should be used, no longer purchased brushes and canvas." What happened during his action entitled *Zerreissprobe* which took place in 1970 in the "Aktionsraum München"

> A man, naked except for panties, silk stockings and suspenders, kneels on a white cloth. He reaches for a razor blade and cuts his thigh. Then he takes a glass, pees into it, and drinks his urine. He strips stark naked, facing away from the audience he slides to the floor, then ties his ankles together. With slow movements, he carves the scalp of his shaven skull with the razor blade. The audience sees the blood running in a line down to his buttocks. Suddenly, the artist jumps up and twists his body in wild rotational movements. He pants excitedly and beats himself. In the end, he gasps and remains as if frozen. (Mießgang, 2018).

The second performance is *Non-Anesthetized Climb* (1971) by Gina Pane. Her feet bare, the artist climbed a ladder whose rungs were studded with sharp metal protrusions, stopping when she could no longer endure the pain. The work was first 'tested' in her studio, with only a small group of friends present, and then in a public gallery. Pane explains her action thus: "My real concern was to constitute a language through this wound that became a sign. Through this wound I tried to convey the loss of energy. For me, physical suffering is not only a personal problem, but a linguistic problem. Inflicting wounds on myself constituted a temporal gesture – a psycho-visual gesture which leaves traces." Finally, the performance *Rufen bis zur Erschöpfung* from 1972, in which Jochen Gerz shouted "Hello" very loudly until his vocal cords failed. The performance took place without an audience but was recorded on black-and-white film stock with a duration of 19 minutes. The fact that no audience was present during this action is due to the intention of the performance, because the senselessness of this lonely call only arises when no other person hears it, and the caller is no longer capable of any vocal communication at the end.[7]

The examples I have just given make it clear that the artist performs such an event as an artistic staging precisely in order to test the conditions and limits of the body. Let us not forget that the central agent of almost every performance is the human body. Violence and passion, dissolution of boundaries and nightmare, standing still and hysterical body choreography – everything can come together in body art pieces which are hard to stomach. The borderline experiences of such experiments must be endured by both the performers and the participants.

4.3 The Mediation of the Ephemeral

The thesis that an event must not proceed according to plan, because it would then at best be a simulation of one, does not exclude the possibility of creating a framework and possibilities which can increase the probability that something will happen under these conditions. The artist exposes him/herself to his/her own conditions created specifically for the performative situation, but only partially controls the stages and the process in the course of performing the actions. Such artistic laboratory situations can lead to the recipients having the impression that nothing happened in the performance or that it had failed. The former should be excluded as a judgement, because even if the artist simply stands still, it is successful: the fact of the performer's presence in a certain place during a certain time can already *be* the performance. A performance

---

7 The film is available as a video file and is in the archives of the ZKM in Karlsruhe.

cannot fail as such, because the apparent failure of an action is a possibility of the set conditions under which the performance takes place. Strictly speaking, only the performer him/herself can decide whether the performance has failed to achieve the desired goal, because it is also possible that the only thing which matters is that the action takes place at all.

One of the most mystical artists of the 20th century was the American James Lee Byars. I found a reference to one of his most minimalist actions quite by chance while reading the book *Why is Landscape Beautiful* by the sociologist Lucius Burckhardt (Burckhardt, 2006). Two black and white photographs are published in it, one a double portrait of the sociologist with the artist and then the artist in one of his typical suits in the mountains. He is standing as a small figure in the picture on a meadow, in direct sunlight, his face bathed in black shadow, in the background, a valley with remnants of snow – it is probably early summer. On this we read the following text by Burckhardt:

> Wearing a golden robe, James Lee Byars dripped a drop of black perfume onto a stone in the rough and stony surroundings of the Furka Pass in 1983. A seemingly senseless action in the storm and between scents of Männertreu and Steinraute. But for those who were there, the landscape of the Furka had changed forever. Through the most minimal of interventions in the landscape, a 'shifting' set in, a transformation of meaning.[8]

If we extract the pseudo-cultic aspect from this action, we are still left with the reception-theoretically exciting question of what the participants could have possibly seen given their distance from the artist? Consider this: it is a drop of a black liquid that is supposed to have fallen in the storm from a bottle or pipette – we don't know – onto a stone in front of the artist. Here, it is already questionable whether the act of dropping could have been seen. But it goes further than that: even if Burckhardt's thesis is correct that the action plus the marking or the signifying act of James Lee Byars had made the landscape more significant, either a material artefact must be perceptible, or it must be possible to tell or read the story of the – let us call it transitory – process. Only those people who see or know that this place, this square of ground, is a prominent one through the acting presence of the artist and that it is not a normal landscape or any other place in a city. This prerequisite is generally valid for action art, and it clarifies the difference from performances in a theatre, because the institution and the apparati – i.e. the context – around and with

---

8   Burckhardt: 16, original in German, translation by author.

the performance are the guarantors that what is performed is per se significant material, or, in Burckhardt's words, that a *shifting* has taken place.

The not particularly exciting action entitled *Inert Gas Series*, which Robert Barry carried out in 1969 far away from people in the Mojave Desert, is only recorded in a few colour photos taken by Barry himself. Alexander Alberro gives the following information on how the action began: "On 3 March 1969, Barry and the patron went to a scientific supply shop and bought one litre of argon and one of krypton, then travelled to an undesignated site and released the gases. The next day the two repeated the procedure, this time with one litre of xenon, on 5 March they released one cubic foot of helium." (Alberro, 2003: 198). A few cubic centimetres of inert gases were released into the atmosphere from commercially available bottles – otherwise the artist did nothing. But let us hear the artist himself speak, how he interprets his work and what the motivations were for this minimanistic action. From an interview with Holger Weh: "The Inert Gas pieces were an attempt to use material – inert gas – which is undetectable, you can't smell it or see it, and use it to create a kind of large environmental sculpture, if you will. It was one of the last works that I did in '69, where I actually used physical material. And so it was a kind of transitional work, in that I was still using material, even though one's understanding of the work and appreciation really had to be totally mental. One would have to use one's imagination."[9]

The show was widely published in the form of a 30 × 45" poster, which Siegelaub mailed to a long list of people and institutions. This was a blank sheet of pure white paper, except for a single line of text in capital letters that ran along the bottom: "ROBERT BARRY / INERT GAS SERIES / HELIUM, NEON, ARGON, KRYPTON, XENON / FROM A MEASURED VOLUME TO INDEFINITE EXPANSION / APRIL 1969 / SETH SIEGELAUB, 6000 SUNSET BOULEVARD, HOLLYWOOD, CALIFORNIA, 90028/213 HO 4-8383". (Alberro, 2003: 118). The address was not a gallery or the curator's private abode, but only a post office box, and when anyone dialled the number they heard a description of the action on a tape.

> Accordingly, Barry's Inert Gas series foregrounded the procedural as much as the innate forces of matter as the determining morphological and structural aspect of sculptural work. Since the inert gas is not only formally unstable but also invisible, the photographs Barry took of the

---

9 ref: http://archives.carre.pagesperso-orange.fr; the original source ot the interview is not indicated; 23. 08. 2021.

site in the Mohave Desert occupied by the gas represented nothing more than desert landscapes. Paradoxically, then, Barry made the photographs to deny the existence of visual evidence. (Alberro, 2003: 118)

As Barry explained to Norvell, "you see, I sort of allow photographs because they sort of prove the point that there was nothing to photograph." (Alberro, 2003: 199)

It should be stressed, however, that Barry did not allow any photographs to be shown at the initial exhibition of the series. Barry tries everything to ensure that nothing material remains of his performances that could be perceived by the senses, and yet he makes a point of ensuring that the message continues to exist as a text and narrative. The end of his strategy could in turn be the beginning of an imaginary play, bringing the discourse full circle in an unpredictable way.

Bibliography

Alberro, A. (2003) *Conceptual Art and the Politics of Publicity*. MIT Press.

Atkins, R. (2013) *A Guide to Contemporary Ideas, Movements, and Buzzwords, 1945 to the present*. Abbeville Press.

Battcock, G. and Nickas, R. (1984) *The Art of Performance: A Critical Anthology*. New York: E. P. Dutton.

Battersby, C. (1989) *Gender and Genius: Towards a Feminist Aesthetic*. Bloomington: Indiana UP.

Baudson, M. (1985) *Zeit – Die vierte Dimension in der Kunst*. Weinheim: VCH Verlagsgesellschaft.

Burckhardt, L. (2006) *Warum ist Landschaft schön? Die Spaziergangswissenschaft*. Berlin: Martin Schmitz Verlag.

Butler, C. and Gabrielle, L. (2007) *WACK! Art and the Feminist Revolution*. Los Angeles.

Carlson, M. (1996) *Performance: A Critical Introduction*. London and New York: Routledge.

Carr, C. (1993) *On Edge: Performance at the End of the Twentieth Century*. Wesleyan: University Press.

Celant, G. (2013) *When Attitudes Become Form Bern 1969 / Venice 2013*. Venice: Fondazione Prada Ca' Corner della Regina.

Charles, D. (1989) *Zeitspielräume. Performance. Musik. Ästhetik*. Berlin: Merve Verlag.

Documenta 5, Exhibition Catalogue (1972). Befragung der Realität – Bildwelten heute. Kassel: documenta GmbH / C. Bertelsmann Verlag.

Dreher, T. (2001) *Performance Art nach 1945. Aktionstheater und Intermedia.* Munich: Fink.

Fischer-Lichte, E. (2004) *Ästhetik des Performativen.* Frankfurt, Edition Suhrkamp.

Goldberg, R. (1998) *Performance: Live Art Since 1960.* New York: Harry N. Abrams.

Isaak, J. A. (1996) *Feminism and Contemporary Art: The revolutionary power of women's laughter.* London: Routledge.

Lippard, Lucy R. (1997) *Six Years: The dematerialization of the art object from 1966 to 1972.* Berkeley and Los Angeles: Univ. of Los Angeles Press.

Mießgang, T. (2018) *Was der Körper so alles hergibt.* Time online, 03 February. Available at (consulted August 2nd 2021): www.zeit.de.

Musée d'Art Moderne (2012) *Fiat Flux. La nébuleuse Fluxus 1962–1978.* Saint Étienne.

Nochlin, L. (1973) Hess, T. (ed.). *Why Have There Been No Great Women Artists?.* New York: Collier.

Nochlin, L. (1971). *Art and Sexual Politics: Why Have There Been No Great Women Artists?* (1971, edited by Thomas B. Hess and Elizabeth C. Baker). New York: Macmillan.

Pollock, G. (1996) *Generations and Geographies in the Visual Arts: Feminist Readings.* London: Routledge.

Parker, R. and Pollock, G. (1987) *Framing Feminism: Art and the Women's Movement 1970–85.* New York: Pandora Press.

Richter, P. (2000) *Mit, neben, gegen. Die Schüler von Joseph Beuys.* Düsseldorf: Richter Verlag.

Sahn, H. (1970) *Happening + Fluxus – Materialien.* Cologne: Kölnischer Kunstverein.

Schimmel, P. (ed.) (1998). *Out of Actions: Between Performance and the Object, 1949–1979.* Los Angeles: Thames & Hudson.

Szeemann, H. (1969). *Live in your head. When Attitudes Become Form.* Bern: Kunsthalle Bern.

Van Leeuw, M. and Pontégnie, A. (1997) *Origin and Destination. Alighiero E. Boetti. Douglas Huebler.* Brussels: La Société des Expositions du Palais des Beaux-Arts.

CHAPTER 5

Urban Environment, Places for Performance
A Groundbreaking Experience: Renato Nicolini and Estate Romana *(1976–1985)*

Raimondo Guarino

5.1   A Performative Turn in Urban History

In August 1976, Renato Nicolini (1942–2012) was appointed Councillor for Culture in the City Council of Rome led by Mayor Giulio Carlo Argan. As a young militant of the Italian Communist Party, he had witnessed the turmoil and transformations within the Italian Left between 1968 and the mid-1970s. As an architect and an architectural historian, he had studied construction sites and projects for Rome by architects and urban planners. With the rise of the Movement of 1977, Nicolini invented a new collective and creative dimension of urban life. At the time, the city was the centre of change, a contended field where the term 'culture' was acquiring a specific and urgent socio-anthropological meaning. Under the young councillor, Rome awoke as a workshop for urban-scale experiments on artistic production in mass culture. His starting point was the critical experience on the fundamental contradictions of building and, more generally, of that field of practices and theories which, in the public sphere, had broken the boundaries between artistic creation, everyday life and political activism. Nicolini was one of the protagonists of a performative turn in urban history. The most distinctive and ambitious of his projects was *Estate Romana* (Roman Summer), a festival which turned a programme of summer entertainment, touristic and festive events into a complex multimedia and transmedia project involving the transformation of places and areas in the territory. This project conveyed an idea of the city that would become a model for Italian and European cities in the following decades. *Estate Romana* began in 1977, towards the end of August, with the first cycle of film projections in the archaeological site of the Basilica of Maxentius. Similar theories and ideas had been developed, and even sectorially experimented with, earlier, from Debord to Fluxus, to European and American interpretations of happenings and street performances (regarding their multiple implications, see Nicolini, 2011; Fava, 2017; Guarino, 2008; 2020). However, mobilization counted more than mere assumptions and intentions. Rallied by Nicolini, movements, associations and

© RAIMONDO GUARINO, 2023 | DOI:10.1163/9789004529816_006

institutions discussed new criteria to locate and plan creative and cultural productions, changing the relationship between centre and periphery, commissions and vocations. The multiplication of presences and languages, and the experiments of 'urban revolution', or 'production of space', to use the Marxian definitions of Henri Lefebvre (1974), generated a new form of festival as a powerful community time and emphasized the categories of the 'ephemeral' and the 'urban wonder' as transforming factors in the uses of public space. At the same time, the effort to implement these ideas had deep, lasting effects on principles and invention in the relationship between local authorities, public resources, and cultural centres. As for the participation of theatre groups, the avant-garde of experimental performance was driven out of alternative scenes, art galleries and the limited but protected world of the underground movements, to intervene directly in the experience of public space.

In the years around 1980, through facts and ideas, an increasing awareness spread of the possibility to change the space of everyday life through interventions and strategies of a collective creation. Nicolini's view on the ephemeral was related to an analysis of the intersection between powers and visions in urban space made by architectural historian Manfredo Tafuri (Tafuri, 1980). Meanwhile, the meaning of 'scene' and 'representation' in the interplays and processes of urban communities was central to the research of theatre historian Ludovico Zorzi (Zorzi, 1977; for urban history and the performative turn, see Guarino, 2019). In a fundamental study by Fabrizio Cruciani, the theatre space was no longer a mere place for performances, but a living dimension of the relationship between theatre people and human communities (Cruciani, 1992). In this perspective, a performance becomes an experiment on contacts, exchanges and conflicts developed and condensed within a shared context. Theatre spaces and places of performance are concrete factors of social history. These insights correspond, directly or implicitly, to the studies on the human environment related to the global process described in *The Fall of Public Man* (Sennett, 1977; 1994). The change in the criteria of analysis and in the material conditions of functional and symbolic behaviour contributed to a radical transformation of that terrain defined as 'public space'.

It is interesting to further explore Nicolini's 'ephemeral city'. In the summer of 1979, as part of a project of *Estate Romana* called *Parco Centrale* (Central Park), the theatre companies of the Roman avant-garde were called to act in the spaces of the *Città del Teatro* (Theatre City), designed and set up by architect Franco Purini in a residential area of the city centre. The extension and reinvention of certain sites prompted theatre groups to experience public spaces through the framework of a complex system of structures modelled on a hypothesis of transformed theatre architecture. *Città del Teatro* appealed to the sensibility and inclinations of the protagonists of the Roman scene, inviting them to adopt a firm position on the sphere of theatre, and engaging them in a profound dialogue between places and identities. This appeal was met by rapid and diverse responses which, in some cases, appeared reluctant. It was an experiment on the perception of performance spaces from the point of view of theatre professionals. On the problematic outcome of that invitation, critic Giuseppe Bartolucci wrote an incisive report, portraying a whole generation, in *Avanguardia alla prova* (Avant-garde to the Test) (Bartolucci, 1981). In the same book, through autobiography and urban anthropology, Nicolini explains the substance and genesis of the ephemeral, and the motives behind the strategy adopted in Rome in 1979. He describes and defines the theory of the "Urban Wonder" through the eyes of an architect who has recreated a living city, going beyond the limits of theatre and architecture.

> The endless game of possibilities of life compared to the poverty of architecture: recognizing 'Wonder' means accepting this limit, its extent, and its contradiction. The Urban Wonder is for me, as an architect, that which is 'beyond' architecture, which cannot be reduced to architecture; for a director or an actor, it could be that which is 'beyond' cinema or theatre. In other words, it is whatever appears to be different from me, something that cannot be limited to professionalism or a job and that leaves the possibilities of cinema, theatre and architecture suspended but open.
> NICOLINI and PURINI, 1981: 67

5.2 From Settings to Settlements: Experiments in Rome

Nicolini's ambitious vision clearly indicated that it was necessary to go beyond the acts and years of his mandate to question the continuity of central issues related to performance and public space. Over the past decades, the relationship between scenes and spaces in Rome has translated Nicolini's legacy into multiple, yet clear, widespread and profound terms.

At the beginning of the 21st century, the directions of research on the spaces in Rome highlight two recognizable processes. As regards the discovery of protected and separated spaces, it is possible to observe and measure how often and for how long abandoned spaces were occupied and revitalized in the name of political antagonism and 'conflict of life models'. One of the numerous episodes that can be ascribed to this process was the occupation of Teatro Valle (2011–2014), which was amplified by the media due to the historical and architectural prestige of a theatre that had been operating since the 18th century. Started in the 1990s, the parabola of settlements and performance projects in social centres has been studied in its peculiar aspects of alternative culture and continuous negotiation between autonomous communities, informal associations and local institutions (Marenzi, 2013). This scenario of tensions and interactions has redefined the substance of public relations.

The strategy of occupations has interacted with another area of practical research: the discovery of alternative routes thanks to the art of walking and the observation of the post-industrial urban and suburban landscape. The former experiences of land art, situationism and anthropological field work inspired a group of architects called *Stalker – Osservatorio Nomade* (Stalker – Nomadic Observatory). Founded in 1995, the Stalker group has carried out a systematic practical, aesthetic and social investigation of the territory of Rome and other European and American cities (Careri, 2002). In 2009, by explicitly referring to and reinventing Nicolini's *Estate Romana*, it created *Primavera Romana* (Roman Spring), a series of excursions exploring the margins and boundaries of the inhabited space marked by the *Grande Raccordo Anulare* (Great Ring Road), the highway which encircles the universe of the city with a visible and multidimensional line. Stalker's *Primavera* originated an individual journey which resulted in the book *Sacro Romano GRA* (Holy Roman Great Ring Road) (2013) by Nicolò Bassetti. This book was loosely adapted by Gianfranco Rosi into a film with almost the same title, *Sacro GRA* (Holy Great Ring Road) (2013), which was awarded a Golden Lion at the Venice International Film Festival. In 2012, a few months before Nicolini's death, Rosi had made the documentary film *Tanti futuri possibili. Un incontro con Nicolini sul raccordo anulare*, (Many Possible Futures. With Renato Nicolini on the Great Ring Road), in which the architect and former councillor talked about and commented on the new horizons of the city.

From the overall dynamics of Roman spaces, characterized by settlements of political antagonism, positions of performing groups and collectives of architects, new synthetic solutions emerged that defined the new horizons of performance as original experiences of appropriations and explorations of common spaces. In the wake of *Primavera Romana*, the project *Mamma Roma* (Mother Rome) by DOM, started in 2014, redefines not only spaces, but also themes and terms of coexistence through long walks and collective meetings, reshaping empty spaces on the borders between known and unknown, public and private, ownership and exclusion (for descriptions of walks and settlements, https://www.casadom.org/about.html).

The events in Rome are emblematic of a significant process which has taken place over the last forty years: from the spaces invented in *Estate Romana*, based on the idea of city and cultural production, to the conflict over autonomous and creative territories and a conscious redefinition of the range of action of artists, performing groups and city communities in the rediscovery and transformation of the limits and values of public spaces.

5.3 Towards a Site-Specific Performative Ecology

Inspired by situationism and Stalker's *Primavera*, with references to the strategies implemented by other creative enterprises, in Italy and elsewhere, the excursions of DOM into urban landscapes reshape mobility, topography, and settlements. The criticism of lifestyles generates different styles of critical intervention: from the experiences of narration and guided exploration of 'ambulatory audiences' (Rimini Protokoll and similar approaches; for the German group Rimini Protokoll, see Schipper, 2021), to the re-enactments of political demonstrations or revisions of popular participation, such as the gatherings of the 'democracy of gesture', invented by choreographer Virgilio Sieni (Palma, 2019).

The whole question of performative research associated with analysis and intervention in the spaces of life requires hypotheses of autonomous sovereignty of the territory involved. The experiences of the Roman spaces cannot be properly understood without shifting attention from the connection between site, physical space, and performance to deeper levels of relationship. The experience of the site-specific performance, in its extent and variety, has left economic, linguistic, historical and social traces (Pearson, 2010; Crisafulli, 2015). It has testified to a constant and objective expansion and a differentiation of the field. Searching for unusual places to create and set a performance in means searching for uncommon places or ways of placing actions in space. By searching for unusual places and actions, it is possible to discover other places and other uses of space. As a result, the perception, knowledge and definition of spaces change. This process increases awareness of the relationship between communities and environments, and among communities within shared environments. Therefore, the issue of the connection between performance practices and shared spaces not only concerns the formulation of languages and economies in symbolic production and cultural consumption, but more directly the conditions of presence and the forms of life. The topography of presences and actions, bodies and thoughts has established local connections between political activism, social invention, and participatory performance (Nield, 2012).

The relationship between environment and performance – the place where the performance happens – has a systemic dimension, on an urban scale and beyond, which accounts for the original contribution of performative cultures and their settlements to the awareness of social practices and the critique of everyday life. It is an extensive, established conceptual framework. The experimentation with the settlements characterizes not only the contents and condensations of creative projects, but also the development and selection of skills and competencies interacting with communities and territories.

Nicolini's experience has shown possibilities and conflicts related to the interaction between the transformation of space and performance cultures and media on an urban scale. In the first decades of the 21st century, it is unimaginable to study performance without studying life forms and, consequently, also assumptions and consequences on the environment, the general economy, and the local and global relationship between biology and techniques. Therefore, it is not possible to neglect the active role and the profound influence of performative practices on an encompassing notion of ecology and on a redefinition of both the common environment and the public sphere.

Bibliography

Bartolucci, G. (1981) *Avanguardia alla prova*. In Nicolini, R. and Purini F.: 47–66.

Bassetti, N. (2013) *Sacro Romano GRA*. Macerata: Quodlibet.

Careri, F. (2002) *Walkscapes. Camminare come pratica estetica*. Turin: Einaudi.

Crisafulli, F. (2015) *Il teatro dei luoghi. Lo spettacolo generato dalla realtà*. Dublin: ArtDigiland.

Cruciani, F. (1992) *Lo spazio del teatro*. Rome-Bari: Laterza.

Fava, F. (2017) *Estate romana. Tempi e pratiche della città effimera*. Macerata: Quodlibet.

Guarino, R. (ed.) (2008) *Teatri luoghi città*. Rome: Officina Edizioni.

Guarino, R. (2019) Storia dello spettacolo, storia delle città. Guarino legge Ventrone. *Storica*, XXIV, 72: 143–152.

Guarino, R. (2020) *Renato Nicolini e Roma. Lo sguardo lungo dell'estate*. In Beronio, D. and Tafuri C. (eds.), *Teatro Akropolis. Testimonianze Ricerca Azioni XI*. Genova: Akropolis Libri, 146–154.

Lefebvre, H. (1974) *La production de l'espace*. Paris: Anthropos.

Marenzi, S. (2013) Teatro, occupazioni e istituzioni. Geografia romana di un decennio. *Teatro e Storia* 34: 229–240.

Nicolini, R. (2011) *Estate romana. 1976–85: un effimero lungo nove anni*. Reggio Calabria: La Città del Sole (1 ed. 1991).

Nicolini, R. and Purini F. (1981) *L'effimero teatrale. Parco centrale. Meraviglioso urbano*. Florence: La casa Usher.

Nield, S. (2012) *Siting People. Power, Protest, and Public Space*. In Birch, A. and Tompkins J. (eds.) *Performing Site-specific Theatre. Politics, Place, Practice*. Houndsmill: Palgrave Macmillan, 219–232.

Palma, M. (2019) *Dizionario minimo del gesto. Corpo, movimento, comunità nella danza di Virgilio Sieni*, Milan: Fondazione Feltrinelli.

Pearson, M. (2010) *Site-Specific Performance*. Basingstoke: Palgrave Macmillan.

Schipper, I. (ed.) (2021) *Rimini Protokoll 2000–2020*. Cologne: Walther König.

Sennett, R. (1977) *The Fall of Public Man*. New York: Knopf.

Sennett, R. (1994) *Flesh and Stone. The Body and the City in Western Civilization*. New York: Norton.

Tafuri, M. (1980) *La sfera e il labirinto. Avanguardie e architettura da Piranesi agli anni '70*. Turin: Einaudi.

Zorzi, L. (1977) *Il teatro e la città. Saggi sulla scena italiana*. Turin: Einaudi.

CHAPTER 6

The Theatre as the Stage of an Elusive Further Society

Mariselda Tessarolo

6.1 Foreword

Art has always had a social character, given that it contributes to showing the various forms through which it can be experienced: architecture, sculpture, painting, dance, poetry, literature, music, and theatre.[1] In choosing theatre, a discrimination is made regarding what has been conceived through writing, along with an architectural form and a representation on stage.

A further characteristic peculiar to this art is that it requires the presence of viewers, not one person at a time but all together – an auditorium, a hall, a tiered seating space, so that the artist can embody a certain character for the audience.[2] The initial core of the theatre was the semi-circular *orchestra* where the chorus performed. The various modifications made to the architectural structure of the theatre have been academic interpretations carried out subsequently, such as those which appeared during the 19th century.[3] They can be regarded as the summary of an experience which, since its beginning, has never been pursued with exactly the same purpose.

In addition, Pierre Francastel foresaw that "we face the same historical reality of a profound change in civilization"[4] (Francastel, 1987: 233). This scholar highlighted that the expression "theatrical space" relates not only to the material container within which the performance takes place, but also to a mindset: the evocation or re-creation by the viewer of an image that was previously in the soul of the author, the director, and the actors; and which ultimately

---

1 The word 'theatre' comes from the Greek *theasthai*, meaning to look at, to watch.
2 In the beginning, spectators would participate directly. Their contribution was slowly reduced to simply clapping, crying, laughing and dissenting.
3 The separation between the hall and the stage dates back to around 1830, when Renaissance theatre made way for another type of theatre (Francastel, 1987).
4 Francastel prophetically said this in 1965, in the first edition of his book, when there was no Internet.

reaches the soul of the audience. "Such a place is imaginary in its essence" (Francastel, 1987: 225).

One of the problems of theatre revolves around the psychological and material distance which exists between the various participants in the performance, the actors and the viewers. Such a problem is mostly down to the fact "that theatre is basically a visual art, and is also an event taking place, not simply a show" (Francastel, 1987: 233). Francastel observed that one of the essential "arguments in contemporary debate is that an imaginary place is necessarily prior to the real place that has to be built" (Francastel, 1987: 225). This does not mean an absence of masterworks to be performed in existing theatres, waiting for more appropriate theatres to be set up. The forms of architecture have always been the forms of the future. Francastel reminds us that it took 300 years to know what a violin should be like and, in the meantime, various instruments were built and works were conceived, imperfect from a theoretical point of view but perfectly effective aesthetically. What he sought to demonstrate is that it is not possible to conceive in advance an instrument (in this case, a theatre) which corresponds to a new system of signification (Francastel, 1987). (In my own opinion, it is practically impossible to know in advance what kind of theatre buildings should be constructed.)

6.2   Theatre as Stage

Theatre is included by Brandi in *astanza* (a pure immaterial presence, disconnected from time) of the linguistic sign related to its being optically delivered, and therefore to *flagranza* (the form of being of the real object which can be perceived). The basic ambiguity of *astanza* had already been noticed in the Greek theatre, since it would mitigate the actor's *flagranza*. For this reason, a detachment was created between audience and stage, and a diction different from common speech was adopted. These requirements grew increasingly stronger until they were reflected in the spatial structure which was intended to contain both the actor and the spectator.

The theatre departs from the novel in the fact that the characters presented on stage, regardless of who they are, do not represent a certain character; rather, each of them is *that* character. The actor, as a human person, conveys his/her being on the scene in the referent of an agent and, as such, is an actor.[5]

---

5   "In theatre, the Titus who existed in Roman history will optically existentialize before the eyes of the viewer, thus giving *flagranza* to the referent's *astanza*" (Brandi, 1975: 216).

This specific quality also seems to be the reason for the primacy of theatre over other arts, since it stems from an obscure intelligence of the very essence of art as a *presence*. "Not even in the figurative arts is presence determined in such an unmistakable and aggressive way as it occurs here, where the physical person in action is ascribed an intentionality as the very *astanza* of the work, while actually being its support" (Brandi, 1975: 217).[6] In theatre, the text fades into the background and what matters is the character acting on stage and the situation in which he/she is acting.

Any art is a sensible form expressing the nature of human feelings, the rhythms and connections, crises and fractures, complexity and richness of what is usually called a person's "inner life", the flow of direct experience, life as it is perceived by a living being (Langer, 1957: 19). Each art has an 'import', i.e. an effect corresponding to its essential characteristic. In fact, Susanne Langer talked about a virtual space for the plastic arts: the import of sculpture is its virtual kinetic volume, that of painting virtual space, that of architecture the ethnic sphere, that of music virtual time, that of dance virtual power and that of poetry virtual life. As regards narration, Langer separated the dramatic illusion of tragedy from the comical rhythm of comedy.

Oddly enough, she made no distinction between theatre and narration, since any narrative writing is *poesis* and, as long as it operates with words only, it creates the same illusion, meaning a "virtual memory" or "history in the mode of an experienced past" (Langer, 1965: 307). Langer dealt with narrative in prose and therefore with the theatre almost incidentally when she observed that a character stands in front of us as a consistent whole. What applies to characters also applies to their situations: both are made visible on the stage, transparent and complete – unlike their counterparts in the "real" world (Langer: 340).

6.3 The Advent of Technology: Cinema

The arts have always used technique to find new forms of expression. Nonetheless, the technical reproduction of works of art is something relatively new, following the discoveries of the last two centuries whose impact on social life has been felt in numerous areas. Photography is one of the most relevant technologies and closest to us, followed by cinema, which originates from a

---

6 "Theatre sees the primacy of character and plot, as compared with the text. This is what made Commedia dell'Arte possible" (Brandi, 1975: 217).

series of images in motion. The film spectator's point of view moves with the camera. A story that is being told does not require a radical 'break' in order to become a cinematic apparition because, unlike the theatre, it does not have an intended spatial structure. The reality that is dreamed of on the screen can go forward as well as backward because it is in reality a virtual present. Instead, the action of drama goes forward since it is creating a future: the dream mode is an endless present.[7]

What audiences seek at the cinema nowadays was previously found at the theatre, for a number of generations. However, locating the audience and actors within the same space does not solve the problem of renewing the communication. It may be a medium, but communication depends on the container as much as on its imaginary contents. The container, i.e. the instrument, provides a solution only with contacts which are effectively generated. "With the emotion engendered in the audience, cinema does not really foster the community of presence but rather the community of the imaginary" (Francastel, 1987: 230).

The performance of a cinema actor is never unitary, given that it consists of a number of single performances (shots and frames) which are then edited. Close-ups expand the space and shed light on completely new structural formations of matter; slow motion lets almost supernatural flowing movements appear (Benjamin, 1998). Slow motion dilates movement, showing that there is a different nature appearing to the camera from that appearing to the eye.[8] Television shooting shows us things we do not normally see in our daily life: one example is a singer's throat shot with a movie camera, and thus a video shooting technique. The essential distance between the stage and the viewer is not respected, and this signifies a very different point of view between the two arts.

The cinema's technical structure is complete and does not undergo any variation in relation to the presence or absence of an audience. In theatre, the co-presence of the audience within the same space constitutes the dialectics of the process underway (Riccioni, 2020: 20). Unlike the artistic performance of a theatre interpreter, who acts on stage in person at that moment, in cinema an actor's performance is taking place on a screen through the projection of edited material, chosen from footage of the various scenes which have been edited to make the final cut of the movie.

---

[7] This accurate observation is by Susanne Langer and appears in the appendix to her book *Feeling and Form* (1992: 451). The author identifies the primary illusion of cinema, i.e. its import, as "virtual life".

[8] The pre-industrial perception of depth was already lost with train travel, since speed makes near objects volatilize (Schivelbrusch W.,1988).

In his book *Dentro lo sguardo* (literally, Within the gaze), Francesco Casetti shows how a film constructs its spectators, fixing a place for them and leading them along a pathway.[9] The viewer is regarded as an accomplice of what is moving on the screen, and is called upon to follow the plot's threads (Casetti, 1986: 15). If we consider the separation between screen and auditorium, we cannot speak in terms of text and interlocutor. This situation also applies to all spatial or temporal mass media. The viewer, however, does not enter the field 'unarmed', but actively contributes to building what belongs to the screen with conscious engagement, watching and taking responsibility. Like the reader of a text, the spectator is compelled to make a reasonable choice at every moment in the 'narrative woods'. There are two possible ways of being a reader or viewer: the model reader of a story is not an empirical reader. The latter is one who is actually reading a text (or watching a film): there is no right or wrong way to read or watch. If there is something wrong, it is not related to the model reader, meaning the typical reader the writer or director had in mind, and whom the text or film requires as a collaborator capable of playing the tale's game (Eco, 1997). All filmed material, whether for cinema and video, is enjoyed by a single viewer (on DVD, a computer, YouTube, etc.) as well as by an audience in a cinema, at home, or elsewhere.[10]

6.4 Performative Arts

In the current age, we are witnessing the condensation of diverse arts which utilize technology. In particular, this is true of the technology relating to video filming. This is very important because besides being conservational[11] it has developed, concurrently with the advent of the Internet, a series of new forms to present the same arts. We are also witnessing the need to narrate/represent for an audience who are fragmented by television media and the Internet. The possibilities offered by the current technological instruments are leading to technical experimentation in every area. Many scholars have found that new electronic media face the need to serialize and gather the performances of

---

9 The points of view identified by Casetti F. are: the objective shot, the interpellation, the subjective shot (seeing with you, and you are aware of it) and the unreal objective shot (from above).
10 A subscription to Netflix gives access to a streaming service offering a wide variety of TV series without commercials.
11 'Conservational' means that it can always be reproduced as a non-performative art, but in a very similar way to autographic art.

multiple arts, especially allographic ones, in the concept of performance.[12] Laura Gemini has studied the basic mechanisms and taken the notion of "actual" from Richard Schechner (1984), who distinguished performative events based on the common features of different performances. However, not all performative arts can be transferred onto the 'electronic stage', where the relational dynamics are no longer of the 'face-to-face' type. Theatre, ballet, opera and concert cannot disregard the physical co-presence of participants, nor the presence of actors (musicians, dancers) and spectators in the same location. The reception of each art has its own specific and autonomous construction of meaning, and the new forms of arts that are appearing will certainly find a space of their own, suitable for their particular *astanza*.[13] Arts which require the presence of an audience and can also be recorded will live a double life, one on the stage in the presence of the audience, and another on various screens or displays in the presence of viewers.

Collective practices include not only the allographic arts which need to be performed (and are therefore performative), but also ludic festive practices belonging to popular tradition. These, however, may not be considered artistic practices.[14] For Richard Schechner (1984), every form of social action is a "performance"; and in the visual society it integrates a significant and communicative form connected with the form of action being enacted. The time of a performance is the subjunctive mood of dreaming, 'as if'. It is transformed into an indicative mood by the performance, when it becomes the 'is' of the body's action. But this means that a theatrical piece, when filmed, no longer has the characteristics of presence, contact with the audience, and the actor's spontaneity. When filmed, it will always be the same as itself: an eternal present, just like a movie, from which it does not differ.[15] Arguably, modernity – among other things – means an exaltation of what Victor Turner called "culture's indicative mood" (Turner, 2014: 141), although some see a return to the subjunctive mood in the postmodern.

---

12 The etymology of 'performance', as is the case for many other English words, dates to the ancient French *parformer* which, in turn, has its roots in the Latin *performare*: to give form, complete or accomplish. A performance is therefore the suitable completion of an experience.
13 Over time, these new genres will each be defined by a specific name.
14 Social theatre could be discussed, in which different forms of active citizenship, social responsibility, ideation and activation are tried out. In order to be considered "theatre", though, it ought to fulfill the requirements described so far.
15 However, the filming of a theatre piece with a camera is not based on editing but on a continuity of filming.

6.5   Serialization and Target Viewers of Works

With all the tools specifically prepared for 'narrating', it has become necessary to continue a certain tale with further events, the story of other characters, etc. Life itself unfolds through many tales. Popular literature had already explored the publishing of novels in instalments with the *feuilleton* (also by major authors).[16]

Besides the advancement in technology leading to the creation of such 'new' arts as cinema, video filming also covers all the arts that need to be performed.[17] Music needs a composer and a performer (alone or in an orchestra); dance needs music, choreography and dancers; finally, the theatre needs a writer, a director and actors. The public is an element that all forms of art need: performative arts certainly need an audience if a performance is taking place live, meaning 'in the viewers' presence'. However, if we consider purely technological instruments, performances can be recorded and broadcast using a variety of means.[18]

The theatre may be closer to life than most other performative genres since, in spite of its conventions and the spatial limitations of its physical possibilities, "it is literature that walks, and talks before our eyes". It is meant to be acted, not as marks on paper to be perceived by our eyes, but as sights, sounds and actions occurring physically on a stage (Boulton, 1971: 3). The data of experience themselves enclose a 'tendency to a form', and the task of thinking is to develop a 'natural understanding' inherent to every unit of observable experience. Needless to say, knowledge is a key aspect, an important dimension for any structure of lived experience, but it is steeped in sentiment and willpower, which are sources of value judgements and norms, respectively.

Every type of artistic performance, including theatre, is an explication of life itself. Wilhelm Dilthey (1999) agreed with R. Schechner in considering performance as attributable to a personal experience which is "pressed or squeezed out" during the performative action. Therefore, what remains hermetically sealed in normal conditions and inaccessible to observation and daily thinking, is experienced directly by a playwright or poet.

---

16   Dostoevsky's novel *Crime and Punishment* was originally published in monthly instalments in 1866. See also Tessarolo (2016[a]).
17   Following Goodman's theory (1976) of allographic and autographic arts. The latter, once completed, are autonomous and no longer need execution: painting, sculpture and architecture.
18   Technological video filming can also concern autographic arts: remote guided visits, for example, at museums which offer the audience this type of service.

In the Web 2.0, where consumers of information are not distinguished from consumers of entertainment, both participate in the production and distribution forms developed and led by a driver: the cultural convergence of mainstream media and bottom-up conversations. "[This] is a state of connection that creates a mediatized environment of culture, whose change involves a non-dichotomous and non-confrontational logic" (Boccia Artieri, 2012: 12). The connection could allow creativity, but maybe not greater creativity since it is increasingly difficult to emerge and become known, regardless of the thousands of followers one might have.

In artistic communication, the target viewer of a concert, theatre piece, etc., recreates the composer's or author's experience to a degree, not only as an expression of their musical or narrative thinking, but also as a communication project cutting across different times. The activities of acting, making music, and listening, occur in a time dimension which is external to the individual, while the experience of sharing an event occurs in the irreversible direction of inner time, involving the recalling of a flow of memories, tendencies and anticipations for both the artist (actor or musician) and the recipient. The performer or actor generally stands as an intermediator between the artist (composer, writer, etc.) and the listener/viewer.

A prerequisite of all human communication is the mutual attunement that is established in the relationship and implies varying degrees of immediacy (Schütz, 2015). The "We" constructed with the experience of interpersonal communication allows the "I" to meet the "You", leading to meaning being shared and perspectives being brought closer. In all performances, the author, director, actors and viewers together pursue the making of sense, each with their own sensibility (Barba and Savarese 1996: 256).

All arts refer to a universe of meanings which become intersubjective. Nonetheless, no dialogic relation can generate meanings that are totally shared, given that the levelling of differences would entail a levelling of people (Tessarolo, 2021). An adjustment to social expectations never occurs in a complete manner; some leeway for irregularity always remains in the enactment of roles and is socially accepted. It reveals the compensation due to the individual's subjectivity and the different contemporaneity of events and generations. The individual always and necessarily absorbs, in the structure of their self, the general model of experience and activity that is expressed in the social life of the specific historical time in which he or she is living. This is precisely where the difference between generations lies, and therefore between the different historical and current pasts. The study of society is the study of social change: society is tendentially centripetal and demands balance and homologation of the individual to the rules. But such a desire for stability clashes with the centrifugal forces coming from the individual, who adapts poorly to homologation (Tessarolo, 2012).

Between artwork and user, a space opens up concerning the interpretative effort by the user. This is due to the fact that 'new pathways' open with each fruition, keeping the process of image construction ongoing. Over time, different users (but also the same user at different times), will understand and interpret things in ways that differ from previous occasions (Iser, 1987; Tessarolo, 2021). In spite of an artwork's variability, its materiality remains the same and it traverses time as it is.[19] This can take place because the typification of social relations undergoes a continuous transformation due to the instability of purposes and the orientation of subjects towards the purposes. In turn, the change in orientation among actors has led to an inconstancy of tastes and a fluctuation of audiences.

Theatre performance is based on a ritual process and participative dynamics. It materializes as an artistic presentation, bringing continuous renewal by adjusting to interactional and interactive multimedia spectacularization.[20] Gemini has observed that the communication pathways of theatre performances, starting from the historical avant-gardes, were able to shake up art's social system as well as middle-class sensibilities. Nowadays, any performance can be thought of as a product and therefore reproduced on video and rendered an object, like a painting or a statue: in this case, the director of the video will be the co-author alongside the author of the theatre piece. Creating means projecting into the future, being bold and going against a pre-established order, but with the aim of pointing to a new way, a new order. There is an ability to transform, to bring 'form' to a new order in which other people, aside from the individual who is the creator, can recognize themselves (Mclucci, 1994: 29). What Gemini has called the "game of uncertainty" is in fact humankind's condition in the world, the contingency of what is modern, where everything is presented at the same time as not necessary nor impossible. It is the character of social complexity, paradoxically multiplied by the spreading of cognitive artefacts which originated with the purpose of reducing it (Gemini, 2020: 15).

---

19 This is much more so in the autographic or presentational arts than in allographic or non-presentational arts. The former are less affected by the passing of time. Even though painting, for example, eliminated the obligation to imitate reality and offered the avant-gardes the possibility of taking action (as in Expressionism, Futurism, Cubism, etc.), sculpture also followed the path of painting but took a different turn (e.g. Henry Moore or Giuliano Vangi, to name but a couple). Finally, modern architecture, which is offering large cities around the world a futuristic look through new materials and technologies.
20 Starting from the orthodox form of Greek theatre, to the current forms of experience: body-art, happenings, to video and on-line performances (Gemini, 2020).

6.6 Conclusions

Language can be understood from two different standpoints. Firstly, in interpersonal communication, as a 'primary orality' based on a co-participation of speaker and listener face-to-face, where communication is performed on the memory of an unwritten narration. We can also speak of 'secondary orality' when written texts are involved. This second mode of language stands at a more complex level of communication since the sender becomes an 'author' who transforms the narrative material, with the support of an instrument, into works and texts which, in turn, take on a life of their own. If an action of decoding is not performed, we cannot speak of communication as such, but rather 'social memory'. The author may be absent, have lived centuries ago and, at any rate, have no relation with the reader-interpreter: the product (text) is sufficient for communication to occur.

Time is virtually non-existent in a linguistic act, while it is required in writing, so much so that writing has a value starting from the moment when it is performed. Unlike dialogue, writing is not interactive in interpersonal communication. A written dialogue, even more than an actual dialogue, expects the single listener to incarnate the universal audience. In art, therefore, a channel is not used to make the message known, but instead identifies with the artwork, thereby becoming a message. The overlaying of form and channel leads to the function of symbolic consumption, which in turn leads to the communicative function being reflected on itself. The ability to produce (poietic) has no communicative function, but is mostly organizational. Which is why a work of art does not say more than what it is, and is contemplated or interpreted by the viewer when reading or enjoying it (aesthesic function). For storytelling and other forms of fabulation, creating is a collective fact and is in any case understood and performed for a viewer who is actually present.

Like every art that needs to be performed, what the artist creates is not automatically visible – and therefore intelligible – but is proposed as "something" that is to be staged from time to time, and thus re-elaborated.[21] Live theatre (or theatrical theatre) is personally re-elaborated by the person who acts (by each single actor, by all the actors together, with the assistance of a director who offers/discusses the scenes and the acting). It is the actor who creates the theatrical moment; and since as an actor the person is limited in time, he/she uses the text as an instrument to accomplish the work within his or her specific contemporaneity. The text is always contemporary relative to the reader

---

21   What is mentioned for the theatre applies to concerts and other performative arts as well.

or actor, because contemporaneity lies midway between the past (no longer) and the future (not yet). It is something elusive that moves with humankind, "because it concerns a sphere that is infinitely broader than the individual person" (Duvignaud, 1969: 11).

Reflecting on art leads to staging certain ways of building a conscious contemporaneity. Each art renews itself through successive eliminations, with fragmentary transformations which will allow the system to be rebuilt little by little – and only in the future. However, the system will never be sufficient or complete. If we already knew of such a system, it would be incommunicable: what we expect from an artist is their involvement, participation in an experience, and not merely the creation of museum pieces (Francastel, 1987; Tessarolo, 2021). Every society provides and allows room for movement within the cultural and social order, since this is useful for maintaining a partial indeterminacy which has taken on great importance nowadays. Art is, from time to time, a mode of understanding and a mode of action that distinguishes the entire experience. It conforms to a material and symbolic activity that processes original objects, and through such objects it shows a historical and social reality which nonetheless expresses an individual sensibility (Francastel, 1987).

Theatre moves forward with its own plots, but what will be staged tomorrow is going to be understood, followed, and recomposed – predictably or unpredictably – by an audience who will be participating as a "future community". The previous audience will have contributed to the birth and progress of the later audience, with new interpretations, thus allowing the "social substance" to crystallize (Duvignaud, 1969: 14). "The imagination is much more than the imaginary, it embraces the entire existence of man, at all levels: we participate through the symbols offered to a potential society that lies beyond our grasp" (Duvignaud, 1969: 12). The expression "beyond our grasp" defines the moment when we think we understand, but our understanding is whole and profound, personal and subjective. The fact of being "in-between" is a situation which confuses us or prevents us from understanding what, and how much, we share with that future invisible community. The interstitial dimension[22] is by definition a dynamic and centrifugal space.

A work of art has the capability of recomposing the fragments of a divided humanity – not a vague and absurd idea of humankind, but a participation, in a viable communication, where our freedom can find its place. Furthermore, "the artist seemingly includes in their work an invisible community, the

---

22   The dimension 'in-between' or 'interstitial' is discussed by Merleau Ponty, M., 1989 and Hannerz, U., 2001.

spirit of society, in which this social substance is crystallized, an authentic 'mana' which makes the weft of our future existence" (Duvignaud, 1969: 11). This grants us the possibility to consider those who came before us and their interpretations.

In contemporary sociology, collective action recedes in favour of mass individual action. So we witness the progressive disappearance of the collective phenomenon in favour of a private reality which has been transforming and moving onto digital platforms; social networks emerge as and continue to be communities marked by individuality. In this panorama, the theatre – similarly to the museum – takes on a novel functionality (Riccioni, 2020). The eye of the theatre viewer has a complex cinematic and television background, allowing that viewer to choose the theatre, whether live or recorded – and the theatre may well be the art which, more than the other arts, can continually establish a relationship with current social forms (Abruzzese, 2017).

Our contemporaneity shows that artists are indeed our contemporaries given that, as such, they can see into the darkest corners of our time (Agamben, 2008). The artist of our time has to live on credit, because the practice brought to life by their creative action may not yet be recognized, not even in its aesthetic value. Posterity will be the judge.[23] "That uncertainty also affects the viewers who find themselves not understanding, but intuiting that something is different there and has brokwn with the past; and such a break may well prove problematic since it is both wished for and rejected at the same time" (Tessarolo, 2016[b]: 211).

Bibliography

Abruzzese, A. (2017) *Il dispositivo segreto. La scena tra sperimentazione e consumi di massa. Scritti teatrali (1975–1980)*, A. Amendola, V. Del Gaudio (eds). Milan: Meltemi.

Agamben, G. (2008) *Cos'è il contemporaneo?* Milan: Nottetempo.

Barba, E., Savarese, N. (1996), *The secret art of the actor. Theatrical Anthropology Dictionary*. Lecce: Argo.

Benjamin, W. (1998) *L'opera d'arte nell'epoca della sua riproducibilità tecnica*. Turin: Einaudi.

---

[23] There are examples in musical history. For instance, Bach was only remembered by the public for 50 years following his death. Vivaldi, during his life, struggled a great deal because of his music (music which Bach greatly appreciated), died abroad in 1739, and was only re-discovered by chance in 1945, two centuries after his death.

Boccia Artieri, G. (2012) *Stati di connessione*. Milan: FrancoAngeli.
Boulton, M. (1971). *The anatomy of drama*. London: Routledge and Kegan Paul.
Brandi, C. (1975) *Teoria generale della critica*. Turin: Einaudi.
Casetti, F. (1986) *Dentro lo sguardo. Il film e il suo spettatore*. Milan: Bompiani.
De Matteis, S. (1986) *Introduzione a Victor Turner, Dal rito al teatro*. Bologna: Il Mulino, 7–23.
Dilthey, W. (1999) *Esperienza vissuta e poesia*. Genova: Il Nuovo Melangolo.
Duvignaud, J. (1969) *Sociologia dell'arte*. Bologna: il Mulino.
Eco, U. (1997) *Lector in fabula*. Milan: Bompiani.
Francastel, P. (1987) *Guardare il teatro*. Bologna: il Mulino.
Goodman, N. (1976) *I linguaggi dell'arte*. Milan: Il saggiatore.
Gemini, L. (2020) *L'incertezza creativa*. Milan: FrancoAngeli.
Hannerz, U. (2001) *Diversità culturale*. Bologna: il Mulino.
Iser, W. (1987) *L'atto di lettura*. Bologna: il Mulino.
Langer, S. (1957) *Problemi dell'arte*. Milan: Il Saggiatore.
Langer, S. (1992) *Sentimento e forma*. Milan: Feltrinelli.
Melucci, A. (1994) *Passaggio d'epoca, il futuro è adesso*. Milan: Feltrinelli.
Merleau-Ponty, M. (1989) L'occhio e lo spirito. Milan: SEI.
Riccioni, I. (2020) *Teatro e società: il caso dello Stabile di Bolzano*. Rome: Carocci.
Schechner, R. (1984) *La teoria della performance*. Rome: Bulzoni.
Schivelbrusch, W. (1988). *Storia dei viaggi in ferrovia*. Turin: Einaudi.
Schütz, A. (2015) *Fare musica insieme. Uno studio sulle relazioni sociali*. Rome: Armando.
Tessarolo, M. (2012) L'arte come comunicazione tra individuo e società. In Farneti A. and Riccioni I., eds, Arte, psiche e società. Rome: Carocci, 44–52.
Tessarolo, M. (2016[a]) Seriality and globalization of fairy tale narratives in postmodern culture, 1–22. E. Polyudova, (ed.), *Once Upon a Time in the contemporary World. Modern vision of old Stories*. Newcaste Upon Tyne, UK: Cambridge Scholars Publishing.
Tessarolo, M. (2016[b]) La creatività e l'innovazione come collegamento tra artista e pubblico. *Cambio. Rivista sulle trasformazioni sociali* VI, 12: 203–214.
Tessarolo, M. (2021) *Artist and Public in Non-representational Arts: Collaborative Aspects*. Învăţământ, Cercetare, Creaţie Vol. 7 (1): 537–545.
Turner, V. (1986) *Dal rito al teatro*. Bologna: Il Mulino.
Turner, V. (1993) *Antropologia della performance*. Bologna: il Mulino.
Turner, V. (2014) *Antropologia dell'esperienza*. Bologna: il Mulino.

CHAPTER 7

Paris and Popular Theatre in Robert Michels

La foule *and the Audience in the Years of Classical Sociology*

Raffaele Federici

7.1   Michels Rediscovered[1]

As a classical exponent of sociological thought, Robert Michels is a complex, challenging, and arguably outmoded author, in whom it is always possible to measure some interpretations of modernity and see how some of these interpretations and feelings still seem to flow in the never-ending definition of sociology as an autonomous science.

This Rhenish author still challenges the contemporary reader, his words and reflections continually adding words, drawing on an endless quest which constituted an impendent system and field of inquiry. For him, comprehension of the complexity of human behaviour arose out of the complexity of a boundless knowledge. Michels offered dense suggestions which are still useful in the general contemporary impoverishment of expression; of course we sometimes face some "hostility to the study of the sociological classics" (Turner, 1999: 8) but Michels, who loved "no-man's lands, in the place of great road junctions, where sciences, ideas, parties and people meet mix and enrich each other" (Einaudi, 1936: 74–75) can be a solid help in understanding the complexity of the contemporary world.

I began reading and studying Michels many years ago, almost by chance, with an approach which began from a heterodox anthology edited by the author in 1934, in which many significant writings of Labriola, Loria, Marx, Pareto, Simmel, Sombart and Weber had been collected, accompanied by an essay which was almost heretical for the dominant mainstream of that time. In these writings, which manifest a certain intellectual courage, and above all, a great attention to detail, Michels gave his readers the opportunity to compare the links of economic theory with certain social facts (Michels, 1934: IX). For Michels, the interpretation of social facts as social and cultural events also underwent a meticulous analysis aimed at building an idea of their internal

---

1   Raffaele Federici, Department of Civil and Environmental Engineering, University of Perugia.

mechanism and the implications that they can cause and provoke. A challenge which Michels did not limit to his writings on political sociology or economic theory, but also to the sociology of arts, architecture, urban planning, theatre, music and popular song.

He was unquestionably a complex author, a supreme example of elitism in action (Tuccari, 2012: 55–84), who crossed different paths with a sensitivity which was often not easy to read but remained intriguing also from a contemporary perspective and of a specific scientific interest. And this latter aspect is the more interesting: a challenge for every single word which a sociologist might employ, even within the status of knowledge of the sociology of theatre.

Within this frame, Michels's intellectual adventure can be understood against the background of a rich and complex biography, at times even contradictory, involved in a network of economic, political and cultural interests, all designated differently: a truly cosmopolitan critic. And, as often happens in such complex cases, numerous interpretations have arisen around the motivation of Michels' thought which, in the end, risks complicating the figure of the author himself, leaving an unresolved image. And then there were Michels' many masters, including Pareto, Weber, Sorel, Labriola, Lagardelle, who affected his life with different emphases, different specificities, different telluric strengths. Above all else, and this is the period on which much of my research has focused, his observations on the dynamism and complexity of many European cities was a source of continuous analysis for an understanding of architecture, urban planning, and any forms of social aggregation within the metropolitan space, and, within these spaces, which forms were visible, in an almost Simmelian sense. Let me recall here that Michels was well acquainted with Simmel's works and maintained a close correspondence with both Simmel's wife, Gertrude, and Simmel's publisher (Michels, 1934: XXXIII–XLI). These observations were both structural and interpretative, and in them he analysed a series of direct experiences in which his own *Zeitgeist* as a wandering cleric converged with his being "the most cosmopolitan of the main intellectuals of the 20th century ..." (Stuart Hughes, 1958: 252).

However, it is not easy to fully understand the meaning of Michels' work, nor to try and unravel the contradictions and ambivalence, without referring to his intellectual profile. A historian, economist or sociologist, three vocations are perhaps too many, it would be better to call him a sociologist, as Giuseppe Braguier Pacini did in memory of another author regarded as outmoded: Sombart (Sapori, 1944: 18), a sociologist with a complex cultural background, as suggested by his niece Maria Costanza Gallino, the daughter of Daisy Michels; that Daisy who, for two years from 1927 to 1929, worked at the

League of Nations in Geneva in a biographical path which seems straight out of a Thomas Mann novel.

In 1936, Dino Camavitto insisted on his purely sociological attitude:

> Robert Michels, it may be said, was a sociologist by virtue of his temperament. His intuitive character made him a stranger to and an enemy of *Homo Economicus*. He never had faith in the economic sciences, and this lack of faith is well illustrated in his numerous writings. It is especially marked in his *Economia e Felicità*, where he refuses to believe that the economic and spiritual welfare of a people are related. He points out that *Homo Economicus* is not only an abstraction but also an absurdity that in no way corresponds to reality. Michels did not trade economics for sociology; he was always a sociologist. He believed it impossible to reduce the complexity of human phenomena to theories or systematization. He was neither an organismic nor a mechanistic interpreter of human conduct. If Robert Michels had a theory regarding social phenomena, it was that human behaviour, especially in its collective manifestations, is derived from a multiplicity of factors. To consider this behaviour from a predetermined point of view would result in particularism and categorical synthesis. This attitude of Michels was not based on scepticism, for scepticism had no place in his exuberant spirit. In fact, he was moved by his intuition and, to a degree, by his conscience, to concede to spiritual and idealistic factors an important place in his conceptual structure. This made him refuse to construct a reality in which the dominant place was occupied by an enigma of human relations. He was convinced that it is necessary to approach the study of social phenomena with a sense of modesty and understanding. In order to describe phenomena it is necessary to feel them. He was not interested in the evaluation of social phenomena but in understanding them. Knowledge of Michels' life makes it understandable why he chose to work in those fields in which controversy prevailed. He was particularly interested in those zones in which sciences and doctrines meet and clash, revealing their inability to offer adequate explanations of phenomena.
>
> CAMAVITTO, 1936: 797

Among Michels' many interests we might recall here his works during the Basel years from 1915 to 1925 as an academic heritage of his overview of major European towns; in particular, he held a series of lectures in various cities around Switzerland which were subsequently published in the *Revue International de Sociologie* and later republished in Italian by Corbaccio in 1926

(Michels, 1926). These essays were a solid intellectual journey which represent a real social critique of the process to modernize Paris following Hausmann's urban planning and the upsurge of the Parisian bourgeoisie.

7.2 Borders and Border Crossings

Michels developed and reworked Sorel's observations, something visible mainly in his *Sociology of Paris* (Michels, 1926/2013).

Michels' scientific interest and approach in these writings on Paris could be characterized as an open methodology in which converge the very idea of power, the new forms of social stratification, the role of migrants, the urban layout, and the fact that Paris was, as an intellectual centre, capable of attracting professionals, scholars and artists from far and wide.

These writings, which belong to the time of the Great War, provide us with some key elements:

> Although the stance he took between 1914 and 1918 might appear controversial in many respects, there is no doubt that, also on a practical level, Michels strove to remain faithful to the democratic ideals of his early youth, trying both to ceaselessly mediate among the parts and to avoid falling prey to the opposing ideological exasperations.
> TROCINI, 2014: 188

In fact, if there is one experience which Michels rejected, it is the one which most comforts us, namely his belief that the world is exactly the way it is observed. Also for this specific reason, Michels offered and developed a system of observation on the main European cities, oriented towards an understanding of the constituent character of each single identity. And it was precisely in Paris that the theme of identity most often emerged, starting from the Latin historical sphere, what Michels called 'neo-Latinity' as a non-genetic cultural theme (Michels, 1926: 11–12). For him, the metropolis, in a quasi-Simmelian sense, was the ideal place to summarize social and cultural change: his sociological research did not have the task or objective to elaborate systems, "but rather [that] of increasing knowledge"; it did not intend to "discover solutions" but should "describe with the utmost care the complex of tendencies and countertendencies, of causes and contributing causes, or, in short, the structural form of social life" (Michels, 1966: 7–8). Thus, it is understood that his works went towards a systematic search for the interrelationship of the various factors, without indicating any primary or secondary causes (Michels, 1913).

Michels crossed the social space with energy, developed his own methodology and style, in a vast, impassioned process which ranged from fine art to statistics, from morality to medicine, from philosophy to history, and from history to psychology. He expressed himself in a fluid, eloquent, and changeable way in the wake of a process named 'modernization'; the study and observation of modernization. For him, modernity imposed itself on Europe as an innovative energy: on the one hand, it was a historical and technological evolution; on the other, it was a change of mentality. A complex and inextricable cultural process which was taking place in all possible fields: the modern state, technique and technology, the arts and entertainment. A modernity whose gravitational centre seemed to lie in the phenomenon of urbanization. What happened in the metropolis was no longer simply a stable concentration of people and residencies, of markets and social activities, but was felt as the centre of assimilation, something which remains a cornerstone of contemporary sociological analyses.

Throughout this path, Michels' ability consisted in developing a complex, dense, and articulate system, far from obvious, to bring together opposing dimensions and feelings, emphasizing the centrality of the metropolis as a place of ambivalence and antinomies, as also observed by Scipio Sighele (1903: 87) and, of course, Georg Simmel (1903/1957); a place of crowds, the masses and, of course, the public.

7.3   *Le fait Social* of the Popular Theatre

In this light, the first question which seems to arise from Michels' observation of Paris's public supports the idea of the centripetal role which European cities could have. The Haussmann-designed boulevards, with their cafés and theatres, fused the public and private spheres with a certain spectacular flair just when *flânerie* was becoming the normal "cultural activity for a generalized Parisian public".

A social and cultural change which could be observed in architecture, urban style, within the arts, in theatres (with popular theatre as both a place and a medium) and in literature. In particular, Michels recalled the importance of the founding of popular theatre at a time which he called the 'Great Revolution' as a sound practice for the Republican cause. Michels retraced the formation of the new theatre, in particular through the figure of Jean Sébastien Mercier, a pupil of Diderot, who tried to found permanent repertory theatres as a suitable tool to enlighten the popular classes and teach them the concepts of dignity and freedom. Here, for instance, the term 'popular' did not have the meaning of an autonomous artistic production for the popular classes, as happened afterwards with the birth of Vaudeville, but was a somewhat political action, a solid location and a means for political discourse. Something which targeted an audience and seemed to be an accomplishment, also thanks to the simulacral and spectacular dimension of the bourgeoisie.

Among these suggestions was a complex cultural transition between different representations, with regard to the theatre as a place as well as a form, a transition which affected the 'fourth wall', the public in search of new forms of entertainment, and of new words – relevant to the new social times. Within this research and observation, Michels exploited the expression of social theatre directly from the writings of Armand Kahn:

> Si par un miracle renouvelé de Lazare, les contemporains des Corneille, des Racine, des Molière, des Voltaire, des Hugo et des Vigny «se réveillaient d'entre les morts » et qu'ils assistassent à l'évolution à laquelle le théâtre, de nos jours, se voit soumis, leur stupéfaction toucherait, à n'en point douter, à un effarement voisin de l'incompréhension. [...] Enfin le théâtre social est sorti de ses limbes. Il commence par la description aussi exacte que possible du milieu bourgeois où l'on se meut chaque jour ; puis il s'attaque aux tares que semble lui présenter ledit état des choses, – de là des comédies telles que Le Demi-Monde, La Question d'Argent (A. Dumas fils). Le Mariage d'Olympe, Les Lionnes pauvres (E. Augier), Les Filles de Marbre (Th. Barrière), – il s'occupe des questions familiales, reproche au bourgeois borné et superstitieux son pharisaïsme, s'en prend au Code, réclame des réformes et devient, suivant la formule d'Alexandre Dumas fils, le théâtre utile.
> KAHN, 1907: 7–10

Michels developed these reflections while observing Paris, the place of a hundred thousand novels, in a definition of Balzac, for whom the capital was "toujours cette monstrueuse merveille, étonnant assemblage de mouvements, de machines et de pensées, la ville aux cent mille romans, la tête du monde" (Balzac, 1973: 95), a summary of the emerging effects in the relationship between social actors in which cultural processes were the presuppositions of a social relationship. Sudden changes and a process which Balzac himself termed 'psychological', one which showed the formation and expansion of the masses, but also the affirmation of the audience (Balzac, 2019).

Also Victor Hugo (1963), mentioned several times by Michels in the pages of his works on this topic, set in motion the entire semantic range of the term *la foule*, (the crowd, t/n) using it at different times to indicate the mass of dispossessed, the slum dwellers, the rioters at the barricades, or the entire Parisian population: in his eyes, the masses were, above all, "the crowd of customers, of the public" (Michels, 2013: 97). And it was the works of Victor Hugo that suggested to Michels his analysis of literature and theatrical pieces as a form and a tool for the social sciences, a theme which would become fundamental in Merleau-Ponty's *Phenomenology of Perception* (1945).

Here, Michels' analysis was aimed not only at *la foule* per se, but, above all, the audience. In his readings of the popular theatre experience and of the everyday life of the *café concerts,* created by the spread of the popular press as a medium, he hunted for the relevance of the audience, in whom the imitative faculties of social actors found an unprecedented development toward a sacralization process. If *la foule* could therefore be defined within the conceptual frame of Gabriel Tarde's works (Boudon, 1979), the audience would become a spiritualized flow. An audience of the theatres, the arts, and popular concerts who symbolized a new community, in which Michels had sensed that the meaning of the theatrical scene varied continuously not only as a mirror of the social facts but also as a prophetic epiphany. Consequently, Robert Michels systematically reconstructed the path of the birth of the popular theatre experience in Paris within a broader process in which the metropolis was conceived as the elective place of the symbolic forms and the sociopolitical practices connected to them. Indeed, the Paris of the many theatres described by Michels seemed to concentrate the social dynamics of change, in which the theatrical reform consisted "in facilitating attendance at existing theatres; in the realization of new theatres based on *la comédie de l'art*; in the realization of new theatres to welcome and develop new artistic forms" (Michels, 1926 (391).

The author tried to identify a dividing line between the *Ancien Regime* theatre and popular theatre. A demarcation which determined the birth of a modern audience and such new ideal types as the bohemians to whom Michels dedicated a little-known work (Michels, 1932). Precisely the idea of 'bohemian' seems to have been located between the bourgeoisie and the proletariat. The bohemian character could be interpreted as straddling the two afore-mentioned categories, a hybrid of modernity: without associating the bourgeoisie with the proletariat, the peculiarity of the bohemian lies in its hybrid configuration: constituting an aristocrat of knowledge with a *flâneur's* vision of the aestheticism of the aesthete. And it was also within this elitist vision that lay the knowledge with which Michels began to build a reflection on the idea of popular theatre, capable, in that historical moment, of communicating to *la foule* by offering a complex symbolic and liturgical apparatus.

However, Michels also observed the role that the intellectual class, endowed with an aesthetic vision, could play in the nascent mass society: elaborating myths, symbols and rituals for those of *la foule* who were becoming an audience. Nowadays, we are more used to a dialogue with the diverse forms of theatrical performances and with different audiences; yet these forms were already present by the end of the 19th century where the centrality of the spectator was evident as a subject/object of the script, a subject who chose, thought, and even acted in an autonomous way. In this light, Michels had seen and understood throughout the arts, literature, in the new experiences of popular universities, of popular theatre, and music, specific abilities to elaborate mythologies and liturgies, communicating via a system of symbols, relying on paths which were emotional and therefore nonlogical, having the possibility, in various ways, to come into direct contact with the multitude. This interpretation seemed to offer the best tools for taming the "modern monster": *la foule*. In this regard, Michels focused on the idea of the Roman Musical, or rather Charpentier's *Louise*, intending to refer precisely to the main form of literary naturalism: the novel. The use of such characters taken from the humblest classes of the population, the workers and bohemians, was fundamental. In fact, this specific form characterized the setting of a script which appeared faithful to reality but actually represented an idealized transfiguration of everyday life, a further vision of a possible social reality. What such a script proposed to the audience was a portrait of the metropolis as the result of a collective mythological vision, coinciding with the bourgeois ideal. A path which, as was the case for Giovanni Papini in those same years (Papini, 1912/1974: 116), defined both ambivalence towards *la foule* and the relationship with the audience.

To understand the origin of these reflections, it is necessary to remember how much the development and success of the press had changed the relationship between the audience and theatres by the end of the 19th century. In this scenario, the theatre was no longer merely the space of a stage, but also an object of controversy. At that time, dramatic criticism was perceived as a sort of extension of the theatrical stage. Émile Zola was the precursor of such dynamics, the intellectual "le plus lu et le plus écoute", an "idole de la foule" thanks to a strong interaction with the audience (Niceforo, 1911: 245–249). Of course, there are several underlying assumptions within this view that are problematic: that public opinion was definable and hence could be articulated; that it was homogenous, or at least not especially heterogeneous, and possessed an insatiable appetite for radical positions. A change grafted onto a wider renewal in which the laws of the theatre were no longer only those of theatrical convention but also those of a certain representation of the *truth:* the 'fourth wall', the audience, the image which highlighted the reality of the scene as separated from the auditorium, summoned up new laws of the acting system, changed the conventions of dramatic writings, modifying the habits and being of the audience during a theatrical show. One example was that of the so-called 'naturalist theatre' which was moving towards a new form of dramaturgy. This was an effervescent world, in which Eleonora Duse was acting in Italian (Signorelli, 1938: 221), when the theatre was becoming a major cultural industry, part of an increasingly incisive economic system. These were the years in which Georg Fuchs (1903–1988) published *The Stage of the Future* and *The Revolution of the Theatre*, writings which Michels seems to have known: Max Fuchs, a disciple of Gustave Lanson, and by extension Emile Durkheim, introduced the teaching and research of eighteenth-century theatre history to the French university system in the 1920s on the precept that theatre must not be studied merely as a genre of literature nor as a venue for performances, but as a *"fait social"*. In this context, Michels swung and moved like a pendulum between an attempt to grasp and describe the momentum, and what he called "the extreme morality" of these attempts, towards *la foule* who were already becoming also an audience, indeed, a large archipelago of audiences, a change which Michels had understood by listening to what came from the pavement and on the pavement.

An archipelago in which the theatre was seen by Michels as a challenge; a challenge which he called "of immortality" because the attempts to make arts available to everyone would always be in vain, but would still prove necessary. Attempts which, however, did demonstrate a certain tenacity and would therefore be endowed with immortality. Here, Michels retrieved his first lesson, namely, that certain objectives might be unattainable but should not be abandoned for this reason. Objectives which could be understood from everyday experiences, especially when theories become inadequate.

Bibliography

Balzac, H. de (2019) *A Parigi!*. Bagno a Ripoli (Florence): Passigli.

Balzac, H. de (1973) *Le Colonel Chabert, suivi de Ferragus, chef des Dévorants*. Paris : le Livre de Poche.

Boudon, R. (1979) Présentation, in Tarde G., *Les lois de l'imitation*, Paris-Geneva: Slatkine.

Camavitto D. (1936) Robert Michels. In Memoriam, *American Sociological Review*, October, Vol. 1, No. 5: 797–799.

Einaudi, L. (1936) Robert Michels, *Rivista di storia economica*, I, no. 1, March.

Fuchs, G. (1988) *La scena del futuro*, in Fazio, M. *Lo specchio, il gioco e l'estasi*. Rome: Levi.

Kahn, A. (1907) *Le Théâtre Social en France de 1870 à nos jours*. Lousanne : Ami Fatio.

Hugo, V. (1963) *I Miserabili*, Milan: Rizzoli.

Merleu-Ponty, M. (1945) *Phénoménologies de la perception*, Paris: Gallimard Paris.

Michels, R. (1934) *Politica ed economia*, Turin: Unione Tipografica Torinese.
Michels, R. (1926) *Francia contemporanea. Studi, ricerche, problemi, aspetti*, Milan: Corbaccio.
Michels, R. (2013) *Sociologia di Parigi e la donna francese*, edited by Federici R., Perugia: Morlacchi.
Michels, R. (1966) *La sociologia del partito politico nella democrazia moderna*. Bologna: Il Mulino.
Michels, R. (1913) *Saggi economico-statistici sulle classi popolari*, Milan: Sandron.
Michels, R. (1932) Zur Soziologie der Boheme und ihrer *Zusammenhänge* mit dem geistigen Proletariat, in *Jahrbuch für Nationalökonomie und Statistik*, Bd. 136: 801–816.
Niceforo. A. (1911) Parigi. Una città rinnovata, Torino: Bocca
Papini, G. (1912/1974) *Un uomo finito*, Florence: Vallecchi.
Sapori, A. (1944) *Werner Sombart (1863–1944)*, Florence: Felice Le Monnier.
Signorelli, O. (1938) *La Duse*. Rome: Signorelli.
Sighele, S. (1903) *L'intelligenza della folla*. Turin: Bocca.
Simmel, G. (1903/1957) Die Großstadt und das Geistleben. In, *Brücke und Tür*, Stuttgart: K.F. Koehler.
Stuart-Hughes, H. (1958) Consciousness and society: the re orientation of European thought, 1890-1930, New York: Knopf.
Trocini, F. (2014) Ubi bene. Ibi Patria, Patriotism, Nationalism, and Internationalism *in Robert Michels' Reflection*, in *Classical Sociology beyond Methodological Nationalism*, Pendenza M. (ed.), Leiden/Boston: Brill.
Tuccari, F. (2012) Le radici, le ragioni e l'inattualità della Sociologia del partito politico di Robert Michels, in *Annali della Fondazione Einaudi*, XL, VI.
Turner, B.S. (1999) *Classical Sociology*. London: SAGE.

CHAPTER 8

The Undone Discipline
A Historical and Critical-Theoretical Account of the Sociology of the Theatre

Marco Serino

8.1   Prologue: What about the Sociology of the Theatre?

Nowadays, the phrase 'sociology of the theatre' sounds quite peculiar and singular. A few scholars – including the current author – have used it from time to time, but at present it seems largely outmoded. It was not by chance that, about fifteen years ago, a roundtable entitled *Où en est la sociologie du théâtre?* was held in July 2006 in Avignon, France (this location too was far from accidental), promoted by the section "Sociologie des arts et de la culture" of the French Sociological Association (*Association Française de Sociologie* – AFS).[1] Due to a lack of knowledge and much debate around the theme, that particular roundtable was an occasion to discuss the current state of the sociology of the theatre, bearing witness to the fact that the French community of sociologists still regarded the subject as one of interest, even in the absence of any development of it as a discipline, along with the attention paid to it by the French-speaking world at large (see below).

An inquiry into what has happened to the sociology of the theatre might thus begin by asking the question: 'What about the sociology of the theatre?' At first, it seems that the answer would be simply 'it has never existed', since it has never reached the status of a truly autonomous academic subject. Indeed, since the very beginning of the sociology of the theatre with Georges Gurvitch's fundamental essay-programme published in France in 1956 (*Sociologie du théâtre*), during the second half of the twentieth century the discipline[2] traversed a period of dissemination, with publications coming out in France, Italy, Belgium, the UK, and Australia. Meanwhile, the USA produced relevant studies from different perspectives, which I shall deal with later on, and international

---

[1]   I am grateful to professor Serge Proust (Centre Max Weber, Université Jean Monnet, Saint-Étienne, France), for this information.
[2]   The term *discipline*, along with *field*, and the like, are used here only for the sake of clarity, since the main thesis of the current essay is that the sociology of the theatre has never presented itself as a discipline (see De Marinis, 1991, and below).

conferences were organized in Italy and Portugal between the late 1980s and early 1990s. It was, however, in the latter timespan that some critical interventions appeared. A number of authors have, in fact, insisted on the uncertain status of the discipline.

First and foremost, Maria Shevtsova, who devoted much effort to provide the discipline with a fertile terrain for sociological research,[3] and issued a trio of articles in 1989 attempting to frame the question: "As far back as 1955, George[s] Gurvitch set a modest plan of action for the sociology of theatre. Yet an account of the subject today will still have the contours of a project for the future rather than the bold lines of achievements past and present" (Shevtsova, 1989[a]: 23).[4] On the same note, Marco De Marinis wrote:

> Within the limits of the social sciences, it is the sociological perspective that has been that most extensively applied to the study of the theatrical event in its numerous aspects. This is not surprising when one considers the social characteristics of the theatre and the evidence that the theatre is a phenomenon deeply rooted in the fabric of a collective existence. Nevertheless, it would be difficult to maintain that there is at present or that there has ever been a sociology (or an anthropology) of the theatre, that is, a true and proper discipline worthy of the name.
>
> DE MARINIS, 1991: 57

Analogously, Atkinson (2006: 41) remarked that "the sociology of the theater remained for many years an underdeveloped research field" (see also Tota, 1997). Indeed, this lack of development persists, not because sociology itself has failed to study the theatre as an artistic, social, and professional world, but for it failed to organize this study systematically as a discipline with its own contours and a definite identity. It remains today, as Shevtsova has said (see above), and even many years after her statement, "a project for the future", albeit with much work already done. While different projects, manifestos,

---

3 Maria Shevtsova has published an exhaustive and updated book which includes her essays on the matter issued from 1983 to 2008 (Shevtsova, 2009). To date, and to the best of my knowledge, this is the only recent book entirely and explicitly devoted to the sociology of the theatre (and performance).
4 Gurvitch first presented his work on the sociology of the theatre at a conference titled *Le Théâtre contemporain et ses publics*, held in 1955 in Royaumont, France. His talk was, however, titled *L'expérimentation sociologique et le théâtre*, which clearly meant that his primary interest was to propose a methodological framework for sociological data collection and analysis rather than a programme for the discipline which was to appear later in his seminal article "*Sociologie du théâtre*" (Gurvitch, 1956). See Serino (2011) and Meldolesi (1986).

programmes or schemas are available (e.g., Gurvitch, 1956; Duvignaud, 1965[a]; Pavis, 1996; Shevtsova, 1989[a]: 30–33),[5] disparate work has been done on the lines provided by these programmes, but cannot be acknowledged as a proper sociology of the theatre. At most, we can speak of a corpus of sociological studies of the theatre, but often by scholars active in other fields. As Shevtsova put it in the early 1990s, the "sociology of the theatre is still beleaguered by problems of status, even though an increasing number of scholars are working in the field or in closely related areas not claiming the title as such" (Shevtsova, 1993: 21). In fact, one of the most salient traits of the discipline is its fragmentation, as is true also when it comes to the specialities and topics which many authors have dealt with when studying the theatre from a sociological perspective.[6] In addition, the fact that diverse scholars involved in such studies have never formed a 'scientific community' has caused rifts and stopped the discipline from developing (see Shevtsova's discussion of the "restriction on growth" in Shevtsova, 1989[a]).

Hence, the problem of absence or inconsistency is the first and arguably the most important one which this essay needs to deal with. However, I shall discuss the reasons why the sociology of the theatre did not become a discipline later on. In this section, I would like to clarify the purposes of the present work and introduce the journey into the discipline that I am presenting to the reader.

This essay is concerned with the sociology *of* the theatre and not with sociology *and* the theatre.[7] Notably, while the former has not fared well, the latter perspective has been rather more successful, since "the use of dramaturgical ideas was more widespread" in sociology (Atkinson, 2006: 41) than using the latter to understand the theatrical world as a distinct domain of activity. The so-called 'dramaturgical sociology' – of which Erving Goffman's (1959) *The Presentation of Self in Everyday Life* is the most famous example (see also Burns, 1972) – "is not, strictly speaking, the sociology of theatre", in that it takes "the theatre to be the prototype of society" and is, therefore, concerned with society *as* theatre (Shevtsova, 1989[b]: 181, 190). Instead, what is at issue here

---

5 For a detailed 'review' of Gurvitch's (1956) programme, see De Marinis (1991). It should be noted that all programmes follow the trace left by Gurvitch.
6 However, delimiting the range of interest to sociology would be neither easy nor fruitful since the work done on the theatre-society nexus or the theatre in society (Shevtsova, 1989[a]) is rather vast and composite. It would, in fact, be more opportune to speak of social sciences in a broader sense than that of sociology – for instance, this is one of the concerns of the sociocultural analysis of the theatre and theatre performances (Shevtsova, 2001[a]) – but this would exceed the limits of the current essay.
7 I have borrowed the use of italics for 'of' from Shevtsova (1993).

is the sociology of the theatre as a matter explicitly addressed to the study of "theatre *in* society", as Shevtsova (1989[a]) has firmly stressed: "the sociology *of* the theatre targets all aspects of theatre in society. It therefore understands theatre to be a specific collective activity involved in a network of economic, political and other activities, all designated differently, that are brought about by social agents" (Shevtsova, 1993: 21).

The aim of the present essay is to offer a systematization of the literature which pertains to the sociology of the theatre understood as above. This means dealing with a multitude of works belonging to various research areas and covering a timespan of several decades, these studies sharing an interest and a focus on given aspects of the theatre in society. In the face of a scarcity which, according to Annalisa Tota (1997: 79), "appears undeniable", these works provide the sociologists' community with a plentiful body of research, which nonetheless needs to be carefully sorted out. No matter what, this attempt will not allow us to derive a unitary theoretical framework from these works.

8.2   Pioneers and Founding Fathers

In line with De Marinis (1991), hence, to the best of his knowledge and mine, the first work where the phrase "sociology of the theatre" was to appear was Gurvitch's homonymous article – already mentioned above – published in the literary review *Les Lettres Nouvelles* in 1956. Indeed, Gurvitch should unreservedly be considered the founding father of the discipline. A later founding father – perhaps more frequently acknowledged as such than Gurvitch – was another French sociologist and Gurvitch's pupil, Jean Duvignaud, whose famous book *Sociologie du théâtre: Essai sur les ombres collectives* (Duvignaud, 1965[a]) represented a breakthrough, albeit not contributing much to an advancement of the discipline, nor helping to overcome the faults of the discipline that Duvignaud himself denounced therein – which did, however, partly replicate Gurvitch's complaints.[8]

---

8   "In spite of being under-developed to date, the sociology of the theatre has already gained a bad reputation because it has left its doors open to many confusions and misunderstandings. The very intensity of the relationship between social life and theatre is responsible for the superficialities and the exaggerations which are often brought about. In this way, we usually feel satisfied simply reflecting the general social conditions in the dramatic creation while establishing a mechanical connection between cause and effect and between the appearance of collective life and dramatic experimentation. [...] Without doubt, the sociology of the theatre suffers from an extreme mediocrity since it is pleased with the parallels that it has

However, it could not be said that the sociology of the theatre was 'born' with Gurvitch's essay – as Tota, for instance, has pointed out (Tota, 1997: 91). Before Gurvitch, other writers had provided noteworthy studies about the theatre-society nexus (but not in terms of an analogy between the two). Initially, at the beginning of the twentieth century, reflecting on the relationship between theatre and the social world was not properly the concern of sociologists. On the one hand, this might have been related to the situation of sociology (and thereby of the sociology of the arts) at that time. On the other, theatre was a matter of speculation among philosophers and literary critics who belonged to the European intellectual tradition. As a sociologist, but above all as a philosopher, Georg Simmel was among the first intellectuals to reflect upon the place of art and specifically the theatrical art and acting in society. His two essays on the philosophy of the actor *Zur Philosophie des Schauspielers* (Simmel, 1908) and *Zur Philosophie der Schauspielers. Aus dem Nachlaß herausgegeben* (Simmel, 1920/21), along with *Der Schauspieler und die Wirklichkeit* ("The actor and reality"; Simmel, 1912) were important elements of Simmel's work on art, aesthetics and society, and addressed "themes lying at the centre of both his theoretical sociology and his important analyses of modernity", such as "the relationship of the individual to his roles" or "the difficulty of playing a role that does not correspond to one's personality" (Thomas, 2021: 239).

Marxist philosopher and literary critic György Lukács, a renowned student of Simmel and a leading figure in twentieth-century European philosophy, also contributed to this early elaboration. Lukács' *Zur Soziologie des modernen Dramas* appeared in German in 1914 but was originally included in his vast and notable study of modern drama, finished in 1909 and published in Hungarian in 1911 under the title *A modern dráma fejlodésének története* (I shall make use here of the English translation by Lee Baxandall, titled *The Sociology of Modern Drama*, 1965). This work can be regarded as one of the very first aimed at understanding theatre in society, albeit through the form of the dramatic text (see also Shevtsova, 1989[b]). It focused on 'new' drama, namely, bourgeois drama – such as the works of Goethe or Schiller – which was new because of the novel social conditions of modernity, in contrast with the 'old' drama of the Renaissance: "The drama has now taken on new social dimensions. This development became necessary, and necessary at this particular time, because of the specific social situation of the bourgeoisie. For bourgeois drama is the first to grow out of conscious class confrontation" (Lukács, 1965: 147). The change

---

established between a static society and a dead theatre, that is, two abstractions" (Duvignaud 1965[a]: 37, cited in De Marinis, 1991: 57; see also Faye and Duvignaud, 1966).

in dramatic form identified by Lukács is thus a change intimately linked to a social change, that is, the emergence of a new class but also of a novel aesthetic manifestation of unrest perceived at a societal level. The rise in the rationalization and intellectualization of social life – the concerns of Weber and Simmel, respectively – due to Capitalism and industrial as well as bureaucratic developments, accompanied new stances in dramatic productions, which highlighted the subtleties of the psychological aspects of the characters and the play as a whole. This was chiefly a resonance of individualism – "The new drama is nevertheless the drama of individualism" – but, at the same time, of a crisis in individualism, with "the beginnings of new drama [being visible] at the point where individualism commences to become dramatic", whilst "the old drama, by which we mean here primarily that of the Renaissance, was drama of great individuals" (1965: 151, 154; cf. Shevtsova, 1989[b]: 187–188).

The legacy of Lukács informs the work of his pupil, Lucien Goldmann, who moved onwards in investigating the modes of theatrical representation and imagery with reference to social classes (Goldmann, 1959): "What concerns him is how and why Racine's tragedy articulates the feelings, ideas and aspirations (world view) of Jansenists, who largely constitute the new class of functionaries (*noblesse de robe*, mainly administrators, managers, and lawyers) at the court of Louis XIV" (Shevtsova, 1989[b]: 188–189). His "'genetic structuralism' [...] assumes that since texts are never created in a vacuum, explanation is available in the concrete realities of given societies"; hence, Goldmann "historicize[s] structures, social and textual, at one and the same time" (Shevtsova, 1989[b]: 189). That of Goldmann was a historical sociology (Shevtsova, 1981), but also a sociology of the literature and a sociology of knowledge (Tulloch, 1976), to the extent that drama was created out of material linked to social structure and an expression of it. Put more simply, Goldmann's sociology of drama was a sociology of the traces that theatre leaves through the related literary work.

Lukács' as well as Goldmann's works were, therefore, a sociology of knowledge applied to theatre, as Gurvitch (1956) pertinently noted. Along with Simmel – whose reflection was far more philosophical and notably much less structuralist – these three thinkers were among the pioneers of the sociology of theatre.[9]

---

9   It should be noted that Goldmann's *Le Dieu caché* (1959) appeared a few years after Gurvitch's seminal essay (1956), hence the former cannot be considered a pioneer to be distinguished chronologically from the latter. In fact, Goldmann had also organised together with Gurvitch the conference *Le Théâtre contemporain et ses publics*, from which Gurvitch drew his *Sociologie du théâtre*. In addition to Lukács and Goldmann, I refer the

In fact, when Gurvitch published his 1956 article, the achievements of philosophers, historians and critics towards the study of the theatre in society were still focused upon a limited understanding of theatre as a literary work and not as a complex activity. The above-mentioned thinkers pursued *interpretive* approaches to the arts, "which replicate traditional humanities procedures in their focus on cultural objects in all their complexity and richness of nuance, produce striking insights into cultural phenomena, but they do not encourage generalization or testing" (Griswold, 1987: 2). Instead, Gurvitch's programme was intended to move forward with the emerging discipline in general and to provide some guidelines to research the theatrical world in its entirety, taking into account the trend described above but also other issues which pertain to *institutional* approaches to art and culture, "which emphasize collective action and the organization of social resources in the production of symbolic goods" (Griswold, 1987: 2).

In this sense, Gurvitch's article was a breakthrough, but also a false start (Serino, 2011), since the sociology of the theatre as he attempted to delineate it had been practised in almost every specialist programme (cf. Shevtsova, 1989[a]; Pavis, 1996) by different scholars, but had nevertheless never been fully actualized.[10] Nor was Duvignaud able to move upward in driving the discipline onto a concrete and clear path (see also Duvignaud, 1955). This ancillary founding father of the sociology of the theatre indubitably provided the discipline with a masterpiece and landmark with his *Ombres Collectives* (Duvignaud, 1965[a]), but, in reality, this book was not effective in nurturing the sociology of the theatre. The same holds true for his *L'acteur: Esquisse d'une sociologie du comédien* (Duvignaud, 1965[b]). According to Atkinson (2006: 41), these "two monographs on the theater and on the actor trace mainly historical trends in theatrical institutions and the sociopolitical contexts in which they occur". Harsher, but absolutely correct, was Atkinson's contention that "there was a marked absence of detailed analysis of the practicalities of theatrical work and performance" (Atkinson, 2006: 41). Along with its abstractedness, this lack of empirical work is among the shortcomings of the beginning of the discipline,

---

reader to Shevtsova (1989[b]: 187 et seq.) for more references about the thinkers who pursued the above-mentioned inquiry into "why dramatic texts are social texts".

10   For Atkinson, Gurvitch's article was "a manifesto for a hypothetical research program rather than the realization of empirical inquiry" (Atkinson, 2006: 41). So it was, however, since Gurvitch was both a pioneer of and a founding father for the discipline and had no interest in pursuing empirical research on the subject. Interesting reflections on that article can be found in Meldolesi (1956). On the motives of Gurvitch's proposal – mostly originating from a methodological debate on sociology – see also Serino (2011).

even though both Gurvitch (1956) and Duvignaud (1965[a]) contended that overcoming the pragmatism and excessive superficiality of empirical studies of the theatre (like those of audience composition) was necessary. Ultimately, Duvignaud's approach was mainly historical (Burns, 1972: 6), when not akin to literary critique.[11] In this respect, according to Meldolesi (1986), his *Ombres Collectives* was nothing less than a "false history of theatre" which replicated the key areas of Gurvitch's programme.

8.3   Dissemination, Effervescence and Diversification

During the 1960s, the sociology of the theatre therefore began to derive mainly from Duvignaud's and Goldmann's works. The discipline was, in fact, still rooted in the historical-critical perspective typical of European philosophers and sociologists. Goldmann and his genetic structuralism and *vision du monde* were a point of reference for analyses of theatre plays in relation to a given social structure, for example the theatre of Genet or Ionesco (Goldmann et al., 1968; Tarrab, 1967). This kind of sociological analysis of dramatic texts (Shevtsova, 1989[a], 1989[b]) did not disappear in the subsequent decades (e.g., Shevtsova, 2006), while attention to actual performances (Shevtsova, 1989[c]) had not yet arisen as one of the branches of the sociology of the theatre – albeit already being touched on by Gurvitch (1956). In addition, studies of theatre audiences also began to appear (Mann, 1966, 1967).

In this decade, however, complaints about the poverty of the sociological approach to the theatre still arrived from sociologists:

> The sociologist has few credentials for writing about the theatre. In his private life, he is apt to be as suspicious of artists as he is of intellectuals – when they are not politically subversive, they are hopelessly Bohemian. In his professional life, he has few incentives and even fewer tools for understanding the expressive categories of artistic language. They simply do not translate into the rationalized, quantitative concepts of his basically positivistic science. The two cultures *are* antithetical.
> HORTON, 1969: 367

---

11   Shevtsova (2001[b]: 131) argued that, by "situating sociological analysis historically, he [Duvignaud] comes closer to Lucien Goldmann's 'historical sociology', Goldmann's safeguard against a purely descriptive positivist sociology, or what might also be termed 'slice-of-life-in-the-moment' sociology, like naturalism in the theatre".

In a footnote, Horton continued: "The professional sociological studies of theatre are non-existent" (Horton, 1969: 367). Observations like these not only remind us of the gap "between the 'two cultures' of the sciences and the humanities [that] has handicapped the sociology of culture" (Griswold, 1987: 2), where the science in question is sociology, in its most objectivist fashion,[12] but also of the necessity of reaffirming the very existence of the discipline.

The 1970s were not so productive in this sense, with several studies akin to the historical, critical, mostly theoretical tradition initiated by Duvignaud, but without the original vitality; such as, in Italy, Mango (1978) – who contributed to both the Italian edition of Duvignaud's main works – or, in France, a book by the theatre director and theorist Richard Demarcy (1973). Apart from the latter, which was concerned with a more systematic discussion of theatre genres and trends, with its main focus on audience reception, these works did not help the discipline to overcome that "impasse" which Duvignaud had spoken of (Faye and Duvignaud, 1966). Duvignaud himself authored two books which also made the discipline more of a theoretical speculation than a social science (Duvignaud, 1970, 1971; see also De Marinis, 1991; Meldolesi, 1986). What is more, these authors – except for Duvignaud – were not sociologists.

Actually, after Gurvitch's and Duvignaud's first 'gestures', the greatest attention to the subject was concentrated in the 1980s. This decade was, in fact, a period of rebirth and effervescence of interest in the sociology of the theatre. Two international conferences took place in Rome in 1986, and Bevagna (Perugia) in 1989, again in Italy, and one in Lisbon, Portugal, in 1992. These conferences were all organized by Roger Deldime, a Belgian scholar and one of the most active figures in the field. Deldime, who passed away in 2015, also made an attempt to frame the discipline from the point of view of creation and the reception of theatrical performances (Deldime, 1990, 1995; Deldime and Pigeon, 1988). His perspective was rather original, in that it concerned the mnemonic traces of theatre performances for the spectators, which was the object of some research conducted in France in the mid-1980s by the Centre de Sociologie du Théâtre of the Université Libre of Brussels among young spectators but also adult ones, who had attended the performances of the Théâtre des Jeunes Années/Centre Dramatique National of Lyon in the period between 1968 and 1984.

A lively debate characterized the 1980s and partly lasted into the 1990s. Shevtsova's writings on the sociology of the theatre appeared in the late 1980s

---

12   Even if sociology has also been considered 'third' between the two: neither science nor literature, but instead both (Lepenies, 1988; see also Bourdieu and Wacquant, 1992: 208).

and left a mark on the discussion with the key articles already cited (Shevtsova, 1989[a], 1989[b], 1989[c]). The 1986 conference in Rome (Deldime and Di Meo, 1988) welcomed renowned scholars from around the world and, consequently, the sociology of the theatre seemed to have arisen as a rich and active field of study. In the same decades, North-American sociology became to develop empirically but also theoretically informed approaches to the arts, including the theatre (Becker, 1982; Griswold, 1986; DiMaggio, 1992). These approaches were only apparently a matter of positivistic sociology (cf. Shevtsova, 1989[a]); they were, more precisely, *institutional* (Griswold, 1987) and can be considered an important piece of the sociological study of the theatre in society. The same holds true for Bourdieu (1992), whose attention to the theatre was limited in extent but insightful.

Finally, since the late 1990s, there has been an age of differentiation, with the emergence of a sociology of the theatre as an artistic profession (Menger, 1997; Proust, 2003, 2019; Serino, 2020) – although this inevitably meant problematizing the boundaries shared with the sociology of work (cf. Shevtsova, 1989[a]) – plus a sociology of audience attendance (e.g., Chan and Goldthorpe, 2005; Grisolía et al., 2010), and a firm sociology of theatre performances and stage productions (anticipated by Shevtsova, 1989[c]; see Shevtsova, 1997, 2001[a], and the essays in Shevtsova, 2009), accompanied by a dialogue with Bourdieu's work (Shevtsova, 2001[b], 2002).[13] In one of these essays, Shevtsova (2002) criticized Bourdieu's idea of field position and position-taking – which Shevtsova names "taking-position" – with regard to the alleged determinism that informs Bourdieu's theory and seemed to recover the agent's creative will in an analysis of the theatrical field, namely the director's agency as not being a direct result of the field's influence on one's own perspective of the field itself:

> Directors' creative choices, intentions, pursuits and decisions may be reactive to the field to a certain degree, but are *proactive* above all else. And this proactivity, which is embodied through the bodies of actors in a production, is rarely as cognitively-based, rational and rationalized as supposed by Bourdieu's three-pronged schema of position-disposition-taking position.
>
> SHEVTSOVA, 2002: 48

---

13 For recent applications of Bourdieu's theoretical framework to the theatre see, among others, Petrikas (2019) and Serino et al. (2017).

Interestingly, in this article, the well-known critique of Bourdieu's objectivism and deterministic vision is concerned with the theatrical field and takes seriously one of the most subtle issues of Bourdieu's sociology of art, namely the freedom of one's creative intention from the constraints of one's position in the social space. This is one of the issues a sociology of the theatre should be concerned with.

8.4   Epilogue: Where (and What) Is the Sociology of the Theatre?

Shevtsova (1989[a]) aptly described some of the factors which caused the growth of the discipline to be severely hindered: "The discipline's origins in the social sciences, instead of in the arts and the humanities, have to date restricted its movement – doubtless an eccentric statement, for where else can social study, the very definition of sociology, be grounded?" (1989[a]: 23). Indeed, this is one of the trickiest aspects of the question, which pertains to the differences between theatre studies and sociology and their idiosyncrasies with regard to theatre as a matter of inquiry. The sociology of the theatre has been an orphan of both the social sciences – where it has not been able to find a place – and "the discipline we know as theatre studies [which] has considered sociology to be alien to it, a perception that goes hand-in-glove with the idea that theatre art and sociology are so different from each other as to warrant mutual exclusion" (1989[a]: 23). It seems, here, that this contrast parallels the one which Pierre Bourdieu attributed to the interplay between art and sociology:

> Sociology and art do not make good bedfellows. That's the fault of art and artists, who are allergic to everything that offends the idea they have of themselves: the universe of art is a universe of belief, belief in gifts, in the uniqueness of the uncreated creator, and the intrusion of the sociologist, who seeks to understand, explain, account for what he finds, is a source of scandal. [...] But it's also the fault of sociologists, who have done their best to confirm received ideas about sociology and especially the sociology of art and literature.
>   BOURDIEU, 1993: 139

This quotation also relates to the way that the two domains of theatre studies and sociology have dealt with the theatre itself. The posture of sociologists towards the arts has often been problematic. Although there is no room here to discuss this point, it is a fact that dealing with the aesthetic, creative, imbued-with-meaning characteristics of arts and artists was a key concern in the sociology of the arts (Zolberg, 1990). Scholars working in theatre studies have engaged with theatre and its social context with more ease than sociologists and have deployed the social surroundings as a conduit to better understand the theatrical art in its uniqueness, without forgetting that it is the social context which allows certain forms, styles and condition to arise in drama and performance. After all, this was the core business of the history of theatre as a good example within theatre studies: the latter's identity "is not destabilized by the contact [between theatre content and the social context], not least because works on content/context can be assimilated in the familiar domain of the history of theatre" (Shevtsova, 1989[a]: 23).

In any event, dealing with the 'social context' with an eye on theatre content – that is, juxtaposing the two – does not mean elaborating a sociology of the theatre, at least in the sense of adopting the theoretical and methodological apparatus of sociology as a discipline for studying how theatrical activity is produced and reproduced *in* society:

> Here it is important to note that the conventional dichotomies of theatre *and* society are inadequate from the perspective of the sociology of theatre whose premise of *in* society is irreducible: theatre is social through and through. Sociologists like Gurvitch refer to nothing less when they say theatre is a social phenomenon. The discipline's task, however, is explaining how and why the network of actions we call theatre – including its aesthetics, its most problematic area – is social and not, say, as in the case of its art, solely a matter of individual genius, or individual inspiration and invention.
>
> SHEVTSOVA, 1989[a]: 24

Considering the purely social aspects of the theatre means investigating everything concerned with it *in* society, but only in so far as it is concerned with activities that can be considered as a concrete artistic field. Nevertheless, my argument clashes with Shevtsova in this respect: I do not believe that "any research involved with theatre *in* society, theatrical or academic, is appropriate to the sociology of theatre and should allay doubts about what the discipline can legitimately encompass" (1989[a]: 24). Instead, I consider that only academic research is to be intended as belonging to sociology – if we maintain that sociology is an academic discipline with its own theoretical and methodological tools – while theatrical research legitimately belongs to theatre's theories and practices. In this sense, I agree with Shevtsova that "the sociology of theatre has not clearly defined its objectives with respect to the research and theories of people working in the theatre" (Shevtsova, 1989[a]: 24). It ought to clarify its range, scope and disciplinary status as distinct from – albeit in a dialogue with – the disciplines of the theatre, namely with the latter's own artistic research and also with theatre studies. Indeed, these disciplines too should be a chief object of study for the sociology of the theatre, which is – or should be – a discipline belonging to the social sciences, and certainly not to theatre studies, where too often – legitimately or otherwise – it has been found.

Bibliography

Atkinson, P. (2006) *Everyday Arias: An Operatic Ethnography*. Lanham: AltaMira Press.
Becker, H.S. (1982) *Art Worlds*. Berkeley: University of California Press.
Bourdieu, P. (1992) *Les règles de l'art: Genèse et structure du champ littéraire*. Paris: Editions du Seuil.
Bourdieu, P. (1993) *Sociology in Question*. London: Sage.
Bourdieu, P. and Wacquant, L.J.D. (1992) *An Invitation to Reflexive Sociology*. Cambridge: Polity Press.
Burns, E. (1972) *Theatricality: A Study of Convention in the Theatre and in Social Life*. London: Longman.
Chan, T.W. and Goldthorpe, J.H. (2005) The Social Stratification of Theatre, Dance and Cinema Attendance. *Cultural Trends* 14(3): 193–212.
De Marinis, M. (1991) Sociology. In: Helbo A., Johansen J.D., Pavis P. and Ubersfeld A. (eds) *Approaching Theatre*. Bloomington-Indianapolis: Indiana University Press, 57–74.
Deldime, R. (1990) *Le quatrième mur: Regards sociologiques sur la relation théâtrale*. Carnières (Morlanwelz, Belgium): Promotion Théâtre.
Deldime, R. (1995) Lo spettatore teatrale: un approccio sociologico. *Lo Spettacolo* 45(1): 11–16.
Deldime, R. and Di Meo, E. (1988) *1 er Congrès mondial de sociologie du théâtre, Rome, 27-28-29 juin 1986*. Rome: Bulzoni.
Deldime, R. and Pigeon, J. (1988) La mémoire du jeune spectateur de théâtre. *Jeu: Revue de théâtre* 46: 88–100.
Demarcy, R. (1973) *Elements d'une sociologie du spectacle*. Paris: Union Generale d'Editions.
DiMaggio, P. (1992) Cultural Boundaries and Structural Change: The Extension of the High Culture Model to Theater, Opera, and the Dance, 1900–1940. In: Lamont M. and Fournier M. (eds) *Cultivating Differences: Symbolic Boundaries and The Making of Inequality*. Chicago: University of Chicago Press, 21–57.
Duvignaud, J. (1955) Recherches pour une description sociologique de l'étendue scénique. *Cahiers Internationaux de Sociologie* 18: 138–159.

Duvignaud, J. (1965[a]) *Sociologie du théâtre: Essai sur les ombres collectives*. Paris: Presses Universitaires de France.
Duvignaud, J. (1965[b]) *L'acteur: Esquisse d'une sociologie du comédien*. Paris: Gallimard.
Duvignaud, J. (1970) *Spectacle et société*. Paris: Denoël-Gonthier.
Duvignaud, J. (1971) *Le théâtre, et après*. Paris: Casterman.
Faye, J.-P. and Duvignaud, J. (1966) Débat sur la sociologie du théâtre. *Cahiers Internationaux de Sociologie* 40: 103–112.
Goffman, E. (1959) *The Presentation of Self in Everyday Life*. Garden City, NY: Doubleday.
Goldmann, L. (1959) *Le Dieu caché*. Paris: Gallimard.
Goldmann, L., Dreyfus, P. and Schechner, R. (1968) The Theatre of Genet: A Sociological Study. *TDR (1967–1968)* 12(2): 51–61.
Grisolía, J.M., Willis, K., Wymer, C. and Law, A. (2010) Social Engagement and Regional Theatre: Patterns of Theatre Attendance. *Cultural Trends* 19(3): 225–244.
Griswold, W. (1986) *Renaissance Revivals: City Comedy and Revenge Tragedy in the London Theatre, 1576–1980*. Chicago: University of Chicago Press.
Griswold, W. (1987) A Methodological Framework for the Sociology of Culture. *Sociological Methodology* 17(1): 1–35.
Gurvitch, G. (1956) Sociologie du théâtre. *Les lettres nouvelles* 35: 196–210.
Horton, J. (1969) The Re-Professionalization of the Theatre: Some Thoughts on Joining the Educational Establishment. *Educational Theatre Journal* 21(4): 367–377.
Lepenies, W. (1988) *Between Literature and Science: The Rise of Sociology*. Cambridge: Cambridge University Press.
Lukács, G. (1965) The Sociology of Modern Drama. *The Tulane Drama Review* 9(4): 146–170.
Mango, A. (1978) *Verso una sociologia del teatro*. Palermo: Celebes.
Mann, P.H. (1966) Surveying a Theatre Audience: Methodological Problems. *The British Journal of Sociology* 17(4): 380–387.
Mann, P.H. (1967) Surveying a Theatre Audience: Findings. *The British Journal of Sociology* 18: 75–90.
Meldolesi, C. (1986) Ai confini del teatro e della sociologia. *Teatro e storia* 1(1): 77–151.
Menger, P.-M. (1997) L'activité du comédien: Liens, indépendances et micro-organisations. *Réseaux* 15(86): 59–75.
Pavis, P. (1996) *L'analyse des spectacles*. Paris: Nathan.
Petrikas, M. (2019) Bourdieusian Concepts and the Field of Theatre Criticism. *Nordic Theatre Studies* 31(1): 38–57.
Proust, S. (2003) La communauté théâtrale: Entreprises théâtrales et idéal de la troupe. *Revue Française de Sociologie* 44(1): 93–113.
Proust, S. (2019) Portrait of the Theatre Director as an Artist. *Cultural Sociology* 13(3): 338–353.

Serino, M. (2011) Introduzione: tracce di una sociologia del teatro. In: Gurvitch G. *Sociologia del teatro*. Calimera (Lecce, Italy): Kurumuny, 9–22.

Serino, M. (2020) Continuity, Change and Transitions of Artistic Professions in the Italian Theatre Industry. *Sociologia del Lavoro* 157: 186–205.

Serino, M., D'Ambrosio, D. and Ragozini, G. (2017) Bridging Social Network Analysis and Field Theory Through Multidimensional Data Analysis: The Case of The Theatrical Field. *Poetics* 62: 66–80.

Shevtsova, M. (1981) Lucien Goldmann: Historical Sociology. *The Australian and New Zealand Journal of Sociology* 17(3): 44–52.

Shevtsova, M. (1989[a]) The Sociology of the Theatre, Part One: Problems and Perspectives. *New Theatre Quarterly* 5(17): 23–35.

Shevtsova, M. (1989[b]) The Sociology of the Theatre, Part Two: Theoretical Achievements. *New Theatre Quarterly* 5(18): 180–194.

Shevtsova, M. (1989[c]) The Sociology of the Theatre, Part Three: Performance. *New Theatre Quarterly* 5(19): 282–300.

Shevtsova, M. (1993) *Theatre and Cultural Interaction*. Sydney: Sydney Association for Studies in Society and Culture.

Shevtsova, M. (1997) Sociocultural Analysis: National and Cross-cultural Performance. *Theatre Research International* 22(1): 4–18.

Shevtsova, M. (2001[a]) Sociocultural Performance Analysis. In: Berghaus G. (ed) *New Approaches to Theatre Studies and Performance Analysis: Papers Presented at the Colston Symposium, Bristol, 21–23 March 1997*. Berlin, New York: Max Niemeyer Verlag, 45–60.

Shevtsova, M. (2001[b]) Social Practice, Interdisciplinary Perspective. *Theatre Research International* 26(2): 129–136.

Shevtsova, M. (2002) Appropriating Pierre Bourdieu's *Champ* and *Habitus* for a Sociology of Stage Productions. *Contemporary Theatre Review* 12(3): 35–66.

Shevtsova, M. (2006) The Theatre of Genet in Sociological Perspective. In: Finburgh C., Lavery C. and Shevtsova M. (eds) *Jean Genet: Performance and Politics*. London: Palgrave Macmillan, 44–53.

Shevtsova, M. (2009) *Sociology of Theatre and Performance*. Verona: QuiEdit.

Simmel, G. (1908) Zur Philosophie der Schauspielers. *Der Morgen* 2: 1695–1689.

Simmel, G. (1912) Der Schauspieler und die Wirklichkeit. *Berliner Tageblatt und Handelszeitung* 41(2, 1. Suppl.): 5–6.

Simmel, G. (1920/21) Zur Philosophie der Schauspielers. Aus dem Nachlaß herausgegeben. *Logos* 9: 339–363.

Tarrab, G. (1967) Essai de sociologie du théâtre: *La Cantatrice chauve* et *Les Chaises* de Ionesco. *L'Homme et la société* 6(1): 161–170.

Thomas, F. (2021) Simmel: The Actor and His Roles. In: Fitzi G. (ed) *The Routledge International Handbook of Simmel Studies*. New York: Routledge, 239–247.

Tota, A.L. (1997) *Etnografia dell'arte: per una sociologia dei contesti artistici*. Rome: Logica University Press.

Tulloch, J.C. (1976) Sociology of Knowledge and the Sociology of Literature. *The British Journal of Sociology* 27(2): 197–210.

Zolberg, V.L. (1990) *Constructing a Sociology of the Arts*. Cambridge: Cambridge University Press.

CHAPTER 9

Theatre as Intersubjective Space for the Mediation of Collective Identity
Outline of a Psychoanalytic Perspective

Maria Grazia Turri

9.1 Premise: Asking Not *Whether*, but *How* Theatre Impacts Society

The idea that theatre or 'theatres' have an important social role to play is here not disputed. Theatres of all times have been investigated for their capability to foster collective identity and the inherent political implications of such phenomenon. For instance, scholars have persuasively claimed that "[t]ragedy was a device which allowed the Athenians to come together and collectively think through their problems" (Wiles, 2000: 48) and that it was the common emotional experience which functioned as the mediator of the massification of political will (Wiles, 2000: 56). The Ancient philosophers Plato and Aristotle centred their reflections on the theatre on the assumption that it was the audience's emotional involvement which was responsible for either the dangers (Plato) or the merits (Aristotle) of the theatrical experience (Turri, 2016: 22–23). For Plato, who condemns theatre to be banned from his ideal Republic, shared emotions are like a current whose force is irresistible even for young men of fortitude (Wiles, 2000: 56).

An essential contemporary reference point is Bertolt Brecht's extensive examination, both in theory and practice, of theatre's social implications. Brecht critiques conventional theatre, which he calls Aristotelian theatre, for being first and foremost aimed at creating an emotional identification of spectators with characters "precisely for the purpose of pleasure" (Brecht, 2001[a]: 181). In opposition to the dominant model of theatre for entertainment, he develops the 'epic theatre' (Brecht, 2001[b]), which is characterised by the sustained effort, through its dramaturgical and performative techniques, to break the spectator's direct emotional identification with characters which Brecht (2015: 184) calls, disparagingly, the 'empathy operation'.

If Brecht's championing of the epic theatre is an explicit attempt at creating a socially engaged theatrical practice, equally important is the denunciation of the harmful effects of conventional modes of production. Aristotelian theatre is not neutral with regards society, it is not politically irrelevant: by enticing

© MARIA GRAZIA TURRI, 2023 | DOI:10.1163/9789004529816_010

spectators to empathise with the characters, it lulls them into obliterating their social and political conscience, fostering the making of conformist and unaware citizens, easily swayed into accepting the current social order with its injustices and oppressions (Brecht, 2001[b]). Theatre, in other words, can never be un-political, even when it purports to be 'just' entertainment. For this very reason, researching the '*how*' of theatre's impact on the audience is an imperative, both for theatres whose purpose may be explicitly social and, perhaps even more so, for theatres whose sole claims are to entertainment, escapism or aesthetic pleasure.

9.2 The Importance of Emotional Engagement to Theatre's Social Role

It may be difficult to contest that at least a component of most theatrical experiences has got something to do with emotions. Brecht's long-lasting frequentation of the theatre as a theorist, a playwright and a director, and his preoccupation with the harmful effects of certain forms of emotional engagement, substantiates the urgency of examining the nature of the audience's emotional experience and especially, I claim, of its unconscious dimension.

Not only does Brecht recognise that the quality of the emotional experience is an important mediator of theatre's social impact, he also considers questions of identity as fundamentally linked to emotional engagement. For instance, he particularly condemns empathy because, in his view, it fosters, within the theatrical space, a relinquishment of the spectator's identity as an active citizen of the world outside (Brecht, 2015). Within the theatre, the spectator lives vicariously the characters' actions on stage and in doing so, he adopts a passive attitude which contaminates his way of being when he leaves the theatre and travels in the space of his everyday life. On the contrary, the epic theatre invites the spectator to be a witness of the happenings on the stage and therefore an active participant of social life: a virtuous circle is established between the actor as a witness to the vicissitudes of the character, the spectator as an invited witness in identification with the actor, and the forming of an identity of spectators as active citizens who observe social reality, question and critique it (Brecht, 2001[c]).

In my previous work (Turri, 2016: 1–16), I have analysed Brecht's theories of emotional engagement in acting and spectating, and his definitions of the passive and active spectator, katharsis, and empathy, showing how his distinction between a passive and an active spectator harbours, at its core, a belief in the opposition between unconscious and conscious emotional engagement. As Brecht returned to Aristotle as a point of reference for his reflections on the theatre, his understanding of what a collective emotional response entails, was not any different from Plato's: the kind of spectating that leads to emotional identification with characters on stage has the force of a current, which engulfs the audience in a passive experience by which they are swept away. Although Brecht's solution was not to abolish theatre altogether, his belief in the socio-political impact of all theatre led him to dismiss, too hastily perhaps, unconscious emotional engagement as a middle-class pursuit which can be easily overcome, providing there is a political will to renew theatre's aesthetic principles. In other words, while Brecht recognised that unconscious emotional responses are central to the way theatre affects spectators, he proposed, at least in some of his most significant writings on the theatre, that such responses can be done away with. It should also be noted, for the sake of completeness, that in his later work Brecht reappraised his view of the place of spectators' emotional engagement, reconsidering, under a more favourable light, the value of empathy (Turri, 2016: 113–114) and pleasure (Turri, 2016: 119–120) for the progressive social function of theatre.

The earlier Brecht, however, with his radical theory of the epic theatre, has exercised a great influence on contemporary scholarship and practice, partly contributing to the antipathy towards studying unconscious responses at the theatre, neglecting their relevance or denying outright their legitimacy as a field of analysis. Erika Fischer-Lichte (2008: 4), in her study of participatory theatre, foregrounds conscious processes of reception, while arguing that "unconscious perceptions remain meaningless for the perceiving subject and cannot be taken into consideration [...] because nobody can claim any knowledge of them". The insurgence of emotions in the audience is seen as secondary either to physical sensations or to a prior cognitive appraisal of the meaning of a certain situation. For instance, when discussing the emotions aroused in an audience witnessing an actor being subjected to self-inflicted injuries or to physical abuse by others, Fischer-Lichte (2008: 153) suggests that "the spectators experienced these emotions because violence against self and others had been charged and connoted with intense emotions for them prior to the performance", discarding the possibility of a primary emotional resonance between actors and spectators. Even more explicitly, Marco De Marinis (1985: 7), in his attempt to formulate a 'cognitive semiotics' of spectatorship, similarly repudiates

> an ingenuous neo-romantic vision of theatrical emotion; a vision according to which it consists of an immediate, primary phenomenon completely independent of cognitive processes that take place during the reception of the spectacle.

Although he acknowledges that there is a complex set of psychic processes that contribute to the experience of the spectator, and that emotive and cognitive aspects do not operate in opposition to each other, he concludes that the emotional experience of the spectator is always regulated by cognition.

Drawing on psychological theories of cognition, Bruce McConachie (2008) privileges consciousness as mediating spectators' responses. For example, he insists on attention as a conscious activity that spectators employ to make deliberate choices about what they watch and see: "At one time or another, all theatregoers have trouble focusing their attention. More than simple awareness, attention requires conscious, selective effort" (McConachie, 2008: 23–24). Although unconscious responses are not altogether dismissed, like when, for example, the unconscious process of cognitive blending is assumed to explain the spectator's ability to "comprehend and negotiate the 'doubleness' of theatre – that is, the fact that a single body on stage can be both an actor and a character" (McConachie, 2008: 7), the unconscious evoked here does not pertain to emotional processes.

9.3 Emotional Engagement and Its Inherent Unconscious Constituent

Psychoanalysis is the scientific discipline which has shown that emotional experiences happen, for the greatest part, at an unconscious level. While in psychology emotions are sometimes defined as those feelings that we have awareness of (and therefore cannot be unconscious), psychoanalysis has been studying unconscious emotional experience for the past hundred and thirty years, since the beginning of Freud's clinical work as an ante-litteram psychotherapist in the 1880s (Freud and Breuer, 1895).

An explanatory note is necessary. Psychoanalysis is misconceived, in certain academic circles, as an abstract and arbitrary construction, devoid of scientific credibility. Instead, it is a scientific psychology which studies the emotional unconscious and its mechanisms in the empirical setting of the clinical encounter. Systematic observation and study of unconscious processes have been carried out on a large scale and thousands and thousands of case studies are collected in the books and journals dedicated to this discipline. This systematic and extensive dataset is comparable to that of modern astronomy, an empirical science which has been largely built on observation rather than controlled experiments (Schwartz, 1996).

When I illustrate the importance of the unconscious facet of emotional phenomena to students, I use the image of an iceberg, with a small fraction of its volume visible on the surface, and the vaster bulk of its underwater portion, invisible to the seafarer's eye. If the naïve seafarer stops at what they see on the surface, not only will they understand very little of the object in front of them, but they will also greatly undermine the object's potential impact and dangers, the tragedy of the Titanic serving as suggestive case in point. Similarly, the naïve scholar of the mind, who does not acknowledge the relevance and import of the unconscious component of emotions, will understand little about their functioning and their beneficial or harmful potential. That is why Brecht's proposition to bypass unconscious emotional engagement as a solution to the spectator's passive suffering of the character's emotions is misguided. Freud himself gave extensive consideration to the predicament of being a passive sufferer of emotional turmoil, but he came to realise that what appear as passive emotional experiences (termed, suggestively, 'repetition-compulsion' to illustrate their ability to impose themselves) are in fact active unconscious emotional processes (Freud, 1920).

Furthering Freud's (1915) work, Melanie Klein and her collaborators showed how unconscious emotional identifications, effected through the mechanisms of projection and introjection, are the active unconscious processes through which the self is constructed. As Klein (1997: 141) puts it: "introjection and projection operate from the beginning of post-natal life and constantly interact. This interaction both builds up the internal world and shapes the picture of external reality". The workings of unconscious identifications may be best understood through the metaphor of the digestive and metabolic functions: like the body ingests, metabolizes, expels, so the mind introjects, processes, projects; in both cases, the transformative function of physiological metabolism and psychological processing is essential to survival, because "[f]ailure to eat, drink or breathe properly has disastrous consequences for life itself. Failure to use the emotional experience produces a comparable disaster in the development of the personality" (Bion, 1984: 42).

9.4 Interlude on Children's Play

I have a memory of a garden chair, upholstered with a fabric depicting small flowers. The image of the blue and green flowery pattern is lucid, the context of the memory vague. I believe it was my grandmother's chair when I was about five years old or younger, and we were sitting outside, I playing, her watching me. In the 'Strange Situation' (Ainsworth and Bell, 1970), an experimental setting designed to measure attachment in young children, firstly the parent, and then a stranger, are asked to sit in a chair next to the child playing. The child's relationship to the observer will determine how she plays: if she is securely attached, she will play happily while the parent is present, but get alerted and upset when the parent has left, and the stranger arrives. The quality of the child's play will drastically change according to who is sitting next to her.

Play is not a casual activity, it is a mediator of identity, too important to be left unframed. In play, the child personifies and impersonates, investing objects with her own unconscious emotions and taking upon herself the emotional processes she encounters in others. For example, a small child may play teacher or mum, impersonating these important figures in her life in order to enter into the unconscious emotional experiences of others as if they were her own. By introjective identifications, the child attempts to understand the other. At the same time, play also involves the unconscious projection of the child's own emotional experiences into inanimate objects, such as dolls or toys, or indeed, into other children or adults who are participants in the game. By projective identification, the child places her own emotional experiences outside of her, so that the 'othering' of her experiences helps her make sense of them. Klein (1998) describes the play of Little Erna, a six-year-old girl whom she was seeing for therapy. During their meetings, Erna would play mother and teacher while she casted Klein in the role of the child, subjecting her to "fantastic tortures and humiliations" (Klein, 1998: 199). In projective identification, Klein inhabited Erna's unconscious emotional experience, while Erna strived to fathom the unconscious emotional experiences of the grown-ups through her impersonations of them.

Freud (1908: 44) highlighted the continuity between the playing of children and the creative process of artists; as I discussed elsewhere (Turri, 2016: 112), playing, art production, and art fruition, all entail emotional investment involving unconscious identifications. The chair of my grandmother watching me play, the chair of the analyst, the chairs of the theatre auditorium are not just places where people sit and make conscious choices. They are anchors from where people, young and old, engage in unconscious emotional identifications. As I discussed in my previous work on the unconscious transpersonal dimension of theatre spectatorship, theatres are places "filled with sparkles of unconscious emotional elements moving across actors' and spectators' minds" (Turri, 2016: 125).

9.5 Unconscious Intersubjectivity and Collective Identity at the Theatre

Unconscious emotional identifications through projective and introjective processes make raw emotional experience available for meaning-making, contributing to one's sense of identity (Turri, 2016: 80–94). Autonomous forms of unconscious emotional processing consist in intrapsychic representations, such as in playing alone with one's dolls or in reading a novel, but at a most fundamental level, unconscious projections and introjections unfold in the transpersonal context of an emotional relationship between at least two subjects. The paradigmatic case in psychoanalysis is the clinical encounter between analyst and patient as it develops in the unconscious communications intrinsic to transference and countertransference. The psychoanalyst Wilfred Bion (1984: 146) describes this dimension as

> a field of emotional force in which the individuals seem to lose their boundaries as individuals and become 'areas' around and through which emotions play at will. Psycho-analyst and patient cannot exempt themselves from the emotional field.

The problem is that the emotional field is opaque to awareness. Like in the vision of a Gestalt shape – take for instance the shape of the vase whose perception can switch to two face-profiles – we must focus on either the vase or the faces to become aware of the figure. Similarly, in the patient-analyst relationship, we may speak of transference if we take the patient to be the subject, or we may speak of countertransference if we switch poles and take the analyst as subject. In reality, the phenomenon is a dynamic emotional 'current' which happens in-between, in the *intersubjective space* between the two poles (Katz, 2011). For this very reason, as Freud (1921: 69) writes in the opening of *Group Psychology and the Analysis of the Ego*: "The contrast between individual psychology and social or group psychology, which at a first glance may seem to be full of significance, loses a great deal of its sharpness when it is examined more closely".

Intersubjectivity foregrounds the relational space as the primary area for the emergence of the self (Turri, 2016: 88–90) and psychoanalysis has shown that this relational space is populated by unconscious identifications. The discovery of mirror neurons has brought forward empirical proof of the existence of neurological mechanisms through which emotional experience can be transmitted directly from person to person, without the need for cognitive mediation (Gallese et al., 2007: 144):

> The other's emotion is constituted, experienced, and therefore directly understood by means of an embodied simulation producing a shared body state. It is the activation of a neural mechanism shared by the observer and the observed that enables experiential understanding.

Although the specific processes of projective and introjective identification, and their working through into self-awareness, cannot be simplistically reduced to the function of mirror neurons (Alford, 2016), these illustrate how "an automatic, unconscious, and noninferential understanding of another's actions, intentions, emotions, sensations, and perhaps even linguistic expressions" (Gallese et al., 2007: 144) operates as a transpersonal dimension which allows for the direct transmission of unconscious emotional states between subjects. This transpersonal dimension is both 'passive', if by passive one intends unconsciously generated and hence unmediated by awareness, choice, or cognitions, but 'active' if one understands it as a communication that inevitably triggers unconscious and conscious responses, including self-awareness. Most importantly, it constitutes a primary component of emotional experience, not something one can choose to obliterate.

Although not uncontroversial with regards the specifics of its characterisation, intersubjectivity is acknowledged as a fundamental dimension of the psychoanalytic encounter, with the analyst's expertise in recognising and handling unconscious emotional identifications put at the service of the patient's self-reflexivity (Renik and Spillius, 2004). If the self emerges out of the encounter with the Other and "[a]nother person is needed to experience our own self" (Bohleber, 2013: 800), the analyst is in a privileged position to contribute to the formation of the patient's identity through the analytic work which is based on the function of interpretation (Turri, 2016: 27–29). As the interpretative task of the analyst is put at the service of the patient's self-reflexivity, so the actor's performance of the character is put at the service of the spectator's self-reflexivity and, as I have argued elsewhere, it is salient that the actor's emotional work on the character is also called an interpretation (Turri, 2016: 99–100). Although any artistic process most likely functions on comparable lines, the actor's interpretation of the character seems to work well as a paradigm.

At the theatre, the intersubjective experience has a peculiar feature. Each spectator is involved emotionally with the characters on stage, with whom they engage through projective and introjective identifications: the 'character' can be conceived as the emotional field where the actor's interpretation is applied to the spectator's unconscious identifications (Turri, 2021: 17). At the same time, spectators share, as a group, a common emotional experience, which is not the sum of individual events, but rather a transpersonal dimension where emotional contagion overrides, at least to some extent, individual responses (Freud, 1921: 75; Brennan, 2004: 68). As an emotional field concerning the audience as group, the 'character' is a centre of gravity which channels the spectators' unconscious identifications towards a common transformative process. As such, the self-reflexivity which is generated through the actor's interpretation of the character must have a stake in the construction of a collective identity.

In her seminal work on the sociology of theatre, Maria Shevstova (2009: 15) has called for frameworks of analysis showing how theatres' artistic and social aims are dialectically linked. The intersubjective space of unconscious emotional processing demands our attention within the strivings towards a sociology of theatre. At the level of unconscious emotional processing, the artistic act of interpretation and the social act of fostering a collective identity are truly one and the same: the audience's unconscious transformations impact their beliefs as citizens, as they exit the social space of the theatre and enter into the social sphere of their everyday life.

9.6 Coda: Studying Spectators' Unconscious Emotional Responses through Empirical Research

As part of a larger project aimed at developing empirical methods capable of investigating spectators' unconscious responses, I co-designed, with Bridget Escolme, an audience research project at *Shakespeare's Globe* in London, as part of the theatre's *Research in Action* events. The methodology and results of the project will be disseminated in a forthcoming book. Here I would like to give a first glimpse of how empirical research on audiences may help us uncover areas of theatre's social function so far unacknowledged, by briefly discussing two of the main results in order to illustrate my point.

The audience of 60 present at the *Research in Action* event were shown 4 scenes from early modern comedies, whose protagonists are mad characters. Two scenes were taken from *The Honest Whore Part 1* by Thomas Dekker and Thomas Middleton (1604), first performed and published in 1604, and two scenes were taken from the *Commedia dell'Arte* scenario '*La pazzia di Isabella*', by Flaminio Scala (1976), published in 1611 in *Il teatro delle favole rappresentative*. Each scene was played twice, with the aim to experiment with variations in the interpretative mood, realised by asking actors to modify a certain interpretative element. For instance, two of the scenes were played once in their expected comic mood and once by asking actors to play them exactly the same, but in a tragic mood. I designed a questionnaire aimed at capturing spectators' intuitive responses immediately after each scene. The questionnaires used prompts so to avoid the need for respondents to spend time recalling, considering, reflecting. Spectators were instructed to fill in the questionnaire as immediately and spontaneously as possible, using the psychoanalytic technique of 'free associations' (Freud, 1924: 195–196).

Interesting differences emerged in the analysis of the responses to the scenes played both in a comic and tragic mood. For example, intuitive compassion for the protagonist (tested by answering to the prompt 'I feel for him/her') was reported in 69% of cases for the tragic scenes and only in 23% for the comic scenes, suggesting that interpretation of a character as comic may decrease spectators' sympathy for a certain social type. Moreover, among spectators who rated the perceived power of the protagonist (tested by answering to the prompts 'weak' or 'strong'), 81% rated tragic characters as weak (as opposed to 19% who rated them as strong) while 82% rated comic characters as strong (as opposed to 18% who rated them as weak). Considering that the same characters appeared in both tragic and comic scenes, a pattern emerges whereby the actor's interpretation of a character as comic leads spectators to perceive them as powerful, while an opposite trend is seen for the actor's interpretation of the same character as tragic, which induces spectators to perceive them as powerless. The discussion of the implications and limitations of these data is beyond the scope of this paper. Suffice to say that for those of us who believe in the role of theatre to transform society, the need to research its impact at the unconscious level should not be forgotten.

Bibliography

Ainsworth, M.D.S. and Bell, S.M. (1970) Attachment, Exploration, and Separation: Illustrated by the Behavior of One-Year-Olds in a Strange Situation. *Child Development*, 41(1): 49–67.

Alford, C.F. (2016) Mirror Neurons, Psychoanalysis, and the Age of Empathy. *International Journal of Applied Psychoanalytic Studies*, 13(1): 7–23.

Bion, W.R. (1984) *Learning from Experience*. London: Karnac.

Bohleber, W. (2013) The Concept of Intersubjectivity in Psychoanalysis: Taking Critical Stock. *The International Journal of Psychoanalysis*, 94(4): 799–823.

Brecht, B. (2001[a]) A Short Organum for the Theatre [1949]. J. Willett, Ed. & Trans. In *Brecht on Theatre: The Development of an Aesthetic*. London: Methuen, 179–205.

Brecht, B. (2001[b]) The Modern Theatre is the Epic Theatre. [1930]. J. Willett, Ed. & Trans. In *Brecht on Theatre: The Development of an Aesthetic*. London: Methuen, 33–42.

Brecht, B. (2001[c]) The Street Scene. A Basic Model for an Epic Theatre [1950]. J. Willett, Ed. & Trans. In *Brecht on Theatre: The Development of an Aesthetic*. London: Methuen, 121–128.

Brecht, B. (2015) Short Description of a New Technique of Acting that Produces a Verfremdung Effect [1951]. In M. Silberman, Giles, S. and Kuhn, T. (Ed.), *Brecht on Theatre*. London: Bloomsbury, 184–188.

Brennan, T. (2004) Transmission in Groups. In *The Transmission of Affect*. Ithaca and London: Cornell University Press, 51–73.

Dekker, T. and Middleton, T. (1604) *The Honest Whore – Part 1*, reprint. Gloucester: Dodo Press.

De Marinis, M. (1985) Towards a Cognitive Semiotic of Theatrical Emotions. Translation by Thorn, B. *Versus*, 41: 5–20.

Fischer-Lichte, E. (2008) *The Transformative Power of Performance. A New Aesthetics*. London: Routledge.

Freud, S. (1908) Creative Writers and Day-Dreaming. In *The Standard Edition of the Complete Psychological Works of Sigmund Freud, Volume IX (1906–1908): Jensen's "Gradiva" and Other Works*. London: The Hogarth Press, 141–154.

Freud, S. (1915) Instincts and their Vicissitudes. In *The Standard Edition of the Complete Psychological Works of Sigmund Freud, Volume XIV (1914–1916): On the History of the Psycho-Analytic Movement, Papers on Metapsychology and Other Works*. London: The Hogarth Press, 109–140.

Freud, S. (1920) Beyond the Pleasure Principle. In *The Standard Edition of the Complete Psychological Works of Sigmund Freud, Volume XVIII (1920–1922): Beyond the Pleasure Principle, Group Psychology and Other Works*. London: The Hogarth Press, 1–64.

Freud, S. (1921) Group Psychology and the Analysis of the Ego. In *The Standard Edition of the Complete Psychological Works of Sigmund Freud, Volume XVIII (1920–1922): Beyond the Pleasure Principle, Group Psychology and Other Works*. London: The Hogarth Press, 65–144.

Freud, S. (1924) A Short Account of Psycho-analysis. In *The Standard Edition of the Complete Psychological Works of Sigmund Freud, Volume XIX (1923–1925): The Ego and the Id and Other Works*. London: The Hogarth Press, 189–210.

Freud, S. and Breuer, J. (1895) Studies on Hysteria. In *The Standard Edition of the Complete Psychological Works of Sigmund Freud, Volume II (1893–1895)*. London: The Hogarth Press.

Gallese, V., Eagle, M.N., & Migone, P. (2007) Intentional Attunement: Mirror Neurons and the Neural Underpinnings of Interpersonal Relations. *Journal of the American Psychoanalytic Association*, 55(1): 131–175.

Katz, W.W. (2011) Book Review of: *Intersubjective Processes and the Unconscious: An Integration of Freudian, Kleinian and Bionian Perspectives*, by Lawrence J. Brown. New York: Routledge (2011). *The International Journal of Psychoanalysis*, 92(6): 1641–1646.

Klein, M. (1997) On Identification [1955]. In *Envy and Gratitude and Other Works 1946–1963*. London: Vintage, 141–175.

Klein, M. (1998) Personification in the Play of Children [1929]. In *Love, Guilt and Reparation and Other Works 1921–1945*. London: Vintage, 199–209.

McConachie, B. (2008) *Engaging Audiences. A Cognitive Approach to Spectating in the Theatre.* New York: Palgrave Macmillan.

Renik, O. and Spillius, E.B. (2004) Psychoanalytic Controversies: Intersubjectivity in Psychoanalysis. *The International Journal of Psychoanalysis,* 85(5): 1053–1064.

Scala, F. (1976) *Il teatro delle favole rappresentative* [1611]. Ed. F. Marotti. Milano: Il Polifilo.

Schwartz, J. (1996) What is Science? What is Psychoanalysis? What is to Be Done? *British Journal of Psychotherapy,* 13(1): 53–63.

Shevtsova, M. (2009) *Sociology of Theatre and Performance.* Verona: QuiEdit.

Turri, M.G. (2016) *Acting, Spectating and the Unconscious: A Psychoanalytic Perspective on Unconscious Mechanisms of Identification in Spectating and Acting in the Theatre.* London: Routledge.

Turri, M.G. (2021) Psychoanalysis and Theatre Revisited: The Function of Character in Mediating Unconscious Processing in Spectatorship. *Sinestesieonline,* 32 retrieved:http://sinestesieonline.it/wp-content/uploads/2021/05/maggio2021-09.pdf (consulted on 3. January 2022).

Wiles, D. (2000) *Greek Theatre Performance: An Introduction.* Cambridge: Cambridge University Press.

CHAPTER 10

Historical Reenactment and Theatrical Performance

On New Perspectives of Educational Methods

Elena Olesina and Elena Polyudova

In Russia, historical reenactment as a hobby activity is widely spread in the country. It exists in the form of various social institutions and groups. It could be a social club that involves the local people of a city or a village. It could be a large association that combines smaller branches under one head committee, as on the official website Rosrecon (https://xn--e1akjbcibh.xn--p1ai/). Recently, since the start of the pandemic, virtual groups have become popular and have connected people from different locations, often far from each other (http://livinghistory.ru/forum/52-katalog-klubov/). These groups and clubs have the traditional international structure of vocational organizations when people with the same interests gather to reenact events from the past. The associations conventionally involve groups of adults, and children actively participate with their older relatives. School students and youth are usually involved in reenactment. This chapter discusses several points about historical reenactment in Russian education as developed in the last decades. The first is the nature and definition of historical reenactment in modern Russian education. The second is the current state of the method in schools, its structure, and the teacher's role in the process of applying school content to the interactive engagement. The third is a case study of a historic reenactment which took place in a middle school, with a description of the stages of preparation and execution, with illustrations, and a description of the aftermath of the lesson for the students who participated in it.

10.1 The Nature and Definition of Historical Reenactment in Modern Russian Education

Educators, seeing this tendency of children to participate actively in reenactment, apply the concept to the learning process. Researchers (Glukharev, 2000; Leopa, 2011; Kader, 2013) underline that reenactment is an axiological part of the youth culture, which makes the activity highly important for education.

The main question to be considered is how to adapt a hobbyist activity, which is the origin of reenactment, to pedagogical methods. One basic principle, which makes the approach applicable for educational purposes, is integration of the experience of reenactment with theatrical performance. Theatrical performance, being highly interactive, is a key principle of the phenomenon. Participants use household items of any era to 'live in' and present a time on the stage. When a period of history is presented in the incorporated content, all actions make sense for students. Simple facts become live objects. Sets of knowledge serve the goal of looking at the history as a breathing organism. The reconstructed phenomena of past eras make it possible to be fully immersed in a historical environment, through costumes, household items, weapons and technologies.

Also, it is important to create a term that describes the pedagogical component and keeps the basic idea of the original source. Traditionally, such activities are called 'historical reenactment'. The term includes reconstruction of historical events and making physical objects, duplicating them, based on information found in historical sources. The latter is called 'living history', which has numerous facets and dynamic activities, from making clothes and using recipes to preparing traditional historical dishes and to replicating weapons. If historical reenactment is an interactive method of studying past events, their specifics and problems, then living history is one level of the reenactment. The goal of this activity is to restore parts of a culture in detail. It allows students to learn more about an era and has the effect of visibility. (It can positively affect the learning process just because of its nature of making abstract objects physically real and perceptible). Reenactment involves rebuilding various aspects of a historical period people used to live in. Traditionally in Russian education one term, 'historical reenactment', is used as the umbrella term that embraces all kinds of activities: reconstruction of events, living history, and theatrical performances.

It is more logical not to create different terms, so as to avoid uncertainty in the educational field. Although, for the purposes of school, there is no such thing as exact historical reenactment. Instead, only some elements of historical reenactment should be mentioned. Educators who use the term 'historical reenactment' include all other activities as variations of it; they use this one umbrella term, 'historical reenactment', because of its universal nature. Being complex in its structure, the method itself gives educators the opportunity to combine different approaches as needed for a certain lesson without overthinking about the terms used. The combination might change depending on the needs and peculiarities of a certain class. The universal strategy makes the approach adaptable for different educational needs. Hence, pedagogy actively uses the term 'historical reenactment' as the basis for defining activities related to reconstructing the past in different ways. Variations of reenactment can be developed in different ways, such as historic, ethnic, folkloric, military, and many other ways. The main idea remains the same, with some flexibility depending on educators' needs, requirements and interests. In education, historical reenactment is defined as an educational method based on the pFrinciples of interaction and immersion, when students study a curriculum through the practical activities of reconstruction, living history, and theatrical performances. Mostly, the method is used for studying social science and history to make the learning process more practical and socially oriented (Kotlyarov, 2013; Gobozov, 2015). To incorporate the method into the school curriculum, special administrative and organizational measures should be taken. In interactive learning, communication and collaboration come to the fore, and the teacher organizes the learning environment, contributing to the stimulation of the students' cognitive activity. The main activity is the communication within the class, the dialogue of all groups involved in the process of communication, conversation and interaction.

10.2 The Current State and Structure of the Method: The Teacher's Role in the Process of Applying School Content to Interactive Engagement

Beside the fact that educational reenactment is popular in schools, it would not be completely accurate to state that historical reenactment is a usual method in Russian schools. Because of its specific nature, reaching far beyond the school curriculum, its presence at school is defined by the presence of an enthusiast, an educator who is ready to dedicate his or her time to extracurricular activities. The method exists rather as an informal part of the school program, incorporated in it based on specially organized activities. This means the method is not easy for researchers to observe: they have to find enthusiasts or else traces of the method in a school's activities. However, school enthusiasts pay attention to the activities of the reenactment organizations, to raise the interest of students in school subjects and to share their experiences in research papers, periodicals and internet resources. However, modern education uses the historical reenactment approach as an efficient form of learning. Educational activities personalize the content of history, a school subject full of facts and names. This explains why most research and studies name the method as 'historical reenactment'. Studying history through revitalizing social and cultural phenomena incorporates it into school curricula. When the studying process goes beyond the school, the cooperation of school subjects and cultural institutions ignites a new circle of interest in history. Glukharev (2000) considers the reenactments as a part of the military-historical reconstruction movement. According to Glukharev (2000), historical reenactment at schools exists as a socio-cultural phenomenon. Beginning as an experimental activity, it is becoming more popular because of its effectiveness as a way for students to acquire ample pieces of information in history studies in schools. When planned carefully throughout the entire curriculum, it exists as a set of milestones for students. They know these activities will take place and look forward to them even when studying long paragraphs about events and historic personalities. For students, when a final reenactment event, or a living history presentation, or a theatrical performance is expected in the future, all studying looks like a reasonable preparation for the desired event. It increases students' motivation, in that getting through some hard work studying will be rewarded by a bright conclusion. Bozhok, N.S. (2013, 2015) defines the movement of historical reenactment as a phenomenon of youth culture. Youths not only like to be involved in activities organized by adults, teachers, educators, or reenactors, but also like to create their own costumes and organize their own performances.

From the perspective of a big structural picture, historical reenactment is a combination of research projects, gamification, immersion, and theatrical performances. When blended with theatre, reconstruction becomes goal-oriented and highly attractive for students who are interested in interactive presentations. In Russian education, the theatrical method is not new. It has deep roots in the works of Ershova and Bukatov (2021), who created a special approach in art education based on the application of theatrical technologies and exercises for classes. The core of the approach is to use special scenarios for running lessons, when everyone is involved in interactive activities in different wars. Based on this approach, called 'directing a lesson' ('rezhissura uroka'), lessons become improvisations when students create new reality built on the skeleton of a laconic plot. Creation of this method was centered on the ideas of Lev Vygotsky, who developed the concept of play as a leading activity for the age of childhood. According to Vygotsky (1996), children explore the world through games and role-plays. Changing roles gives children an opportunity to see the world from different angles, adjust it to their developing minds and move forward to the next level of their development. Later, in Soviet and Russian pedagogy, the idea became the core concept in creating the theory of children's development. The method is widely used in educational activities to improve students' social and cognitive skills. Elements of gamification and immersion support the goal of creating approximate models of historic periods. The models need not be an exact replica of history but should generate the idea of it. Meticulous details are not the main goal of this activity, for educational reenactment is supposed to create a broad picture of the epoch. It is not research with certain formalities, but a game with entertainment to reach educational objectives. It exists as a didactic approach, not a professional activity, being rather a socio-cultural phenomenon of modern pedagogy. Educators design it without expecting a serious outcome, but for the pleasure of the students who are playing roles.

Educators who constantly work with students of different ages highlight an effect the theatrical approach has on schoolers. It activates their ability to view events from various perspectives. It leads to strong cognitive results of understanding and knowing a part of historical knowledge. As educators highlight, the most important result is developing students' social skills of working in groups and as a team, forming soft skills of understanding each other and expressing oneself better. Another impact is the sense of self-realization and self-actualization. For schoolers, history as a living organism embodied in personalities becomes the way to express themselves in an individual way. Each student can find his or her own aspect of actualization through both historical material and theatrical performance. This activity is half-factual and half-personal. The therapeutic role of playing games help students to be someone else, remaining inside the school environment. It serves as a hidden support for those who need help but are afraid to ask.

Analyzing the recent experiments, researchers see reenactment as the way to develop the assimilation of cognitive, psychological, and educational spheres, at the cutting edge of efficient and natural personal development. Reenactment that allows observing the life of 'others' plays a complex role not only in students' education, but also in their upbringing. According to Ivanova, Golikov, et al. (2020), reenactment becomes a soft power to develop students' personalities. This conclusion leads in turn to an understanding of school reenactment as a meaningful activity to reach not only cognitive goals, but also psychological and communicational ones. Based on the statements of Ivanova, Golikov, et al. (2020), considering reenactment as a vital part of in-class activities balances the class psychological environment more than any kind of talks on the matter. School students who are involved in reconstruction, a 'cultural heritage event', see history as 'living history'. For them, history is not just a part of the textbook, but revitalized cultural life of the past. Moreover, being presented as theatrical activities, history becomes a part of student life. For school theatrical activities, historical material is presented not as a set of facts but as material for role playing, with all its accompanying aspects such as images of different historical personages, their psychological states, and characteristics.

These personalities have to have a certain pre-history and logic of behavior in certain circumstances. Their interactions with other historical figures must also have a certain sense. Without these factors, any personage from a history book will not be trustworthy. School students could not pretend to be truthful in such a performance, but they touch the subject, discuss the material, research the period, and look through the psychological background. The process becomes more important than the result, although often the result reaches the highest point of quality.

Other scholars ponder on a teacher's role in organizing such activities. As Vyazemsky & Strelova (2001) state, the teacher's role is central in the process of organizing a successful reenactment activity. The teacher, attracting students to reconstruction, arranges the reality of a past era's events. According to Vyazemsky & Strelova (2001), teachers are persons who organize and manage the process. They observe all actions from the perspective of the entire vision, the big picture. As professionals in both pedagogy and the taught subject, teachers have an extended background in the subject, which allows them to choose the most relevant and attractive elements. Such activities as the study of archival sources, the selection of materials and the manufacture of objects is always a practical activity, which at the same time relies on visual means. Educators become mediators between the ocean of knowledge and a group of school students with their personal traits, educational habits and studying interests. Educators plan carefully, turning the historical reenactment into a visual and practical method of teaching where students gain knowledge and develop skills by performing practical actions. Understanding of the method and its benefits was discovered by many teachers in the country. The method, being applied to different groups of students and to different subjects and topics, is becoming more developed in terms of educational instructions. Based on the praxis, teachers are sharing their experience and developing the approach, constantly adding new aspects and features: Dyomina (2012, 2013) – preserving cultural memory; Chyr (2016) - typology of the phenomenon; Kurbatov, Kurbatova (2014) – structure of the phenomenon; Dyachkov (2017) – immersion in history; Ivaschenko (2017) – self-actualization of adolescents; Kader (2015) – forming axiological systems in youths; Mikhalina, Bondarenko, Kryukova (2016) – understanding the historical background of everyday life through creative activities; Mirmanova (2016) – triggering students' cognitive activities. Hence, the educational approach is based on principles of interaction and immersion in the context of educational objectives. As many scholars and practitioners have claimed, special administrative and organizational measures should be planned and executed to make schoolers' experience more systematic and socially oriented. Teachers should develop a specific procedure to make a lesson with historical reconstruction as effective as possible. Altogether with the class management, it includes preparation for this type of lesson. The preparation has a sequence of stages that help in organizing the flow of a lesson: Ivashchenko (2017). Recognizing these stages allows a teacher to prepare a lesson more carefully without forgetting small details. The stages also organize students' attention through clear definition of the steps for the entire time. The following stages for preparation of a lesson with elements of historical reenactment are important for planning:

1) Development of a reconstruction scenario, using archival documents, maps, memoirs, historical materials.
2) Definition of heroes, historical characters, periods.
3) Rehearsal by students of their roles in the reconstruction.
4) Design of the space of the studied period (fields, premises, etc.).
5) Production, preparation of costumes.
6) Rehearsal of historical reconstruction.
7) The course of historical reconstruction.
8) Reflection.

In the third part of the chapter, a practical application exemplifies the stages in the context of studying a period of Russian history.

This approach cannot be so extensive without support from the state. During recent years in Russia, historical reenactment has become not only one of the methods of conveying the material to be studied, but also a socially significant way of getting to know and appreciate the past of the Motherland. It has received support from the government to run several social programs to enhance interest in the country's history. It serves the goal of preserving national history and heritage through the active involvement of youth in the preparation and running of festivals and gatherings. The movement of historical reconstruction is actively supported by the state. One of the examples is support for the military-historical reconstruction of the project "The Great Victory, May 1945". It is a voluminous program of several events for the reconstruction of significant battles and days of the Great Patriotic War (1941–1945). The measures of the Great Patriotic War are still fresh in the memory of the Russian people. It took place not so long ago, and there are still participants in the events who can convey to young people information about the events. The festival was held in the city of Bolgar, in the Republic of Tatarstan. The historical reconstructions were attended by teenagers and young people aged 12–30 years from military-patriotic clubs and educational institutions from different regions of Russia. The importance of the participation of young people in the Festivals of Military Events is unquestionable, in that it allows members of historic clubs to gather and become participants in the historical actions that reflect the Homeland's history. This festival keeps growing year after a year, with a growing number of historical reenactment clubs.

Another historical festival of national importance takes place every year in early September in the Borodino museum-reserve. This large-scale and well-known event is known not only in Russia. The International Military History Festival "Borodino Day" started more than 20 years ago, in 1987, at the celebration of the 175th anniversary of the Patriotic War of 1812. The first reenactors of military-historical clubs and associations came to the Borodino field and created the historical component and colorfulness of the event. The festival is held with the support of the Ministry of Culture of the Russian Federation. The key episode of the festival is the military-historical reconstruction of the combat episodes of the Battle of Borodino.

The festival in Smolensk "Gnezdovo-2014" is held with the support of the Department of Culture of the Smolensk Region. It is a festival of Slavic culture and historical reconstruction, and the only event for the reconstruction of the Viking Age.

The following is a list of other historical reconstruction festivals present in modern Russia:
- Military-historical festival "Kirillo-Belozerskaya siege" in the Vologda region.
- Festival "Persistent Tin Soldier" in the Moscow region.
- International historical festival "Forgotten Feat – Second Shock Army" in the Novgorod region.
- Festival "Siege of Azov" in the Rostov region.
- Military-historical Festival "Gumbinen battle" in the Kaliningrad region.

All these factors, such as the growing popularity of historical reenactment festivals, support by the state, and interactive technologies incorporated in the educational process of Russian schools, make school projects more interactive and spread out into different regions. Such activity connects schools, clubs and projects via the internet, giving schools new ways to communicate, share ideas, and exchange the results their projects.

10.3 Example of Historical Reenactment in a Middle School

As an example of educational historical reenactment, lessons at secondary schools in Odintsovo city, Moscow region, are considered. The activities of the method are applied as auxiliary elements in the classroom at school with the pedagogical modeling of the lesson. The reenactment approach includes elements of living history, theatrical performances and self-actualization. The living history element is conducted as a collaboration between the schools' teachers and the participants of the Odintsovo Living History Studio "Khronotop". The theatrical element is supported by the club members, who were briefed about the lesson's scenario and took part in the play. The self-actualization element is applied at the end of the series of lessons, when students work on their individual projects to make their own personal objects from the studied era.

Before and after the lesson, the teacher analyzes the procedure to create a road map of organizational details. The following are the important details to consider in planning a lesson. In the subsequent description, to exemplify the planning process, the general details are combined with the actual lesson (underlined).

- Define a school grade in terms of understanding the educational and psychological traits of the audience.
  The lesson is designed for students of the 4th grade.
- State the topic of a planned lesson.
  The topic of the lesson is the Old Russian state.
- Outline the purposes of the lesson in terms of its content as well as the adjacent content of the curriculum.
  Lesson: formation of new knowledge.
- Curriculum: The purpose of the lesson is to acquaint students with the era of the formation of the Old Russian state of the 9th to 11th centuries.
- Describe the form of the lesson in terms of the historical reenactment presentation/activity/application.
  The form of the lesson has two elements: presentation of the living history and theatrical performance based on the presentation.
- Explain the correlation between the lesson's content and the reenactors' participation.
  Students study the content during the previous lessons. The lesson involves presentation of living history objects as examples of the pictures and explanations from the textbook. The performance happens during the presentation (partial involvement of students) and after the presentation (based on the scenario).

Another important part of the planning is describing a lesson's objectives in a more detailed way. In the case of the lesson shown above, the objectives are the following:

1) Introduce various handicraft and cultural processes of the considered epoch to the students.
2) Help students learn about the military-squad traditions of Old Russia.
3) Assess students' personal contribution to the reconstruction.
4) Conduct students' personal participation in the event.

The teacher acts as the coordinator of this lesson, but the leading role is given to representatives of the historical reconstruction club (Figure 10.1). For clarity and more convenient work, it is recommended to change the arrangement of desks in the classroom, thereby creating a space in the center for demonstrating reconstructions. During this type of a lesson, students not only act as listeners, but also actively participate in the educational process. They participate in theatrical and role-playing productions planned by the teacher and performed by the club members. This activity gives students the opportunity to try on the image of a resident of the era under consideration (Figure 10.2). Due to the stylized appearance of the club members, the clarity and mainly the game form of the lesson, students are very interested in what is happening.

One of the most important points of these lessons is the summing up, the so-called reflection part. At the end of the lesson, the teacher thanks both the reenactors and the students for the lesson and offers the students a chance to discuss the experience. Students are invited to note the moments of the lesson they most liked. They are encouraged to discuss this format, which things interested them more and which less, and why (Figure 10.3, Figure 10.4).

As a part of the educational method, the reflection part is conducted with the following survey. In the case of the experimental and research work, the survey was offered to the students right after the reflection part (collaborative self-analysis of the lesson). The survey was given in the form of a questionnaire with 6 questions regarding the students' interest, their involvement in the lesson's material, their emotional state and their understanding of the material. The students responded to the following questions. The first one should define the level of participation: high (68%), average (26%), low (6%) (Figure 10.5).

The next five questions are Yes/No questions. The second defined how satisfied (65%) and not satisfied (35%) the students were with the lesson material. The third showed students' perception of the lesson: they were asked whether it seemed short (82%) or long (18%) (Figure 10.5). (It is important to note that, for school students, perception of a lesson in terms of its length is an important complex indicator of how interesting and engaging the lesson was. Usually, when students are completely involved in the study material, they do not rush out when the lesson ends. The researchers did not pick out the level of interest, but intentionally used a word familiar to the students. It helped to save time in completing the survey as well as to avoid unnecessary explanation about a new word that could distract students from their impressions.) The students were deeply involved in the content and did not want the lesson to finish. In this case, the lesson was not a lesson anymore, but a captivating journey with various activities.

FIGURE 10.1   The members of the Reenactment club display details about the living history in Old Russia

The fourth question was designed to show students' tiredness as a result of the lesson: not tired 55%, tired 45% (Figure 10.5). As was predicted, the students were tired although they were deeply involved in the lesson. This fact confirmed the research's suggestion that this type of lesson does not need to

FIGURE 10.2 After exploring the handmade replicas of the ammunition and life of the time, students are eager to take a picture with the club members and the objects

be given on a constant basis. For half of the students, being actively involved is a tiring experience that could be amusing only from time to time. The fifth question asked the students about their emotional state: improved mood (64%), not-improved mood (36%) (Figure 10.5). It demonstrated students' self-perception after the lesson. It was important for the researchers to ask students about it, to ignite the process of self-analysis and see how the lesson material impacted on students' emotions.

The results of the fifth question as well as the fourth one help to avoid overloading the reenactment lessons with extra activities. Based on the results shown (not tired 55%, tired 45% and 64% improved mood and 36% not-improved mood) (Figure 10.5), it would be better to reduce the number of activities and give students more time for self-reflection and simple rest.

The last, sixth, question was designed to gauge students' self-perception of the study material: 72% claim an understanding of the material, 28% – not understanding (Figure 10.5). It was not a formal quiz or a test. On the contrary, the question should demonstrate how students saw themselves in terms of studying. In the future, these results will help the teacher to compare the

FIGURE 10.3   After the presentation lesson, it is the time for self-introspection and analysis. It goes also together with the club representative in a costume of the Old Russia

self-awareness of the received knowledge and the final portion of the knowledge that remains.

Based on the questionnaire, students were keen to have more lessons like that. They were looking forward to studying the subject, knowing about further possibilities to participate in integrative activities with their classmates.

10.4   Conclusions

Based on the current state of praxis in Russian schools, the historical reenactment method is a new direction in the reenacting movement, based on

FIGURE 10.4 The grand finale: creating your own object based on the studied material with guidance and support of the teacher

educational needs. It can be concluded that the use of interactive methods allows students to be more confident in their abilities and skills. The integrative complex of different activities, from cognitive research to social interaction and performance, increases their level of self-esteem and self-confidence. The effectiveness of this interactive teaching method results in the following outcomes:
– Raising students' motivation in studying theoretical and highly factual subjects, such as the history of different time periods.
– Providing extensive opportunities for creativity through interactive activities, exposure to historic objects, communication with people who are

involved in the historical reenactment movement, and theatrical performances based on scenarios of different types.
- Promoting self-realization and self-actualization through pre-planned introspective activities that support the entire process of working on a project.
- Acquiring the study material more effectively and firmly through a complex approach that includes a combination of traditional studies, preparation for and active engagement in theatrical activities, and a special time of self-analysis on the studied content.

Interactively engaged students work independently to finish their individual projects as a part of the common goal. The final theatrical performance provides live experience of learning. Self-reflection helps students to understand the process of individual perception of the study material. The final stage, creative projects, enhances their knowledge through the realization of their personal projects. Although the process of developing the method of educational historical reenactment is not yet widespread in the country, it is getting popular and becoming more developed. With state funding in support of historical reenactment, the educational approach will gain a more practical usage. Educators who contribute to the method's improvement share their experience and expand the areas of its application.

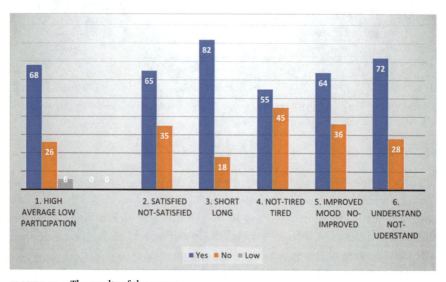

FIGURE 10.5 The results of the survey

Bibliography

Bozhok, N. (2013) Metod living history kak innovatsionny folklorno-etnkgrafochesky komponent istorichesky rekonstrurtsii v kontekste molodezhnoi politiki (The Living History Method as an Innovative Folklore-Enthic Component of Reenactment in the Context of Youth Poitics), *Innotsionnaya deatelnost, 2* (25): 162–169.

Bozhok, N. (2015) Vremya istoricheskoy rekonstruktsii (Time of the Historic Reconstruction). *Sociologicheskie nauki, 4*: 75–80.

Chyr, L. (2016) O raznovidnosti istoricheskoi rekonstruktsii (On the 3 of the Historic Reenactment). In *Sposoby, napravleniya i urovni rekonstruktsii kulturno-istoricheskoi realnosti.* Moscow: IV RAN, 7–15.

Dyachkov, I. (2017) Istoricheskaya rekonstruktsiya kak metod pogruzhenija v istoriyu (The Hisctoric Reenactment as a Method of Immersion to History)етод погружения в историю, *XLV itogovaya studencheskaya nauchnaya konferentsiya,* Izhevsk, 236–237.

Dyomina, A. (2012) Dvizhenije istoricheskoi rekonstruktsii: puti i reshenija. (The Historic Reenactment Movement: Paths and Decisions), *Vestnik KGU* (5): 45–48.

Dyomina, A. (2013) Fenomen istoricheckoy rekonstruktsii kak forma sokhraneniya kulturnoi pamyati. (The Historic Reenactment Phenomenon as a Form of Preserving of Cultural Memory), In *Genesis. Frontir. Nauka.* Astrakhan, 42–48.

Ershova, A. and Bukatov, V. (2021) *Rezhissura uroka. (Conducting a Lesson).* Moscow: Obrazovatelnye proekty.

Glukharev, I. V. (2000) *Dvizhenije voyenno-istoricheskoy rekonstruktsii kak sotsiokulturny fenomem (The Military-Historic Reenactment Movement as a Socio-Cultural Phenomenon).* Moscow.

Gobozov, I. (2015) Istoricheskaya nauka i rekonstruktsiya istoricheskogo proshlogo (The History Subject and The Reeanactment of Historic Past). *Problemy istoricheskogo posnaniya* (1), 65–80.

Ivanova, A., Golikov, A., Skryabina, A., Gogoleva, I., Dabrasova, L. (2020). *pedagogocal Conditions for the Development of Cognitive Independence for Humanitarian Studies in the Process of Mathematical Education.* Retrieved from G ÊNERO & DIREITO: https://doi.org/10.22478/ufpb.2179-7137.2020v9n2.50816.

Ivaschenko, G. (2017, 11 03) *Istoricheskaya reconstruktsiya na urokakh istorii i vo vneklassnoy rabote kak sposob samorealizatsii podrostkov. (Historic Reconstruction for History Lessons and Extracurriculum Activities as the Way of Adolescences; Self-Actualization).* Retrieved from Sovremenny urok (Modern lesson): https://www.1urok.ru/categories/8/articles/3999.

Kader, A. (2013) Istoricheskaya rekonstruktsia kak sotsiokulturny fenomen (Historic Reenactment as the Socio Cultural Phenomenon). *Psohologia. Sotsiologia. Pedagogika.*(6(31)), 20–22.

Kader, A. (2015) Aksiologichesky aspekt istoricheskoy rekonstruktsii (The Axiology Aspect of the Historic Reenactment). *Vestnik MGUKI* (1(63)), 141–145.

Karpenyuk, E. (2017) *Istoricheskaya reconstruktsiya kak pedagogichesky priem orientirovanny na standarty novogo pokoleniya: iz opyta raboty. (Historical Reconstruction as the Educational Method Oriented tothe New Generation's Standards: From the Praxis).* Available at DocPlayer: http://www.gymn2.ru/assets/files/1211_01.pdf.

Kotlyarov, A. (2013) Istoricheskaya rekonstruktsiaya kak fenomen sovremennoy rossiskoy kultury (Historical Reconstruction as the Phenomenon of Modern Russian Culture). *Traditsii i novatsii v sovremennom kulturno-obrazovatelnom prostranstve. Materialy IV mezhdunarodnoy nauchno-practicheskoy konferentsii.* Ed. L. Rapatskaya, 257–262.

Kurbatov, V. and Kurbatova N. (2014) Rekonstruktsia kak deistvenny sposob izuchenia proshlogo. Vidy. Structura. Funktsii. (Reenactment as the Efficient Way of Studying the Past. Types. Structure. Functions). *Konstept, 26*, 261–263.

Leopa, A. (2011) Reconstruktsia istoricheskogo proshlogo kak osnova formirovaniya istoricheskogo soznaniya obschestva (Reenactment of the Historic Past as the Basics of the Society's Historic Self-Assurance) . *Nauchnaya zhisn* (5), 100–105.

Mikhalina, Z., Bondarenko, N., Kryukova L. (2016). Obrazy i smysly povsednevnosti v istoricheskoi rekonstruktsii (Images and Meanings of Everyday Life in Historic Reenactment). In *Rol i mesto informastionnykh tehnology v sovremennoi nauke.* Moscow, 72–78.

Mirmanova, N. (n.d.). *MKOU "Novokrasinskaya OOSH". Istorucheskaya reconstruktsiya kak sposob aktivizatsii poznavatelnoi dejatelnosti obechayuschikhsya (Novokrasinskaya School. Historic reenactment as the Way to Enhance Students' Cognitive Performance).* Available at Solnechny svet. Mezhdunarodny pedagogicheski portal: https://solncesvet.ru/opublikovannyie-materialyi/is.

Vyazemsky, E. and Strelova, O. (2001). *Metodika prepodavaniya istorii v shkole (The Method of teaching History at Schools).* Moscow: Vlados.

Vygotsky, L. (1966). Igra i ee rol v psohicheskom razvitii rebenka (The Game and Its Role in the Child' Psychological Development). *Voprosy psikhologii*, 6, 62–68.

CHAPTER 11

Political Theatre in the 20th Century

Elements for Archaeology

Marisol Facuse

11.1 Introduction

The few authors interested in theorizing on the relationships between art and politics in theatre have mostly come from such disciplinary fields as theatrical studies, aesthetics, and art theory. This issue has also been of interest, albeit to a lesser degree, to sociology researchers who – to approach this relationship – have prioritized it as the object of their studies of the literature (Leenhardt, 1973) or the visual arts (Péquignot, 1993; Halley, 2003). On the contrary, politics in theatre has appealed much more strongly to artists, who themselves were the protagonists of these experiences of convergence between theatre and political activism. Most theoretical texts on the matter have been written by men and women of the theatre who, at different times, have given rise to militant theatre while theorizing with regard to the relationships between the two. Scriptwriters, directors, and actors have theorized on this situation from their own experiences such as the emblematic cases of Brecht, Meyerhold, and Piscator or, more recently, Augusto Boal (Boal, 2006) or Dario Fo. The historical sources of this reflection mostly come from artists from different historical periods who, through their writing, have recognized theatrical experiences implicated in the social struggles of their time.

Although in no way exhaustive, this present work seeks to contribute some elements to a sociological approach to the phenomenon of political theatre in the 20th century. In doing so, we have sought to configure an archaeology of the artistic practices in theatre. The exercise consisted of retracing three historical experiences of discontinued political theatre. These took place in collaboration, but also in dissonance, with other actors of the social struggles and the politics of each context.

In this article, we will examine three historical political theatre experiences separated by cultural context and geographical location: 1) agitprop theatre, 2) the political theatre of Erwin Piscator, and 3) experiences of intervention theatre in France. From there, we propose some elements which, although fragmented and dispersed, can contribute to comprehension of this particular

© MARISOL FACUSE, 2023 | DOI:10.1163/9789004529816_012

form of theatre that accompanied the social struggles of the 20th century. We will encompass the principles of this form of theatre, its singularities, and its contradictions. The objective is to find in this series of theatrical experiences convergences between theatrical and political practices.

11.2 Agitprop Theatre in the USSR

The emergence of agitation and propaganda theatre, known as agitprop theatre, was associated with the social upheaval and specific revolutionary imagery of proletarian struggles, inspired by socialist and anarchist utopias at the end of the 19th century and the beginning of the 20th.

Each of these political, social, and artistic contexts formed these experiences with various effects. An emblematic example in the Soviet Union was Meyerhold, who dared to take theatre from the showroom to the streets, factories, public demonstrations, and strikes; in other words, to the venues of the workers' lives and struggles.

Despite the specific aspects, we can say that agitprop theatre generally signified a disruption of the divisions which predominated over theatrical activity: professional/amateur, spectator/actor, song/theatre, performance/education, and art/propaganda. During a period impregnated with transformative utopias, these theatrical experiences sought to subvert not only the very conventions of theatre, but also the rethinking of genres, form, and dramaturgy, the structure of performances, and the place of the audience. The actors and directors thus sought to realize the utopia of proletarian art as a weapon of struggle that questioned and transformed the logic governing theatrical activity, as well as its audience, purposes, actors, and the motor of its action.

In the proletarian theatre of the day, its various manifestos and documents (as well as its declarations of principles and articles) expressed the search for a radical transformation of theatrical activity (Bablet, 1977). During these experiences, a deep and imperative desire for the reinvention of theatrical works, which invited the audience to participate in the entire process of theatrical production, opened up the whole process of creation. The writing, staging, and rehearsal processes were thus understood as flexible stages of a collective creative process, since "Theatre must not hide any aspects of its production. From the first steps, the process must be accessible to all".

These first disagreements seemed to herald the conflictive relationship between artistic practice and political structures, beginning with the eventual subordination of artistic work to the imperatives, or, on the contrary, to achieve creative harmony between artists and activists. On occasion, this theatre was accused of being too overt and radical in its defended political positions and performances. In terms of form, it was criticized for using blunt formulas to entice the proletariat to revolutionary movement. Meyerhold reacted to these divisions between political and artistic logic by claiming the inalienable need for autonomy in theatrical work, affirming that "in theatre, there is a certain number of indispensable elements which cannot be side-stepped without paying the price of abandoning theatre" (Bablet, 1977).

Despite the existence of a horizon of common values, artists and political structures clashed over various tensions regarding the emphasis and form of expression in these discourses. How could the logic of artistic effectiveness coexist with political logic in a project of common partnership? Where were the limits of artistic autonomy and singularity in projects which exalted the collective?

However, this transformative impulse of theatre and its anchor in collective life at the dawn of revolutionary experiences met its limitations with the conflicts between artists and state and party powers. Agitprop heralded a tension that would return with force some years later: the difficult balance between freedom of creation and the mobilization demands of the parties and movements which led the revolutionary processes.

11.3 The Political Theatre of Erwin Piscator

From 1919 to 1927, the actor and director Erwin Piscator conceived two theatrical experiences in Berlin that qualified as *political theatre* and which he compiled in the emblematic text of the same name years later (Piscator, 1972). Companies such as those of the Proletarian Theatre (1920–1921), the Volksbühne (1924–1927), and the Piscator-Bühne (1927–1929) put into practice a theatre which sought to become a vehicle of social transformation. The experience narrated here is based on the trajectory of a man of the theatre who, shaken by the horrors of war, found a new purpose and meaning in political activism.

Inspired by Meyerhold's agitprop theatre, Piscator initially participated in theatrical experiences during the war years, when soldiers performed for each other to raise morale during difficult times. In contrast with agitprop, which emerged in the context of latent revolution, Piscator's political theatre arose in Germany during the 1920s, as highlighted by the author himself, in the heart of a fully consolidated capitalist society.

Scrutiny was not limited solely to the socio-political domain: it also questioned the role and place of art in society. The program of political theatre sought to, in the words of its creator, "become a medium of social uprising against art and intellectual activities in general". Its author thus sought to evoke the anti-art radicalism present in the Dadaist manifestos: "Let's free ourselves of art by ending it" (Piscator, 1972: 27). The valuing of proletarian culture and agitation took centre stage, i.e., "Less art and more politics".

The objective was thus not only to propagate a political and social message but also to renew aesthetic forms through theatrical, technical, and dramaturgical experimentation. This new form of theatre sought to distance itself from the artistic conceptions of the late 19th century, which Piscator considered to be too captive "in an idea of beauty, grandiosity and truth" (Piscator, 1972: 27). In contrast, Piscator proposed a theatre which, like agitprop, sought to bring to the stage the struggles and conflicts of the workers.

The slogan "art of the people" became more relevant. This meant contesting a cultural terrain which, until then, had been monopolized by bourgeoise culture. For Piscator, the working class had to have access to theatre, which implied the transformation of differing aspects of theatrical activity, from the playwriting to the admission prices. This did not mean neglecting the quality of the theatrical work. As far as Piscator was concerned, "aesthetic critique was impregnated with political critique and as a consequence, poor artistic performance would betray the revolution and end up favouring the counter-revolution" (Piscator, 1972).

Political theatre sought to eschew an idealist notion of art in favour of a theatre which portrayed prisons, factories, stores, machinery, surplus value, and class struggle.

In 1920, Piscator created the Proletarian Theatre, which sought to serve the revolutionary movement and the propagation of class struggle. An important aspect of this project was to transform the principles of theatrical work. Common interest and collective disposition were encouraged based on equality between directors, actors, stage designers, employees, and technicians, as well as the audience itself.

This new project was not well received by all the political actors of the era and tensions gradually began to emerge. The German Communist Party strongly criticized Piscator's work, considering it a mere work of propaganda that did not deserve to be recognized as art. Other criticisms were of the fact that this form of theatre did not emerge from the social struggles: "Art is identified neither with its words or sounds, but with action [...] It is not in the Proletarian Theatre where a new form of art will be made, but in the trade unions and struggles of the street." (Rote Fahne 1920 in Piscator, 1972).

Between 1927 and 1929, Piscator began to direct the Piscator Bühne company, a theatrical project with a wider scope applicable to the new techniques of the Bauhaus movement and the theatrical stage. This implied a series of challenges on the financial plane. On the other hand, the public for whom the plays were intended could not afford to enter the theatre because of the high admission prices. In its final days, the Piscator Bühne suffered a period of 'catastrophe' dealing with artistic, political, and financial demands which ended up suffocating the utopia of proletarian theatre.

The greatest contradiction appeared to be that of a theatrical project which sought to propagate, through the medium of art, the values of a non-capitalist society but needed financial backing to survive. The artistic-political experience of Piscator brought to light the difficulties for a revolutionary theatre in societies that were still unchanged.

11.4 Intervention Theatre Post-May 1968 in France

Born in the context of social revolt and experimentation, intervention theatre after May 1968 in France resumed the initial longing of agitprop to reinvent theatre and its relationship with social reality. In these experiences, the desire to update collective work forms in theatrical production was revisited, as was that of rethinking the place of the director, the relationships with the audience, and the willingness to open the theatre to the workers, with culture transforming through policy coupled with politics, and vice-versa.

According to Philippe Ivernel and Jonny Ebstein, although there are significant differences between intervention theatre and agitprop, intentions common to both experiences can be found (Ebstein and Ivernel, 1991). As we saw in the manifestos of agitprop, in intervention theatre, the intention to transform theatre in both aesthetic (the search for new forms and playwriting) and organizational (the place of the director, the division of labour, and the distribution of salaries) dimensions are explicit, reaffirming artistic practice as a medium of social transformation. Both proposed, like the theatre of Piscator, to invite to the theatrical stage a public who were habitually distant from it: labourers, immigrants, trade unionists, and secondary school pupils.

The programme of intervention theatre seeks to overcome divisions between theatre and music, the streets and the theatre hall, the director and actors, and artists and technicians to work from a new logic based on the idea that "the whole world can get on stage". Artists of the time such as Anne Quesemand and Laurent Berman of the Théâtre à Bretelles recall that the contemporary theatrical practices proposed "making music and doing politics in a different way". Likewise, the initial intention of agitprop to bring theatre to non-theatrical places such as factories, stikes, psychiatric hospitals, and prisons was resurrected.

One of the legendary intervention theatre experiences was the Cartoucherie de Vincennes in Paris (Cramesnil, 2005). At the beginning of the 1970s, five theatre troupes were housed in the abandoned hangars of an old gun cartridge factory, where they built the walls of the theatres. The Théâtre du Soleil, the Théâtre de l'Aquarium, the Théâtre de la Tempête, the Atelier du Chaudron and the Atelier de l'Epée de Bois began their artistic adventure which gave new life to French theatre that continues today.

At the same time, the Brazilian theatre director Augusto Boal published *The Theatre of the Oppressed* which, through various methods such as 'forum theatre', 'invisible theatre' or 'newspaper theatre' proposed new tools and methods with the purpose of "giving the means of artistic production to the people" (Boal, 2006). At the same time, Dario Fo shared the desire to create political theatre and collaborated with the theatres of the Cartoucherie, highlighting the need to create theatrical forms closer to the culture of the people and oriented towards the proletariat: "Speak to the workers! [...] the aesthetic currents of the petite bourgeoisie are nothing but nonsense", (Fo in Cramesnil, 2005) in a formulation which reminds us of Piscator. Thanks to his influence, *commedia dell'arte* became fundamental to the theatrics of intervention theatre.

La Cartoucherie opened its theatres with a strong impulse towards artistic experimentation. The actors used various theatrical forms such as clowns, stories, street theatre, the use of masks, happenings, circuses, and songs. Companies such as Bread and Puppet and Living Theatre have participated in this movement.

Another distinguished intervention theatre company which was also close to La Cartoucherie was Troupe Z, who proposed and were characterized as a community of political and theatrical interests that sought to make this venue "a meeting place for the proletarian left [...] understanding theatre as a medium of combat and not a moment of leisure". (Luc Meyer in Ebstein and Ivernel, 1991: 124–125).

Jean Louis Benoît, director and co-founder of the *Théâtre l'Aquarium*, recalls these years in the Cartoucherie as an extraordinarily creative period in terms of new theatrical forms:[1] "The challenge was to construct a method of working impregnated with the ideas of the May '68 movement". An aspect of great relevance was the combat against specialization: manual/intellectual, master/

---

1 Jean Louos Benoit created the Theatre de l'Aquarium with Jacques Nochet, Karen Renourel, Thierry Bosc and Didier Bezace. The words quoted in this text were expressed in the conference "Building our Theatre" at La Manufacture theatre school in Lausanne, on May 23, 2005.

disciple, etc. This gave rise to new models of functioning. The themes of these performances were related to the occupation of factories, workers, the discontent of the working class, migrants, women, etc. as "the dynamo of this theatre was the desire to move towards the people, towards the oppressed, towards those who lacked the right of the word". The spectacles were conceived as "little battalions in factories and neighborhoods in the struggle". Just like the theatre of Piscator, the aesthetic dimension was never underestimated, as it played the main role in making sense of the performances. L'Aquarium created an innovative method based on the collective writing of texts compiling the lived experiences of the marginalized collected during long periods of on-site research. The actors collected testimonies, speaking to workers, housewives, and immigrant labourers to subsequently create performances based on these social realities. However, they also sought to avoid a romanticization of the world of the workers, likewise highlighting their contradictions. As with the experiences of agitprop, intervention theatre questioned theatrical production forms, the relationship with the press, and critique.

In theatrical organization, self-management and collective decisions were encouraged, in the belief in the importance of transforming the forms of theatrical production: "There is no revolutionary theatre without a revolutionary process".

Another of the companies of that period was Le Théâtre de l'Epée de Bois, which proposed making experimental theatre, based on research, which would function at the margin of the traditional economical logic of theatre. Its founder, Antonio Diaz Florian, affirmed its intention to make theatre political: "It is not through theatre that we will change things. I wish for the members of the company to some day become revolutionaries" (Cramesnil, 2005). Like other theatres of the period, L'Epée de Bois worked based on equality of salaries between members of the company, and implemented an artisanal functioning in which "all of the creations are fruits of the physical, manual and intellectual commitment of all of the members of the company" (Cramesnil, 2005: 193). Diaz Florian affirmed his conception of theatre as "a search for humanity and spirituality where the word 'professional' does not exist and the more senior actors train the newer. [...] All of the company assumes administrative and technical responsibilities" (Cramesnil, 2005: 321).

Georges Bonnaud, an actor of the Théâtre du Soleil, recalls that one of the fundamental principles of intervention theatre was to approach the 'non-audience' in their places of work. In a general way, they sought to respond to new objectives, answering the questions of "why and how do we do theatre?" (Ebstein and Ivernel, 1991: 33).

The question of 'how' was answered with its mode of functioning based on the principles of "equal salary for all, breaking with hierarchies and traditional forms of labour division". However, the desire to bring theatre to the workers had to face the suspicion of the very same proletariat towards a means of expression that had been reserved for a privileged class for decades (Ebstein and Ivernel, 1991: 162).

As a result, intervention theatre proposed the search for a 'pre-audience' in their day-to-day locations: factories, schools, etc. These experiences were not always so well received, as these were spaces that were distant from the theatre. As we have seen in the experience of Piscator and agitprop, it was common for tensions to emerge between the artists and members of political organizations.

During the same period, community theatre emerged in France. As we have seen, intervention theatres brought theatre to the neighbourhood and ran the "risk of becoming performing social workers", thus losing the power of its political intensity (Ebstein and Ivernel, 1991: 33). In contrast, the artistic legitimacy of theatrical practices, which had become distant from the conventional spaces of theatre, came under pressure.

The tensions related to the artistic recognition of this type of theatre, as well as the economic sustainability of the companies in the framework of political and cultural transformations of the 1980s (Abirached, 2005), gradually contributed to the decline of intervention theatre.

Paradoxically, the strength and radicalism of this theatre weakened with the Left coming to power. What started as a movement against the official culture began a gradual process of institutionalization. The companies faced these dilemmas in different ways. Some abandoned the themes related to social struggles to become conventional theatres. Others began to focus on themes of day-to-day life. Contrariwise, some directors became heads of regional *Centres dramatiques nationaux* ('National Drama Centers' or CDN, emblematic establishments for the decentralization of drama directed by the State from 1946).

With regard to the forms of organization, the horizontal models of functioning gradually began to fall out of fashion.

The new government doubled the subsidies to some companies, which caused changes in their organization. The principles that had inspired these theatrical practices, such as equal salaries and self-management, were replaced by more classical forms of functioning and the director once again occupied a central role in decision-making. The theatres thus went from artisanal functioning to the structure of a cultural enterprise.

Meanwhile, contradictions regarding the financing of these theatres emerged. In the 1970s, the budget allocated to culture, and in particular to art, was extremely limited (Abirached, 2005). The intervention theatre companies had demonstrated excellent quality in their work, creating shows and performances in extremely challenging conditions, often with neither theatre halls nor stable workplaces and with almost no public support. Most of the budget was directed towards the CDN and independent companies were forced to work under precarious conditions with their own resources or the sole support of the public.

The new policies of subsidies implemented by the Ministry of Culture in the 1980s caused many changes. A process of liberalization of cultural policies created large transformations in the economy and the functioning of the theatre companies. The grants no longer benefited the companies and began to be awarded directly to the directors who financed projects with rotating actors for limited periods of time. With that, the 'permanent theatre troupe' was no longer the predominant model, as it was overtaken by a model of 'freelance actors' contracted by the directors according to the needs of each specific project. Theatrical activity, like any other domain of society, failed to escape the logic of flexibility and precariousness that began to govern the work economy from that period onwards.

A new tension began to affect the continuity of political theatres, as the dilemma between autonomy or institutionalization in the middle of a period in which the conditions of artistic work carried out beyond the most recognized circuits of theatre began to decline even more, losing prestige and falling out of favour. Intervention theatre had managed to propose a new style of theatre that went against the institutional grain, creating theatrical practices 'interwoven with' the social reality of its time (Proust, 2006). The question was how to continue existing without renouncing the principles that had inspired artistic experiences post-May 1968. The companies found different ways of facing this challenge. Many ended the self-management and equal salary model to resume more classical organizational styles, while others ended up disbanding.

Over time and with the new demands, most intervention theatres ended up abandoning the desire to make the militant theatre that had marked the 1970s. Social exclusion and inequality were far from being overcome. Nonetheless, political and social protest movements had weakened and the theatres no longer put them at the forefront of their mission. Nevertheless, these experiences achieved a theatrical revolution during the 1970s, transforming its organization through self-management and increased equality between members.

During this period, intervention theatre achieved its goal of becoming a tool of transformation, emancipation, and rebellion. With it, traditional forms of organization were questioned. These included the absolute power of the director, the hierarchical relationship between intellectual and manual work, and the distribution of labour, among others. As declared in the manifestos, a double rupture was created: politics with theatre, because it transformed common social struggle strategies, but also of theatre with politics through the convergence of the stage and social conflicts (Ebstein and Ivernel, 1991). Intervention theatre had effectively succeeded in breaking with one order and creating another from the relationship between the theatre stage and real life.

11.5 Conclusions

An overview of some experiences of 20th-century political theatre throughout its history allows us to conclude that the artistic and activist practices are recreated in each era and context. Accordingly, the particularities of the social and political movements to which this art belongs are a repertoire of collective action. The theatres become political action as a function of the imaginaries, political issues, and ideologies that characterize each period. In the case of the intervention theatre of May 1968, the polymorphic and fragmentary nature of the movement gave rise to more diverse theatrical experiences than that of agitprop, which sought to be proletarian theatre according to a socialist utopia. Although both share a desire to bring to life a theatre capable of intervening in political and social problems, a broader range of political demands and discourses can be found in intervention theatre.

Theatrical practices are inspired by different utopian horizons, ranging from universal humanistic values to proletarian revolution, as we have seen in the cases of agitprop and the political theatre of Piscator. Although all three programmes seek to position theatre on the side of the oppressed, intervention theatre appears to have expanded its scope to include women, immigrants, the homeless, the mentally ill, and the incarcerated (Pessin, 1992).

Compared to its predecessors, intervention theatre demonstrates a particularity in its valuing of the micropolitical dimension of the social struggle. Both the conflicts expressed on the theatre stage and the demands of May 1968 span from public to private ("the personal is political") influencing the forms of organization and the relationship between the subjects participating in these experiences. The place of subjectivity and lived experiences of social actors and artists become increasingly relevant, as do the power dynamics in the organization of labour in the companies.

In this sense, in contrast with the programme of Piscator, the dimension of affect and emotion acquire newfound importance. It is no longer a case of "prioritizing the function knowledge and the objectivity of theatre" (Piscator,

1972); on the contrary, it is a case of considering the physical and subjective dimensions of the commitment of the actors and spectators, as well as the effects of the work on the body of artists and the social body. Political theatre has become of increasing importance in what Guattari recognizes as the struggles of desire (daily life, gender relations, the relationship with nature) articulated as struggles of interest (the economic system, salaries, working conditions) (Guattari and Rolnik, 2006). This is an issue that has become increasingly prominent in political theatre and performances of the 21st century, especially concerning the struggles of the feminist movement, which may be the topic of a future article.

Bibliography

Abirached, R. (2005) *Le Théâtre et le prince 1, L'embellie (1981–1992)*. Arles: Actes Sud.
Bablet, D. (1977) *Le Théâtre d'agit-prop de 1917. Tome II. L'URSS. Écrits théoriques, piéces*. Paris: L'Âge d'Homme.
Boal, A. (2006) *Legislative Theatre*. London: Routledge.
Brecht, B. (1997) *Les arts et la Révolution*. Paris: L'Arche.
Cramesnil, J. (2005) *La Cartoucherie, une aventure théâtrale*. Puteaux: l'Amandier.
Ebstein, J. and Ivernel, P. (1991) *Le théâtre d'intervention depuis 68*. Paris: L'Âge d'Homme.
Facuse, M. (2013) *La Compagnie Jolie Mome. Pour une sociologie du théâtre militant*. Paris: L'Harmattan.
Guattari, F. and Rolnik, S. (2006) *Micropolítica. Cartografías del deseo*. Madrid: Traficante de sueños.
Halley, J. A. (2003) Culture, Politique, et Vie Quotidienne: Dada et L'Expérience du Choc. In Deniot J. et Pessin A., *Les Non-Publics: Les Arts en Réception*, Paris: L'Harmattan.
Leenhardt, Jacques (1973) *Lecture politique du roman: la Jalousie d'Alain Robbe-Grillet* Paris: Éditions de Minuit.
Péquignot, B. (1993) *Pour une sociologie esthétique*. Paris: L'Harmattan.
Pessin, A. (1992) *Le mythe du peuple*. Paris: Presse Universitaire de France.
Piscator, E. (1972) *Le théâtre politique*. Paris: L'Arche.
Proust, S. (2006) *Le comédien désemparé: Autonomie artistique et interventions politiques dans le théâtre public*. Paris.

CHAPTER 12

Blast Theory between Public Space and Social Space

Vincenzo Del Gaudio

12.1 Blast Theory space

Theatre is a matter of space, and not only metaphorically, it is always a matter of territorialization, that is to say, it is the child of those social processes through which social actors structure the natural physical space, thereby transforming it into an artefact. Suffice to look at the famous incipit of *The Empty Space* by Peter Brook to realize this: "I can take any empty space and call it a bare stage. A man walks across this empty space whilst someone else is watching him, and this is all that is needed for an act of theatre to be engaged" (Brook, 1968:7). It is clear that the relationship with a space is something innate to the scenic device: there is no theatre without space, yet this relationship is never defined because specified by social and cultural conditions (Cruciani, 1992) and therefore must always be read within a historical horizon. This relationship today becomes even more complex to define because it must also take into account the dilation of space and time produced by the digital media (Manovich, 2001; 2010; Bolter and Grusin, 1999; Boccia Artieri, 2006).

This contribution intends to investigate the relationship between theatre, the performing arts, and public space in light of the work of the British company Blast Theory which, also thanks to a collaboration with the Mixed Reality Lab of the University of Nottingham, since the late 1990s has produced performances which undermine the idea of a defined physical space and work on the boundaries between physical and digital spaces.

The work on space of Blast Theory, in particular on urban space, is configured within a double bisector: on the one hand the company places at the centre of its performances a model of spatial relations that is fuelled by the relationship between performance, media, and audience, in which the public space is a result of a continuous negotiation between the actions of the performers, the actions of the audience, and the particular media involved, while on the other hand it invites the audience to reflect on the growing mediatization of public spaces in general. If it is possible to define the theatrical and performative space as that social space in which the everyday perception of the world is suspended (Ortega y Gasset, 1996; Turner, 1986; Del Gaudio, 2020), and therefore as something opposed to public space – at least on a symbolic and imaginary level, the performances of The Blast Theory, by the admission of Nick Tandavanitj, one of the artists of the collective, tend to weaken this opposition in order to experience an urban scenic space in which: "to let people occupy some fantasy life within public space" (Pereira Dias, 2012: 2). In their relationship with space, the performances of Blast Theory are part of a process of *performativization* of everyday life; which means thinking of public space as a relational space which is the result of an intersection between the social actors involved, the process of production of meaning given by the performance framework and, finally, the hiatus created between the everyday perception of the world and its artistic transfiguration. In this relationship, a decisive function is assumed by digital media, which are both an integral part of the relationship and the object which the group's research focuses on (Del Gaudio, 2021). The urban space thus becomes an ambiguous set in which the everyday perception of the world (always the daughter of deep mediatization processes – Couldry and Hepp, 2016), is put under a sort of magnifying glass whose main purpose is to think on the mixed nature of reality, and ultimately of space. Space, in particular the urban space, becomes the real focus of the performance since it is the condition of possibility of the interaction between the various co-subjects involved (actors, audience, social actors, media, etc., etc.); such an interaction can therefore be considered a kind of performance (Benford and Giannachi, 2012).

A first example of such logic can easily be shown in the 2006 performance entitled *Rider Spoke* (Foster et al., 2014). This performance "invites you to cycle through the streets of the city alone with a smartphone on your handlebars and a voice in your ear. You're asked questions about your life, searching for a place to hide your answer to each one. As you cycle on, you get to choose – answer another question, or look for the hiding places of others and hear what strangers have to say?" (Blast Theory, 2007). Audiences are placed at the centre of a necessary relationship with the space which determines the meaning of the performance. The audience must choose a certain space in which to recount their own little piece of the world, and above all it is the space which holds this for the other spectators, who may or may not have access to the fragments of information. In this way, the performance constitutes a finite narration and at the same time is inaccessible in its entirety both because it is dislocated in space (the different places where the various spectators choose to keep their messages), and because it is constructed in such a way as to produce an enormous network of information in relation to everyone involved but whose totality is not accessible to individual users. The urban space of *Rider Spoke* is also the child of the interaction between the audience and the computer installed on the bicycle, which gives instructions to the user so as to place him/her in a context where the meaning is the child of the relationship between user, space, and media. In this way, the space deflates and expands; not being solely confined to the physical space it becomes a mixed space which is open to the possibility of always being something else depending on the contingent performative interactions.

Ultimately, the space which mainly interests the company is the urban space and the city, since if on the one hand we can see a deep urbanization of the world which can be read through theatre and performance (Harvie, 2009) on the other, urban performances produce new perceptual models related to specific objects whose knowledge is pre-established and whose perception has solidified into shared meanings. In other words, the urban performances of Blast Theory aim to question a certain perception of urban space as well as the position of the social actors within it. This space must be understood not so much and no longer as an empty space, as per Peter Brook (1967), but as an *environment* (Schechner, 2012), a condition of possibility that is delineated beyond its physical status to become a space of relation between different social actors connected both online and offline. This model of space is an open, transportable space (Manovich, 2001) – it is itself a medium – which deflates mediatically and shifts its boundaries to redefine them as jagged coastlines.

12.2   Mixed Reality

The central concept for understanding Blast Theory's work on urban space is that of *mixed reality*. This was formulated for the first time in 1994 by Milgram and Kishino as: "a particular subclass of VR-related technologies that involve the merging of real and virtual worlds" (Milgram and Kishino, 1994: 1321). A mixed reality is one in which real and virtual elements coexist, it should be understood as a space in which different environments coexist in communication with one another and produce a virtual continuum thanks to which the various objects, both physical and digital, are presented within a single display. Useful in this regard is the scheme devised by Milgram and Kishino:

A mixed reality, in an era of digital convergence, and starting off from the pervasiveness of the production and consumption of digital cultures, must be thought of as a space in which the opposition between real and virtual has been eliminated. It is produced where a space of relationship is built between different fragments of the real that are in relation to pieces of communication and digital objects that have their own well-defined reality. This means that

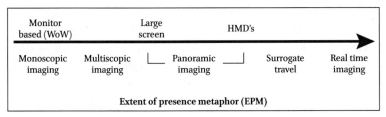

FIGURE 12.1   Extent of Presence Metaphor (EPM) dimension

the experience one has of mixed realities is increasingly pervasive. Therefore, Matt Adams goes so far as to hypothesize that in contemporary reality, due to increasingly smaller mobile devices which are continuously connected to the Internet, we are always experiencing Mixed Reality: every reality today is a mixed reality. For this reason, the works produced by Blast Theory investigate perceptual functions and patterns based on the ever-increasing influence of digital media on and in space. The methodology used borrows tools from the theatre and the performing arts as well as media studies, with particular reference to tools for analysing the videogame medium. (Jayemanne, 2017; Bogost, 2011; Pizzo, 2018). Despite a very strong theatrical and performative component, they rely on functions and tools produced by digital media and the use of digital technology in a creative and innovative function. By 'creative and innovative function' the company and the mixed reality lab mean the idea that digital media can be used for purposes other than those for which they were created and programmed; as if using digital technology against digital technology to make it manifest and understand the function and presence of devices in physical space – particularly urban space. For Blast Theory, thinking about performative mixed reality products means opening up a whole new web of fresh meanings to the everyday experience of urban space.

Thanks to the collaboration with the Mixed Reality Lab, the company has experimented, through mixed reality performances, with new forms of production and the dissemination of knowledge, such as producing not simply transferable knowledge through the verticality of the practices of reading and writing scientific essays, but embodied knowledge (Schneider, 2001; Taylor, 2019; Giannachi, 2021). Embodied knowledge is thus based on a movement of embodiment which travels from the page to the body and in the body becomes sedimented. This body is always at the centre of vectors of forces, is always a cyborg body (Caronia, 2008; Boccia Artieri, 2006) with technological grafts of various kinds, thanks to which the body itself becomes the ground and substrate on which to produce and reproduce knowledge. The body and the urban space are in a close relationship with each other, the space becomes one of the technological prostheses that are grafted onto the body. In the works of Blast Theory, mixed reality represents a model for probing reality in order to serve as a space for analysing the production and communication of knowledge related to digital media and how these influence social relations in physical space. Following Patricia Leavy's intuitions, the work of Blast Theory is based on a particular mode of knowledge transfer: "Importantly, performances constitute an exchange or transfer between the audience and performer(s) (this exchange is mediated in the case of films or written scripts). Moreover, the "exchange" may involve a complex negotiation of meanings. This interaction between the performer and audience also varies depending on the environment and mood" (Lavery, 2020). The work on mixed reality is based on the synergy of production, communication and consumption of knowledge "body-to-body" (Schneider, 2001) which works precisely thanks to the communication between bodies and space. These bodies are always thought of and taken in a close relation with digital media in order to create a true *digital performance social science* (Del Gaudio, 2021).

Mixed reality performances are based on four fundamental elements: 1) Performance as space, 2) Time 3) Interaction 4) Performance roles (Benford and Giannachi, 2013: 15). These four elements are decisive in triggering an open form of performance in which the various elements contribute to the success and negotiation of the meaning of the work as a whole. In particular, the first point focuses on the idea that space is performable in itself (Riccioni, 2020), that urban space is always a potentially performative space which, thanks to a temporal and interactive scaffolding supported by precise rules, places the relationship between social actors and technologies/devices under a sort of magnifying glass. The last point that needs to be addressed with regard to mixed reality is the central role of the viewer/spectator who, depending on hisher choices, sees a narrative and a process of sense production. This means that mixed reality performance models are based on a process of embodying knowledge and experience which works in a personalized way putting the user at the centre of the process as a decisive element for the success of the performance. This again means that, although there is a sort of plot and above all rules which guide the user's choices, what is produced in mixed reality performances is the child of an interaction and is therefore often not predictable (at least not in a schematic way) beforehand. Mixed reality makes every urban space a potential performance space. The spaces of the theatre and the urban space tend to overlap. This overlap produces a short-circuit whereby the urban space instead of being everyday becomes an extra-daily space (Del Gaudio, 2020), which is transformed and regenerated by the performance and shows its other side.

12.3 Can You See Me Now?

In order to fully understand the social logic at the base of the idea of space centred on the concept of mixed reality, it is appropriate to analyse some performances produced by the group. The first example is that of *Can You See Me Now?* (Benford et al., 2006). This performance, given for the first time in Sheffield in 2001 but repeated in many cities around the globe, is based on the principle of the game "cat and mouse". In the game, 15 people were connected online to a virtual model of a city; through a login they were able to access a portal where the basic rules of the performance were explained to them. In the beginning, the participants were asked the name of a person they had not seen for a long time and whom they would like to meet again. At this point, the real game began and then developed across about 500 – 1,000 metres of the city. In a virtual model of the city some avatars controlled by the online users could move, while in the urban space some 'runners' or 'searchers', equipped with a handheld computer featuring GPS technology had to search and arrive at least 5 metres away from the participants to consider them having been 'found'. When a certain person was found, he/she left the game, and the score was determined by the time he/she had been able to accumulate without being found. The runners were also equipped with transmitters with which to communicate with one another and cameras through which to take photos and make videos. The participants too could communicate with one another through the game system. All the players could access the others' locations and their communications.

This *pervasive game* (Pizzo, Lombardo and Damiano, 2021) was based on the idea that urban space could be shaped by social interactions both online and offline, that it functioned as a subtle medium (Manovich, 2001), one that could be "squeezed, re-formatted, changed into a flow, filtered, computerized, programmed and interactively managed" (Del Gaudio, 2016: 104). Urban space then becomes the stage for an interactive theatre which nods to video games as a tool for interconnection and the production of new forms of engagement. The architecture of the game also closely recalled that of a videogame, particularly those like the "Grand Theft Auto" series, while the model of the audiences moved from watching an action to performing an actual agency (Lavender, 2016) which, just like in videogames, is measured by the effects it produces on the narrative and the determination of urban space. In *Can You See Me Now?* this becomes an increasingly complex space model made up of coexisting physical and digital realities, a real media space.

Another point to focus on is related to the questioning of the liquidity of digital culture: working in a mixed reality, performances like *Can You See Me Now?*

focus on unmasking the materiality determined by digital media. The latter, far from being immaterial, determine their range of action from different layers of materiality ranging from that of the devices to the materiality of the links and servers which serve to operate the links. The performance shows how, starting from these new levels of materiality of information, space is increasingly the child of a negotiation between practices, agency, and a new materiality:

> The affect-production of the piece is bound up in its work across digital and material dimensions. The runners provide a commentary that emphasizes their corporeality and acts as a useful aid for those at the monitors. It conveys in-game information, as they communicate with each other about sightings they have made, or individuals they will track. And it endorses their outdoorsness. One runner comments, 'There's hardly anyone about. And it's getting very cold.' We can also hear their breath on our headphones. Space is physically inhabited and mediated through personal encounter and experience. This particular virtual world is a place of embodiment.
> LAVENDER, 2016: 187

Space, in this case, cannot be defined exclusively by its material qualities and therefore determined once and forever, but is liable to continuous re-significations and remixes, and is the child of social relations and especially by *affect-production*, of the affections and feelings which the agencies of the participants produce (Grusin, 2017). In this way, urban space and theatrical space (the latter understood as a space of suspension of the everyday), dialogue, and the sense of performance space are always linked to a negotiation between these two spatial models? along with? the media which expand both material boundaries and the affections of the users/players. The mixed reality model of *Can You See Me Now?* is based on a space open to possibility, a space which is itself performative since it is the child of an agency of social actors experienced in it, the child of the possibility of sharing a time producing new forms of 'digital liveness' (Auslander, 2012) based in turn on forms of 'nowness' (Del Gaudio, 2020; Gemini, 2016) which is a deep temporal sharing. Such space is based on interactions which are themselves performative forms, concrete actions for a determination of the space (Banford and Giannachi, 2012); and on the rules of performance as a necessary background with which the space must relate:

> It is only in the last couple of years that it has become obvious to us that our interest in locative media and work with mobile devices as in *Can You*

> *See Me Now?* is partly about how we can negotiate our relationship with strangers in the city. How you exist in an urban space, how you find the strength or the mechanism that enables you to have relationships with other people or with strangers, and what the political ramifications of this might be. And I think that they are very strong.
> CHATZICHRISTODOULOU, 2009: 109

Following the reasoning of Matt Adams, one of the founders of Blast Theory, interviewed by Maria Chatzichristodoulou, it is the new locative power of digital media, which become true locative media, that redefines the urban space in which we increasingly exist, on the border between media space and physical space as the rest of a network of forces and relationships.

12.4 *Rider Spoke* and *Karen*

Two other important examples of the relationship between urban space and digital performance in the work are the performances *Rider Spoke* (2007), which we have analysed, and *Karen* (2015). The former was produced by Blast Theory in collaboration with the Mixed Reality Lab at the University of Nottingham for the European project IPerG (Giannachi et al., 2010; Quigley, 2016). The game's performance encouraged participants to cycle around the streets of a given city and to stop at specific locations where they could record some memories. The urban space thus became a kind of memory space on which to engrave their memories which then remained available to the other players. Participants arrived at a fixed location in the evening, registered there, and were instructed by Blast Theory on the rules of the game and how to use the game interfaces. After this first phase, the players departed from the designated location one by one. The entire experience lasted about an hour and a half. After a few minutes, the voice of Ju Row Farr, one of the company's performers, would ask the participants to search for a place. In this way, each message of *Rider Spoke* assumed its own position in the urban space and prompted the players to transform "everyday life occurrences into spectacles" (Giannachi et al., 2010: 356). At the end of the performance, the participants were asked to leave a message with expectations about their future in the city and then return to their starting place. The interaction between the players/users and the technology took place through a headset connected to a touchscreen device. This interface allowed them to listen to messages from other users or record their own, as well as interacting with instructions from company members. The hiding places where the messages were released had a double characteristic: they were real, mixed-reality spaces because they had the characteristics of a physical place combined with the characteristics of a digital place, located through a WI-FI system and through this digitally represented. Following the performative turn (Fisher-Lichte, 2014), *Rider Spoke* transforms the urban space into a performative space by relating it to the personal experiences of the users who assume their own position within it. In this localization process, the everyday experience is transformed into a performative experience which is based on the interaction between user and digital devices on the one hand, and between user and other users on the other. *Rider Spoke* postulates a space which, like a medium, can be engraved with shreds of memory which become an integral part of its locative conformation, of the actual geography of the city. The space is continuously rewritten by the users' experiences which become cardinal points to orientate oneself and move within it: "Each city in which *Rider Spoke* took place thus became a mixed-reality palimpsest, a user-generated repository of more or less 'truthful' ephemeral memories" (Giannachi et al., 2010: 357).

Of a similar tenor is the performance called *Karen* (2015). This too is based on the possibility of performing everyday life and relating everyday space with performative space to measure their nuances and thresholds of incidence. *Karen* is an intermedial dramaturgy that works from an app which is downloaded onto the mobile devices of the participants. Once downloaded, it is possible to interact with the life-coach who bears the name of the app through a messaging system, videos and some questions which *Karen* asks us. While answering the questions, *Karen* collects the answers to create a profile of each user by interweaving the data from the answers and the data the user provided at the beginning in order to profile him/her. Interactions with *Karen* occur throughout the day. The architecture of *Karen* is multi-layered: 1) The text written by the artists on *Karen* hich is interwoven with the profiling questions which the company has adapted from the personality assessments administered to British military (Adams, 2016); 2) A second textual model generated from the interaction between the user and the app (Ilter, 2018); 3) A third text which is an account made by *Karen* from the interaction and is offered at the end of the experience at a price of two pounds ninety-nine. The intermediary process of *Karen* is produced within everyday spaces; it shows how interaction with our devices continually re-signifies the spaces within which we live. "By collecting information about us, Karen also collects information about our relationships in an everyday space". Another interesting thing is that the performance audiences act remotely: "audiences are never present as witnesses – they are asked to immerse themselves in an experience, take an active part in the development of a piece by performing certain actions, making choices, playing a game, making decisions that will shape their own and others' experience of the work" (Chatzichristodoulou, 2015: 238). The users are immersed within the game and determine its meaning and bring it to life by creating a real collective dramaturgy. *Karen* opens up space, shows how it is nowadays increasingly defined by human-device interactions. Public space, in Blast Theory performances, becomes more and more a performative space, as in the neo-avant-garde movements of the 1960s and 1970s, but, unlike the latter, not only is it increasingly complex to distinguish between everyday life space and theatrical space, but this indistinctness opens up thresholds of social experimentation of new forms of relationships that are daughters of the interaction between man, physical space and devices that shift its boundaries: a mixed-reality space. The work of Blast Theory is part of a radical rethinking of the forms of contemporary *performativity* in which space and interactions can be considered models of performativity understood as the ability to redefine and build performative models through the agencies occurring in space which, far from being an empty container in which to insert actions and objects, is always the child of the relationship and therefore never gives of itself once and for all but always in an intersection of forces and vectors in contrast and in agreement with one another (depending on the case). For this reason, in the work of Blast Theory, the theatrical space and the public and urban space are always children of a relationship, are always open to new meanings, as with *Can You See Me Now?* or *Rider Spoke* in which the urban space of the city from being something familiar suddenly becomes unknown and open to possibilities, or as in *Karen* where the everyday space however private it is (our home, the bathroom, etc.) is reconfigured starting from the relationship with the app and the device which allows the interaction.

Bibliography

Adams, M. (2016) *Inteview*, In Ilter, S. (2018) Blast Theory's Karen. *Performance Research* (23) 2: 69–74.

Auslander, P. (2012) Digital Liveness: A Historico-Philosophical Perspective. *Journal of Performance and Art* 34 (3): 3–11.

Benford. S., Crabtree, A. Flintham, M., Drozd, A., Anastasi, R., Paxton, M., Tandavanitj, N., Adams, M. and Row-Farr, J. (2006) Can you see me now? ACM *Transactions on Computer-Human Interaction.* 13 (1): 100–133.

Benford, S. and Giannanchi, G. (2013), *Performing Mixed Reality*, Cambridge: MIT press.

Benford, S. and Giannachi, G. (2012) Interaction as performance. *Interactions* (19) 3: 38–43 (consulted January 11 2022).

Boccia Artieri, G. (2006) *I media-mondo. Forme e linguaggi dell'esperienza contemporanea.* Roma: Meltemi.

Bogost, I. (2011) *How to do Things with Videogames.* Minneapolis: University of Minnesota press.

Bolter, J. and Grusin, R. (1999) *Remediation. Understanding new media.* Cambridge: MIT press.

Brook, P. (1967) *The empty space.* London: Palgrave.

Caronia, A. (2008) *Il cyborg. Saggio sull'uomo artificiale.* Padova: Shake.

Chatzichristodoulou, M. (2009) How to Kidnap your audiences: an Interview with Matt Adams from Blast Theory. In Chatzichristodoulou, M., Jefferies, J. and Zerihan, R. (ets), *Interfaces of Performance.* London: Routledge, 107–118.

Chatzichristodoulou, M. (2015) 'Blast theory'. In Tomlin, L. (ed.) *British Theatre Companies 1995–2014: Mind the Gap, Kneehigh Theatre, Suspect Culture, Stan's Cafe, Blast Theory, Punchdrunk.* London: Bloomsbury Methuen Drama, 231–54.

Couldry, N. and Hepp, A. (2016) *The Mediated Construction of Reality.* London: Wiley.

Cruciani, F. (1992) *Lo spazio teatrale.* Bari-Roma: Laterza.

Del Gaudio, V. (2020) *Théatron. Verso una mediologia del teatro e della performance.* Milano: Meltemi.

Del Gaudio, V. (2016) Remediated Spatiality. Performative and Medial Spaces in the Work of Imitating the Dog, *Anglistica AION an interdisciplinary journal*, 20 (2): 97–107.

Del Gaudio, V. (2021), Interactive Tools Performance: Blast Theory between Media Theory, Performance Studies and Social Research, *Comunicazioni Sociali*, 1: 79–86.

Fisher-Lichte, E. (2014) *Estetica del performativo.* Roma: Carocci.

Fostera, J. Benford, S. Chamberlain, A. Rowland, D. and Giannachi, G. (2014), Riders Have Spoken: A practice-based approach to developing an information architecture for the archiving and replay of a mixed reality performance, *International Journal of Performance Arts and Digital Media*, 6(2): 209–223.

Gemini, L. (2016) Liveness: le logiche mediali nella comunicazione dal vivo. *Sociologia della comunicazione*, 51: 43–63.

Giannachi, G. (2021) *Archiviare tutto. Una mappatura del quotidiano.* Roma: Treccani.

Giannachi, G. Rowland, D., Benford, S., Foster, J., Adams, M. and Chamberlain, A. (2010) Blast Theory's Rider Spoke, its Documentation and the Making of its Replay Archive. *Contemporary Theatre Review.* 20(3): 353–367.

Grusin, R. (2017) *Radical mediation. Cinema, estetica e tecnologie digitali.* Roma: Pellegrini.

Harvie, J. (2009) *Theatre & City.* London: Palgrave.

Ilter, S. (2018) Blast Theory's Karen. *Performance Research*, 23 (2): 69–74.

Jayemanne, D. (2017) *Performativity in Art, Literature, and Videogames.* London: Palgrave.

Lavender, A. (2016) *Performance in the Twenty-First Century: Theatres of Engagement*. London-New York: Routledge.

Leavy, P. (2020) *Methods Meet Arts. Arts-Based Research*. New York-London: The Guildford Press.

Manovich, L. (2001) *The Language of New Media*. Cambridge: MIT press.

Manovich, L. (2010) *Software culture*. Milano: Olivares.

Milgram, P. and Kishino, F. (1994) A Taxonomy of Mixed Reality Visual Displays, *IEICE Transactions on Information*, 12 (12): 1321–1329.

Ortega y Gasset, J. (1996) *Idea di teatro*. Milano: Medusa.

Pereira Dias, M. (2012) A Machine to See With (and Reflect Upon): Interview with Blast Theory, Artists Matt Adams and Nick Tandavanitj. *Liminalities: A Journal of Performance Studies*, 8 (1): 1–8.

Pizzo, A. (2018) L'attore umano nei videogiochi. *Acting Archives Review* 1 (12): 33–49.

Pizzo, A., Lombardo, V. and Damiani, R. (2021) *Interactive storytelling. Teorie e pratiche del racconto dagli ipertesti all'Intelligenza Artificiale*. Roma: Dino Audino.

Quigley, K. (2016) Letting the Truth Get in the Way of a 'Good' Story: Spectating Solo and Blast Theory's Rider Spoke. *Journal of Contemporary Drama in English* 4(1): 90–103.

Riccioni, I. (2020) *Teatro e società: il caso dello stabile di Bolzano*. Rome: Carocci.

Schechner, R. (2012) *Performance studies. An introduction*. London-New York: Routledge.

Schneider, R. (2001) Archives Performance Remains, *Performance Research: A Journal of the Performing Arts*, 6(2): 100–108.

Taylor, D. (2019) *Performance, politica e memoria culturale*. Roma: Artemide.

The Blast Theory (2007) Ryder Spoke

Turner, V. (1986) *Dal rito al teatro*. Bologna: Il Mulino.

CHAPTER 13

Live/Life Sharing

The Use of Social Media by Contemporary Theatre Companies in Italy

Laura Gemini and Stefano Brilli

13.1   Introduction

In this paper, we investigate the use of social media by Italian contemporary theatre artists and companies. The study represents the exploratory phase of an ongoing research project on how performance artists manage the boundaries between online and offline performativity, and between self-narration and artistic promotion. Through a combination of in-depth interviews and content analysis of Facebook profiles, we want to understand how this artistic scene – which has always experimented on intermedial and participatory possibilities – is making sense of social media. This reflection becomes crucial in the present moment. Firstly, because we are witnessing what some have called an 'ephemeral turn' in digital media (Haber, 2019); the shift from content permanence as a default condition to the multiple temporalities of stories and video streams, opens a new strand of possibility for relations between social media and performativity that are to be explored. Secondly, because of the way in which the Covid-19 pandemic centralized relations between theatre organisations and audiences in the online space for more than a year (Gemini et al., 2020); understanding what kinds of communicative practices on social media preceded this migration and how they mutated in the moment of crisis is of paramount relevance for the study of the relationship between theatre, media and the public sphere.

13.2   Theatre and Social Media

For the past decade, the use of social media in the theatre scene has been fuelling debates on the possibility of redefining the performer–audience relationship on a wide scale (Lonergan, 2016). In the context of mainstream-mainstage theatre, this possibility has been initially explored through Twitter in particular. For example, with the experimentation of live tweeting during performances with particular 'tweet seats' (Ahmed, 2011), or through the cross-media transfer of classic drama, as in the often-cited case of *Such Tweet Sorrow* by the Royal Shakespeare Company (2010).

These cases represent an initial phase characterized by a 'fascination' with the medium. However, as Bree Hadley (2017) has analysed, the relationship between theatre and social media now concerns a much broader spectrum of meaning-making possibilities that arise around performance. In her study, Hadley traces at least six areas in which we can currently observe the impact of social media in the theatrical field:

1) in the use of social media for the construction of intermedial performances, 2) in the dissemination of performances, 3) in the processes of audience development, 4) for the public of critics, 5) for documentation and archiving, and 6) in the performative aspects concerning the daily use of social media. To these areas, Crews and Papagiannouli (2019) also added the use of social media in the training phase. Del Gaudio (2021), expanding on the use of social media in intermedial performances, further distinguishes between: 1) Social media logic embedded in the dramaturgical material, 2) The use of social networks in mixed-reality performances, and 3) The staging of online performances which theatricalize digital space.

One of the main themes framing the debate on theatre and social media is the emphasis on the democratizing potential of these instruments, especially on the possibility that they have to reach marginalised audiences otherwise excluded from the orbit of contemporary theatre (Sant, 2014; Walmsley, 2019). Moreover, the theme of democratizing potential has also been explored looking at the role that social media can have in reconnecting theatre to the public sphere, notably by Butsch (2008), Conner (2013), and Balme (2014). In this regard, social media can amplify the range of debates developed within theatre outside the "closed circuit of subscriber audiences, professional reviewers and theatrical unions" (Balme, 2014: XI). Research on the 'expansive' potential that social and digital media could have on theatre have produced contradictory outcomes. The main problem is the actual ability of such media to breach the margins of the canonized networks. For example, O'Neill (2014) noted in his study of Shakespeare's diffusion on YouTube that non-European adaptations were almost absent from search results without racial appellations such as 'African', 'Asian' or 'Pacific'. In analysing the use of digital platforms for dance audience engagement, Walmsley (2016) concluded that these enhance the critical exchange between spectators, but also that such platforms struggle to maintain online engagement over time, especially for non-spectators.

At the same time, we also observe a mutating hierarchy between theatre texts and paratexts (Conner, 2013; Brilli and Gemini, 2022). This process entails the increasing centrality in spectators' meaning-making operations of all those elements which are external to the performance (audience conversations, promotional materials, theatrical trailers, artists' profiles on social media, etc.) but which are becoming more persistent and searchable thanks to the affordances of digital contents.

How the daily online presence of performance artists and companies relates to the paratextual corpus of performance is still a theme barely explored by the literature. Following this path becomes of particular interest in the light of the process of aestheticization of everyday life in which social media participate (Gemini, 2009), which places performance as a pivotal tool in the narratives of the digital self (Lavender, 2016). Observing this process solely as a collapse of the boundaries between performance and the mundane proves to be a short-sighted perspective, as it does not account for the way theatre artists work to establish the margins of their role within a media-based environment. As Nancy Baym (2018) observed in her ethnographic study on how musicians manage the artist-fan relationship, the increasing use of social networks by artists entails an increasingly high level of relational work for them. Such a task means a constant and demanding emotional effort to manage the frontiers between artistic work, private life, and personal exposure. Where the interaction with fans can no longer rely only on the boundaries provided by classic rites and infrastructures of performance (such as the stage, a concert situation, etc.), performers must experiment with the most appropriate ways to control the interaction. Defining the relationships with users, spectators and fans, is now likely to become an integral part of the theatre artist's labour routines.

13.3 Methods

Given that the use of social media by contemporary theatre artists remains a partly unexplored territory, the research presented here adopts a mixed-method approach. Specifically, two research questions guide this study:

RQ1: How do contemporary theatre companies and artists manage the boundary between promotion and artistic experimentation on social media?

RQ1: How do contemporary theatre companies and artists manage the boundary between self-performativity and artistic performativity?

To approach these questions, we conducted 16 in-depth interviews with some of the most significant companies of the Italian contemporary theatre scene,[1]

---

1 We conducted the interviews between July 2017 and November 2019. The length of the interviews varied between 50 minutes and two hours and fifteen minutes. The interviews were part of a larger research project aimed at analysing the relationship of Italian contemporary

as well as a content analysis of all Facebook posts published in the year 2019 by 38 companies or individual artists. The choice of the year 2019 stemmed from the need to analyse a timeframe that is recent, but not yet affected by the Covid-19 crisis, which arguably had a profound impact on the role of social media for artists and theatre organizations. The platform we chose to carry out the content analysis was Facebook since it was and is still overwhelmingly the main one in Italy to promote artistic events.

A key methodological problem was the need to adopt an overall view of the contemporary theatre field. We decided to avoid focusing on single case studies, which can be excellent for studying the more experimental side of social media use but are hardly representative of the whole art system. Mapping the field of contemporary theatre, however, leaves us with the long-standing problem of defining those who belong to this scene without falling into the oft-used approach of 'I know it when I see it', which relies on the authority of the researcher's gaze. We, therefore, had to turn to a criterion of self-definition. Our point of departure was the *Coordinamento dei Festival Italiani del Contemporaneo* (Italian Contemporary Performance Network). We collected all the programmes of the 53 festivals that are part of this network and selected the 38 artists who recurred most often in the programmes of the 2019 editions of these festivals, considering them as a sufficient approximation of the contemporary scene. Using the CrowdTangle[2] monitoring tool, we downloaded and coded all the posts from the year 2019 of the 38 profiles, obtaining 4,118 unique posts. For each post, we coded its prevailing communicative function (promotional, narrative, circulation of appeals etc.), whether it promoted anything, what kind of item it publicized (a performance, a theatre workshop, another type of product), and whether there were any references to other artists and theatre companies.

The choice to focus on contemporary theatre stemmed from the need to deal with artists actively experimenting with media technologies. In this sense, the interviews allowed us to analyse the artists' experiences while benefitting from their theoretical viewpoints, given the premise that contemporary

---

theatre artists with digital technologies, including promotional videos and social media. The selection of the interviewees used purposive sampling drawing on different generations of artists: five companies founded in the 1990s (Masque Teatro, Motus, Fanny & Alexander, Accademia degli Artefatti and Kinkaleri), five companies founded between 2000 and 2005 (Eva Geatti/Cosmesi, Anagoor, Stefano Questorio, Gruppo Nanou and Menoventi) and six companies founded after 2005 (Sotterraneo, Collettivo Cinetico, Babilonia Teatri, Compagnia Frosini/Timpano, Mara Oscar Cassiani and Ateliersi).

2 CrowdTangle is a tool owned by Facebook which tracks publicly available posts on the platform: https://apps.crowdtangle.com/search/.

intermedial performance implies reflexive work on the place of media in society (Gemini, 2003).

13.4 Results and Discussion: Social Media beyond Promotion?

A first issue which emerged from the interviews is that the field of contemporary performance has always paid close attention to the paratextual materials surrounding a theatrical event. Gianni Farina of Menoventi recounts how, before the spread of digital promotional methods, there was a strong commitment to imagining and composing physical folders containing information about the performances which were then sent to theatre organizers. Before the rise of social networks, he says, these became highly elaborate artefacts on which the artistic work on the performance percolated:

> When we started our activity, the companies were very careful in making folders for the theatre operators [...] Now they seem much less careful in the construction of folders, because there is more care in the online promotion. For example, Teatro delle Albe, a company that has always taken great care of communication, has now switched to simple cardboard folders. While once they had golden folders with embroidery. I think that at the same time they have taken more and more care of videos, photos, and Facebook communication.
> GIANNI FARINA, MENOVENTI

Another example of this aesthetic extension of the company's artistic work to performance paratexts is the production of video reductions of a play (Brilli and Gemini, 2022). These were meant to function as promotional trailers for the performance, but they often remained useless in the absence of a circulation infrastructure such as that of the social networks. Nevertheless, theatre artists continued to put much effort into their creation during the nineties:

> It's important to clarify one thing. We had a strong fascination for video because it was something that does not disappear like theatre, but which remains impressed. But in those days, since there was no social media platform at that time, video was a residual object. Either you circulated it in situations like festivals, such as TTV in Riccione, or you didn't really know what to do with it. There was no possibility to use it in a real promotional sense.
> ENRICO CASAGRANDE, MOTUS

Therefore, although digital platforms have redefined the role of media and performing arts paratexts (Gray, 2010; Conner, 2013), theatre artists demonstrate a particular awareness of their role that precedes the digital technological leap.

Looking at the way in which the interviewees conceive their use of social media, what stands out is a predominantly 'broadcast-like' or 'one-way' approach. There is little disposition among the interviewees to enter into a conversational mode or to stimulate user involvement.

> Our communication on social networks is not looking for comments. We would like to stimulate shares more than comments. [...] Conversation is not something we have ever sought much.
> MARCO VALERIO AMICO, GRUPPO NANOU

The expression of such an attitude does not mean that companies reject the interaction with their followers, but that the content they produce on digital platforms is framed in a *pull logic* rather than a *push* one.

> The philosophy of our communication can be summarized as follows: *if you look for us you will find us.* We do everything we can to be there and to be found, but the drive must come from your interest in us or in the themes that lead you to us. I'd rather not come ringing your doorbell every day.
> FABRIZIO ARCURI, Accademia degli Artefatti

In this sense, social media platforms are seen more as destinations for the artists' contents than as areas of relational work; their management, in other words, is not very dissimilar to that of a website. For example, Daniela Nicolò of Motus argues that the Facebook fan page settings allow a certain 'closure' to external interventions which is necessary to maintain control over communication of their artistic identity:

> We are also quite satisfied with the Facebook page setting where others can't put things on your page [...] I understand that personal pages may have other functions, but in order to show the identity of an artistic reality you need a fan page.
> DANIELA NICOLÒ, MOTUS

Another point that the interviewees strongly emphasize is the tendency to question the very concept of 'promotional'. They prefer to speak of 'presentation', 'seduction', 'anticipation', and 'invitation' when it comes to describing their use of social media. The rejection of a purely promotional logic is not merely the reflection of an anti-commercial or snobbish prejudice. It comes firstly from companies' doubts about the effectiveness of social media in broadening the company's visibility and, even less so, in bringing people to the theatre.

> In my opinion, the increase in followers never comes from the work on the Facebook page itself, but from offline things, like people coming to see the performance or from an event you participated in.
> CLAUDIO CIRRI, SOTTERRANEO

Secondly, this rejection comes from the realization that presentation has become a widespread (almost unconscious) habitus, and that it is no longer necessarily a commercial behaviour.

> The moment this idea of publishing material becomes a habitus, it changes what we are and what we do, then it bypasses this strictly commercial idea to become a representation of what one is doing at that moment.
> MASSIMO CONTI, KINKALERI

Thirdly, it also comes from companies' conceptions of their relationship with spectators. What is considered incompatible with the promotional angle is the pretension that they anticipate and satisfy the spectators' tastes. As Fabrizio Arcuri of Accademia degli Artefatti states:

> To me, 'promotional' seems to suggest meeting people's tastes, which is a problematic logic for me. When you're preparing a performance, you're not thinking about the audience's tastes or what they expect. It's a bit presumptuous to think you're able to anticipate people's choices.
> FABRIZIO ARCURI, Accademia degli Artefatti

This quest for artistic autonomy does not seek to sacralize contemporary theatre in opposition to more popular expressions, but rather to recognize and preserve the mutual independence between the artist's labour and that of the spectator (Gemini et al., 2018).

In place of a promotional logic, more than one interviewee opposed the logic of the 'aura'. This term refers to the way in which the online presence is not just a way to promote performances, but to construct a continuous existence of the company, an aura, indeed, which makes the artistic identity persist even outside the ephemeral performance event:

> It seems to me that our online hyperactivity works quite a bit, however mostly on people you've *already entered into a relationship* with, even a minimal relationship. Even at a distance, because you do not wind up in the province of Mantua every day, if it goes well you may find yourself there once every three years, but you give them an element of continuity. [...] Because all in all, be it big or small, *it's the artistic aura that we try to build, but that corresponds to how we are.*
> DANIELE TIMPANO, COMPAGNIA FROSINI/TIMPANO

> There is a *third function* in addition to promoting to organizers and audiences. Namely the function of *building your artistic identity in the social space, with people who may never come to see your play but somehow follow you.* [...] It creates that famous *aura* on which every artist works and then you do not know exactly when you will have the return and in what terms. [...] When you don't tour as much as you would like, the fact of saying 'that dimension exists' also makes you feel more alive. Because we all need people to acknowledge our work in some way.
> ANDREA MOCHI SISMONDI, ATELIERSI

We find an aspiration to use social media as spaces for communicative and artistic experimentation, at least for some of the artists. The interviewees do not seem to rule out the possibility of using such platforms to implement a communication that goes beyond the dichotomy between advertising and performance. However, this kind of use requires financial, temporal, and human resources that companies cannot always invest in.

In the second phase of the research, we therefore attempted to closely analyse which communicative styles the main Italian contemporary theatre companies were using on Facebook.

Figure 13.1 shows the number of posts published on Facebook in 2019 by the 38 companies or artists we brought together. As one can easily notice, there are substantial differences between the companies' posting frequency. A third of the profiles in the 'tail' of the graph make episodic use of Facebook, publishing less than once a week; the group in the middle of the graph publishes 1–3 posts a week; then, at the head of the graph, we find a few companies who generate a daily flow of content, to the point of producing a sort of digital live presence. In one specific case, that of the Compagnia Frosini/Timpano, this frequency

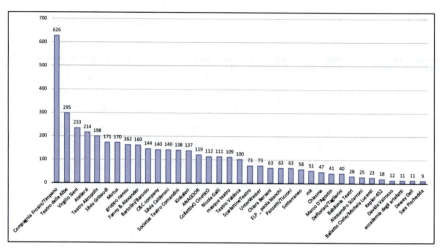

FIGURE 13.1   Number of Facebook posts published in the year 2019 by the 38 profiles we examined (via CrowdTangle)

reaches almost two posts per day, creating what we have named a strategy of 'social logorrhoea' (Gemini and Brilli, 2020).

The results of the content analysis show a somewhat unexpected situation (Table 13.1). Posts with a promotional function – by which we mean posts that communicate the date of a performance or a workshop – are the vast majority (63.6%). Theatre performances are the core of the promotional effort (Table 13.2). Less than a quarter of the posts refer to something outside a specific performance. Most companies follow a fairly standard posting style, which follows the performance life-cycle: posts about the preparation of the play, promotion of the date, gratitude to the audience and organisers, sharing of review article, and back to the beginning. The second most frequent function is a narration of the company's activities – sharing of tour photos, stories about the rehearsals, etc. – and posts sharing reviews. In line with usual social media trends, narrative posts receive significantly higher engagement than purely promotional posts (Table 13.1): if a post that promotes the company's activity has a mean number of 29.2 interactions (calculated from the sum of likes, shares, and comments), a post narrating the company's life gathers a mean of 43.5 interactions.

Contrary to our initial assumptions, self-narration is hardly present and online performances on social media are almost completely absent. Furthermore, we expected to find a dense network of cross-promotion, but despite the communal ethos that animates the scene, there is little reference to other artists or companies (Table 13.3). Only 2.4% of the posts are made to

LIVE/LIFE SHARING

TABLE 13.1 Results of coding a Facebook post's function and mean number of interactions (like + shares + comments) per function

Main function of the Facebook post	%	N	Mean interactions
Promotion of company's activities	63.6%	2,665	29.2
Narrating the company's life	17.8%	747	43.5
Sharing reviews/articles	9.9%	413	30.2
Curating cultural and news contents	3.5%	146	50.9
Promoting other artists' activities	2.4%	101	21.0
Personal narration	1.2%	52	62.4
Circulation of appeals/requests	1.1%	45	44.9
Commemoration/celebration	0.3%	14	38.8
Online performance	0.1%	5	60.6
Total	100.0%	4,188	33.1

TABLE 13.2 Coding of an object promoted in a Facebook post

Promoted object	%
Performance event	78.1%
Other type of theatrical activity	11.5%
Non-theatrical activity	5.1%
Festival/season	4.0%
Other	1.3%
Total	100.0%

TABLE 13.3 Coding of the presence of references to artists or events in Facebook posts not directly related to the activity of the company/artist

Reference to artists/events not related to own activities	%
Not present	89.8%
Theatre artist/company	4.0%
Non-theatrical artist/company	3.8%
Event	0.7%
Artistic community	0.3%
Other	1.3%
Total	100.0%

promote the work of other artists not directly related to the company. Perhaps even more interestingly, when promoting the work of others, there is almost as much reference to non-theatre artists as to theatre artists.

From what we have observed on Facebook, it is still more appropriate to speak of a 'presentational labour' rather than a 'relational labour'. Boundary management with the fans does not appear to be a central aspect.

Albeit in a few cases, some interesting combinations of languages emerge. These combinations corroborate the declarations of some interviewees regarding the attempt to overcome the idea that the online presence is strictly promotional. At least three-quarters of the companies whose profiles we analysed follow a style of promotion on Facebook that could be described as fairly standard. However, among the remaining quarter of companies, we can spot highly distinctive communication styles. Amongst these profiles, we have distinguished five approaches which break down the boundaries between promotion, narration and artistic communication: *paratextual extension, company as a public actor, dilution of the promotional aspect, 'artistic life is personal'* and *'personal life is artistic'*.

The paratextual extension approach is when the Facebook post provides additional elements about the theatre play which feed into the paratextual corpus that surrounds the performance. These elements can be details about the production process, sources used by the performers, extra-theatrical references such as films, songs or visual artwork, or audio-visual fragments that transmedially extend the performance. This approach is often adopted by the Compagnia Frosini/Timpano, one of the most forward-looking companies in Italy when it comes to transmedia experimentation applied to theatre (Gemini and Brilli, 2020). One example is a post (Compagnia Frosini/Timpano, 2019) in which they present a poem by the poet Carlo Bordini as one of the source materials that led to the writing of the text for their show *Zombitudine* (2013).

In the approach which we named 'company as a public actor', the theatre group intervenes on social media as a critical entity commenting on current events and disseminating calls to action. The clearest example of this position is that of the Motus company. Motus's artistic path has always involved establishing a connection between performance and action in the public sphere. This attitude continues on Facebook as well. Motus intervenes as a vocal presence both on current events – as in the series of posts on the Mediterranean migrant crisis and in support of the Open Arms NGO (Motus, 2019a) – and on episodes concerning the artistic community they belong to, as in the case of sexual harassment and bullying allegations against the acclaimed Belgian director and choreographer Jan Fabre (Motus, 2019b).

In the 'dilution of the promotional aspect' approach, the promotional aspect is still present in the Facebook post, but is complemented by a narration of the company's life or by personal reflections from the artists. In this respect, there is a tendency to mitigate the promotional aspect, where information about the show dates is preceded by other kinds of communication. This type of co-presence of communicative functions is found, among others, in the profile of dance and performance artist Marco D'Agostin. One example is a Facebook post, dated 17 May 2019 (D'Agostin, 2019), titled 'BELLA STORIA + COSA SUCCEDE STASERA' [A Beautiful Story + What's Coming Up Tonight]. This title immediately establishes a combination of storytelling and promotion. In the post, D'Agostin recounts how, following a lecture on his work given to a group of high school students, each student sent him a letter signed 'best regards', like the title of the artist's performance. At the end of the post, he writes how he will celebrate this touching event by channelling that youthful energy into that night's performance of his piece *First Love*. Thus, not only does the post contain both a promotional and a personal narrative, but it tries to put these two components in dialogue with each other.

By 'artistic life is personal', we define a style of social media communication where the working routine of the company is described as a way of life. Rehearsals, travel, workshops and moments of leisure are not just the building blocks leading up to the performance event; they also describe a specific way of existing in the world, based on being a group of people affectively and artistically connected. The posts by Collettivo Cinetico are examples of this style. The company associates the hashtag *#becinetico* to its more narrative posts, making explicit the confluence between 'working as' and 'living as' a company. For example, in a Facebook post from 29 June 2019, Collettivo Cinetico published a photo of the company engaged in nude free climbing on the Ligurian naturist beach of Sassoscritto (Collettivo Cinetivo, 2019). This is a moment of leisure, but one which embodies the bodily poetics of their performances.

Lastly, by using the reverse formulation 'personal life is artistic', we mean the way in which an artistic approach becomes a lens for looking at one's personal life. As in the previous style, it is difficult to separate the personal narrative from the narrative of artistic activity. In this case, however, what is narrated is not the company's work, but moments in the artist's life that open up insights into aesthetic and political reflection. In a Facebook post, dated 10 November 2019, performer Silvia Calderoni recounts a moment in which she finds herself sorting out the photographic archive on her computer (Calderoni, 2019). She reflects on how the overload of pictures classified in folders reflects an attempt to give order to the 'schizophrenic multitude' of which each subject is composed. The daily event thus becomes the stimulus for engaging in a subject consistent with one of the topics of the performer's artistic work, without leading to the promotion of a specific project.

In the next stages of our research we should also pursue this 'qualitative' look at social media communication in the contemporary theatre sector. The purpose will be to understand whether these styles we have observed are unique to individual artists/companies or constitute ways of overcoming the promotional logic that is giving rise to new communication practices.

13.5 Conclusions

In this paper, we have seen how the idea that performance artists can have a fruitful dialogue with social media has been present in the academic debate and among artists for years now. Yet this theme has been scarcely investigated.

One of the points which emerges firmly from our analysis is the willingness of artists to distance themselves from a purely promotional intent. Some oppose this aim with a different kind of conception of the company's communication. This conception is sometimes defined in terms of the construction of the aura of the company. The lexicon of the 'aura' appears as a way to extend the autonomy of the artistic field to typically heteronomous components (such as the production of promotional material). This conception also follows the will to cultivate a presence of the theatre company that gives continuity to what is, by definition, an ephemeral appearance linked to the theatrical event. We also find, both from the interviews and from analyses of the profiles, a scarcely interactive usage, which appears more presentational than relational. Is this distance from relational labour part of that logic of overcoming the promotional attitude? Or is the aura discourse used as a way to compensate for the lack of resources and skills needed to implement relational work? Further research is needed to clarify this issue.

Indeed, in some cases, companies seem to experiment in that grey area between the need to be known and performativity. However, this attitude does not emerge as a prerogative of the whole contemporary scene. In other words, we did not find a style that could be described as 'distinctive' for the way contemporary theatre is present on Facebook.

At the same time, contrary to widespread opinion, it is not digital platforms per se that redefine the boundaries between public and private, and between two-way and one-way communication. These boundaries are the product of artists' communication choices. We did not find sufficient evidence to support the hypothesis that online communication has necessarily made artists' exposure more personalised overall. This could, nonetheless, be due to a shift concerning Facebook itself, which has declined in its self-narration function for users compared to a decade ago. For this reason, in the next steps we would like to extend the content analysis to Instagram, where we can expect a higher degree of self-narration. A further step in the research will be to compare the data for the year 2019 with that of the last two years which were affected by the Covid-induced closures.

Bibliography

Ahmed, B. National Public Radio. *'Tweet Seats' Come To Theaters, But Can Patrons Plug In Without Tuning Out?*, December 12, 2011. Available at: https://www.npr.org/2011/12/12/143576328/tweet-seats-come-to-theaters-but-can-patrons-plug-in-without-tuning-out.

Balme, C. B. (2014) *The Theatrical Public Sphere*. Cambridge, UK: Cambridge University Press.

Baym, N. (2018) *Playing to the Crowd: Musicians, Audiences, and the Intimate Work of Connection*. New York, N.Y.: New York University Press.

Brilli, S. and Gemini, L. Trailers as Mediatized Performances: Investigating the Use of Promotional Videos among Italian Contemporary Theatre Artists. *Journal of Italian Cinema & Media Studies* 10, no. 1 (2022): 77–95. Available at: https://doi.org/10.1386/jicms_00103_1.

Butsch, R. (2008) *The Citizen Audience: Crowds, Publics, and Individuals*. New York, N.Y.: Routledge.

Conner, L. (2013) *Audience Engagement and the Role of Arts Talk in the Digital Era*. New York, N.Y.: Palgrave Macmillan.

Crews, S. and Papagiannouli C. (2019) InstaStan – Facebrook – Brecht+: A Performer Training Methodology for the Age of the Internet. *Theatre, Dance and Performance Training* 10, no. 2: 187–204. Available at: https://doi.org/10.1080/19443927.2019.1613260.

Del Gaudio, V. (2021) *Théatron: Verso Una Mediologia Del Teatro e Della Performance*. Milan: Meltemi.

Gemini, L. (2003) *L'Incertezza Creativa: I Percorsi Sociali e Comunicativi Delle Performance Artistiche*. Milan: FrancoAngeli.

Gemini, L. (2009) Stati Di Creatività Diffusa: i Social Network e La Deriva Evolutiva Della Comunicazione Artistica. In *Network Effect. Quando La Rete Diventa Pop*, edited by Lella Mazzoli, 113–36. Turin: Codice.

Gemini, L. and Brilli S. (2020) On Theatre Mediatisation: Exploring Transmediality in Aldo Morto 54. *International Journal of Performance Arts and Digital Media* 16, no. 2: 150–67. Available at: https://doi.org/10.1080/14794713.2020.1773698.

Gemini, L., Bartoletti, R. and Brilli, S. (2018) Il Lavoro Dello Spettatore Dal Vivo: Capitale Culturale Ed Esperienza. Il Caso Del Pubblico Del Rossini Opera Festival. *Sociologia della comunicazione*, no. 56: 43–64. Available at: https://doi.org/10.3280/sc2018-056004.

Gemini, L., Brilli S., and Giuliani, F. (2020) Il Dispositivo Teatrale Alla Prova Del Covid-19. Mediatizzazione, Liveness e Pubblici. *Mediascapes journal* 15: 44–58. Available at: https://rosa.uniroma1.it/rosa03/mediascapes/article/view/16771.

Gray, J. A. (2010) *Show Sold Separately: Promos, Spoilers, and Other Media Paratext.* New York: New York University Press.

Haber, B. (2019) The Digital Ephemeral Turn: Queer Theory, Privacy, and the Temporality of Risk. *Media, Culture & Society* 41, no. 8: 1069–87. Available at: https://doi.org/10.1177/0163443719831600.

Hadley, B. (2017) *Theatre, Social Media, and Meaning Making.* Cham: Springer International Publishing.

Lavender, A. (2016) *Performance in the Twenty-First Century: Theatres of Engagement.* London: Routledge.

Lonergan, P. (2016) *Theatre & Social Media.* London: Palgrave Macmillan.

O'Neill, S. (2014) *Shakespeare and Youtube: New Media Forms of the Bard.* London: Bloomsbury Publishing.

Sant, T. (2014) Art, Performance, and Social Media. In *The Social Media Handbook*, edited by Jeremy Hunsinger and Theresa Senft, 53–66. London: Routledge.

Walmsley, B. (2016) From Arts Marketing to Audience Enrichment: How Digital Engagement Can Deepen and Democratize Artistic Exchange with Audiences. *Poetics* 58: 66–78. https://doi.org/10.1016/j.poetic.2016.07.001.

Walmsley, B. (2019) *Audience Engagement in the Performing Arts: A Critical Analysis.* Cham: Springer International Publishing.

Sitography

Calderoni, S. (2019), https://www.facebook.com/346799346481/posts/10156847358501482, (consulted November 13 2021).

Collettivo Cinetico (2019), https://www.facebook.com/117438244939501/posts/2792549094095056, (consulted November 13 2021).

Compagnia Frosini/Timpano (2019), https://www.facebook.com/compagniaFrosiniTimpano/posts/2171873992835066, (consulted November 13 2021).

D'Agostin, M. (2019), https://www.facebook.com/157798090958238/posts/2677823585622330, (consulted November 13 2021).

Motus (2019a), https://www.facebook.com/93219706774/posts/10156752970886775, (consulted November 13 2021).

Motus (2019b), https://www.facebook.com/93219706774/posts/10157094165291775, (consulted November 13 2021).

CHAPTER 14

Theatre as a Means of "Interpreting" Lockdown
The Case of Staged

Jessica Camargo Molano

14.1 Introduction

The Covid-19 pandemic prompted governments around the world to take all possible steps to counter the spreading of the virus. In most countries, different forms of lockdown were adopted, including short-term or long-term closures of the main activities.

Even in the United Kingdom, after deciding not to adopt lockdown, the government led by Prime Minister Boris Johnson chose to close all non-essential activities to prevent the spreading of the virus. In an address to the nation given on 23 March, 2020, Johnson announced the country's first lockdown, which was followed by a second lockdown which began on 2 November, 2020, since precautionary measures had been relaxed during the summer.

Among the activities closed during the UK lockdown were all indoor entertainment venues, including theatres. *Staged*, a project produced by the BBC, took place against this background. It was created with the aim of meeting the requirement of British citizens to experience theatre despite the closure of physical venues where plays are performed.

Staged is a 'videocall series' of which two seasons have been produced until now, in correspondence with the first and second British lockdowns. As the title underlines, the starting point for *Staged* is theatre: the protagonists of the TV series are two theatre actors who are forced to interrupt the rehearsals of their play due to lockdown. On the director's suggestion, the two actors continue rehearsing the play through a series of video calls even during lockdown. The episodes of the series focus on the video calls that Tennant and Sheen exchange.

The aim of *Staged* is to succeed in performing even when it is impossible to be on a stage in the traditional form. Is it possible to speak of a theatrical form when a play is not performed on a stage, but through video calls broadcast by a TV series? Is it still theatre or is it another means of communication?

14.2 Theatre without Theatre

Staged is a new, different work that cannot be ascribed to a single means of communication. It is a hybrid in every respect, born from the contingent situation determined by the restrictions imposed by the British Government to avoid the spreading of the Covid-19 pandemic.

Staged can be considered a TV series, consisting of episodes (six in the first season and eight in the second). It was produced by the BBC, broadcast on BBC One, and later released on the BBC iPlayer streaming platform. Nevertheless, it is an anomalous TV series, as it was not filmed on a TV set, consisting instead of a series of video calls which the protagonists of the events exchange. Consequently, another means of communication, the video call, is involved. The video call implies modalities of interaction different from those typical of a TV series. The main characteristic of this medium is its static nature: the actors do not have the possibility of moving around as they would on a set, but are forced to stay in front of their computers' webcams. As a result, scene furnishings and scenery become secondary as they are only present as a background to the protagonists' close-ups.

Also the framing is linked to the medium used, i.e. the video call. There is no cameraman behind the camera, frames are shot by a webcam, a fixed camera. The actors are shot almost exclusively in close-up and, when they interact with other characters in the same room, they get out of the frame, as happens in real video calls.

Even the lighting reflects the idea of the video call. The actors' faces are lit by diegetic light sources (lamps, natural light), as happens in real video calls.

The other medium involved in *Staged* is theatre. The two protagonists of the story are theatre actors who play the role of theatre actors. They decide to rehearse their play through video calls, as they are unable to rehearse in a theatre, due to the closure of all theatres. Theatre is the backbone of *Staged*. Although it is not a play and is not performed in a theatre, *Staged* is a form of meta-theatre. *Staged* is conceived, written, and performed as if it were a play.

Therefore, *Staged* can be considered an example of what Bolter and Grusin define *remediation*: "the representation of one medium in another" (Bolter & Grusin, 1999). These two scholars contrast McLuhan's point of view according to which "the 'content' of any medium is always another medium" (McLuhan, 1962).

Bolter and Grusin argue that remediation is a characteristic of the new digital media, "we call the representation of one medium in another 'remediation', and we will argue that remediation is a defining characteristic of the new digital media. What might seem at first to be an esoteric practice is so widespread that we can identify a spectrum of different ways in which digital media remediate their predecessors, a spectrum depending upon the degree of perceived competition or rivalry between the new media and the old." Theatre is not a new digital media; therefore, according to Bolter and Grusin, remediation should not belong to this medium, yet the case of *Staged* shows a different scenario. Television seriality, video calls and theatre intertwine: the result is not a new medium, but a mixture of the present media.

It is possible to discover in *Staged* the crisis of theatre described by Williams in an earlier period: is there a theatre more in crisis than a closed theatre? "The crisis of performance, and of the theatre as an institution, itself affected by new means of dramatic performance in the cinema, in radio and in television, has made the continuing problem of dramatic form especially acute. Certain orthodoxies have hardened, and many damaging gaps have appeared and continued to appear. But also, through and within these difficulties, the energy and power of dramatic imagination have continued to create some of the essential consciousness of our world" (Williams 1954: 11).

Staged is just a product of the crisis of the theatre as a performing space and is a reflection on theatre as an art form and the other media. "The scenic device dialogues with other media fruitfully and borrows not only their téchne but also their logos, working as a metamedial machine, that is, using the scenic device to reflect on the functioning of the media that come into contact with it." (Del Gaudio 2020: 52).

14.3   *Staged*: A Mirror of Britain Fighting Covid-19

As already mentioned, *Staged* appears as a hybrid in all its components, starting with the choice of the protagonists. The main characters are two theatre actors, David Tennant and Michael Sheen, who play the role of two theatre actors.

It is worth noting that two Shakespearean actors were chosen, two representatives of the highest expression of British theatre. David Tennant has often pled the great kings narrated by the Bard, from Hamlet to Richard II, while Michael Sheen began his career giving life to Romeo and continued playing numerous characters from Henry V to Othello, until he acted Hamlet.

Apart from their theatrical careers, both actors can boast numerous performances on both the small and big screen. In 2009 Michael Sheen was appointed Officer of the Order of the British Empire for his artistic achievements, while in 2005 David Tennant became the incarnation of the tenth Doctor Who, a fundamental figure in the British collective imagery, a real recognition of his career.

When analysing a product intended for a British audience, it is also important to highlight the origins of the two actors. David Tennant is Scottish, and Michael Sheen is Welsh: both have always shown a strong attachment to their homelands, choosing on numerous occasions to act with great emphasis in their original accents. Alongside the two protagonists are their respective wives: Georgia Moffett from London, married to Tennant, and Anna Lundberg from Sweden, Sheen's partner. *Staged* was created with the aim of acting as a mirror for the British public of what was happening during the first and second coronavirus lockdowns. Therefore, it was necessary that it represented all the components of Great Britain. Tennant, Sheen and Moffett bring Scotland, Wales, and England on stage (they sometimes joke about and refer to the different origins of the three actors), while Anna Lundberg represents the many foreigners who found themselves stuck on British soil during the lockdown, far from their families of origin. Although Northern Ireland is also a part of Great Britain, it is not represented, since the Belfast Parliament implemented different strategies to contain the pandemic.

The BBC produced *Staged* with the aim of creating a product that could be enjoyed by the entire British public, with which all Britons could identify, and which could unite the population of the kingdom in the face of the pandemic.

The video calls between the two protagonists are interspersed with symbolic images of the lockdown: a deserted London, silent streets, empty supermarket shelves, the "toilet paper hunt" and images of the NHS, the National Health Service.

Just as the origins of the characters are useful for representing the different members of the audience, also the different types of families have the same goal. The Tennants have to look after four school-age children, while the Sheens show what it means to have a newborn baby at home during the pandemic. These two couples are joined by a third made up of the director Simon Evans and his sister. Evans, a theatre director, plays the role of a director of the play which Tennant and Sheen should have performed on stage and is at the same time the real director of *Staged*.

In the series, where Evans appears as a recurring character, he is shown stuck at his sister's house because of the lockdown. He represents the many grown-up people who have been forced to experience an unexpected cohabitation during lockdown.

In turn, the protagonists tell the stories of their neighbours: Michael Sheen has to deal with an elderly woman who lives alone (and who will suddenly be hospitalized), while Georgia Moffett has to assist a friend who is about to give birth. Two stories which represent two other aspects of lockdown: life that goes on, somehow, despite the pandemic, and life that has to face the disease.

THEATRE AS A MEANS OF "INTERPRETING" LOCKDOWN

The Covid-19 pandemic is undoubtedly what prompted the creators to conceive *Staged*. If there had been no pandemic and theatres had not been closed, both the main narrative cue and the goal of the story would have not have worked. Even though Covid-19 is constantly present in *Staged*, it is at the same time the great absentee. There is no introduction explaining why the protagonists are forced to stay at home: the audience know the situation well because they are experiencing it personally.

This is precisely the reason why the scriptwriters chose never to mention what is happening: the words Covid-19, coronavirus and pandemic are not used in any of the fourteen episodes. Only in the first episode do the actors hint at the contingent situation:

TENNANT: "The Welsh must have a good phrase for the end of the world."
SHEEN: "Why do you say that?"
TENNANT: "Dylan Thomas must have written about it. Written a poem or something."
SHEEN: "Of course, he wrote *Do not go Gentle Into That Good Night*."
TENNANT: "Well, there you go."
SHEEN: "I did a bit for the BBC."
TENNANT: "Did you?"
SHEEN: "Rage! Rage against the dying of the light!"
TENNANT: "Do you know what it is in the original Welsh?"
SHEEN: "How do you mean?"
TENNANT: "I thought it was translated."
SHEEN: "Translated?"
TENNANT: "Yeah, do you know what he originally wrote?"
SHEEN: "He originally wrote Do not go gentle into that good night."
TENNANT: "In English?"
SHEEN: "Yes!"
TENNANT: "That's disappointing."
SHEEN: "Cachu hwch."
TENNANT: "What does that mean?"
SHEEN: "Total fucking disaster"
TENNANT: "Kakhee hochhh!"
SHEEN: "Sounds like you're throwing up!"
TENNANT: "Kakhee hoch!"
SHEEN: "Cachu hwch!"
TENNANT: "Kakhee fuckin' hoch!"
SHEEN: "No, now you've gone Scouse!"
TENNANT: "Cachu hwch!"

SHEEN: "Cachu hwch."
TENNANT: "I could be Welsh. I could definitely be Welsh."
SHEEN: "We would never let you in."
TENNANT: "You'd love to have me. You'd beg to have me."
SHEEN: "We have been fighting the Scots off for centuries. We're not going to let you in now."
TENNAT: "Cachu hwch!"

It is worth observing that although there is a veiled allusion to the pandemic in this playful and sometimes ironic exchange of witty remarks between the protagonists about the different nations that make up Great Britain, no known term is used to speak about the contingent situation. Terms such as pandemic, Covid-19 and coronavirus are replaced with a Welsh expression *cachu hwch* (the end of the world).

Staged goes through the different phases of the pandemic: the first lockdown (Season 1), the illusion that the pandemic is over (conclusion of Season 1), the second lockdown (Season 2), the first fearful reopening, and the return to a certain normality (conclusion of Season 2). During these phases, the British people experienced periods of great emotional and psychological stress due to the restrictions imposed by the government. The appeal for national unity was fundamental: the individual's correct behaviour and respect for the rules was essential for the entire community. The symbol of unity for the British people is Queen Elizabeth II: in the most difficult phases of lockdown, the sovereign appealed to her people, trying to infuse them with courage and hope. The presence of Queen Elizabeth II was a fundamental element in the British people's processing of the lockdown. Therefore, *Staged*, too, could not fail to report this situation in its own way.

If Elizabeth II is the Queen of Great Britain, Judi Dench is the undisputed queen of Shakespearean theatre for the British people. Apart from her official recognitions (including Officer of the Order of the British Empire, Lady of Commander of the Order of the British Empire, Member of the Order of Companions of Honour), Judi Dench can also boast a relationship of friendship and esteem with the sovereign, whom she portrayed in the film *Shakespeare in Love*, a performance which won the Academy Award for Best Supporting Actress. Her ten-year role as M in the British film saga par excellence (James Bond), as well as her commitment to numerous solidarity and civic activities, have made the actress a real national institution and, therefore, it is Judi Dench who makes an appeal to the nation through *Staged*. In the middle of the first season, after having spent a first period of lockdown, the two protagonists start to become intolerant to the difficult situation. They no longer have any interest in working, in devoting themselves to rehearsals, they alternate the desire to go out and return to normality with pessimistic and almost depressive moods. The emotional swing experienced by the two characters represents the same mental and psychological fatigue experienced by all citizens during that period, a situation that can only be overcome thanks to the appeal of the Queen, or Judi Dench.

14.4 *Staged*: Theatre as a Mission

Judi Dench's presence within the story is a moment aimed not only at uniting the British people during the pandemic, but also underlining the very significance of theatre in British culture. When the protagonists, mentally exhausted by lockdown, decide to stop rehearsing their play, the director calls Judi Dench to the rescue. The actress invites the two colleagues to resume rehearsals, because, as soon as lockdown is over, citizens will be faced with a necessity: theatre. Theatre is not a pastime, something that can be present or absent in people's lives, theatre is a need inherent in every individual. From this point of view, Judi Dench's words define the profession of the actor as a real mission: the artist is called upon to satisfy this need for theatre that human beings have. The actor, therefore, cannot shirk his/her task; even during a moment of crisis, and according to Dench, especially during a moment of crisis, the actor should be at the service of citizens because only theatre can be the support necessary for the overcoming of the crisis.

The importance of theatre as a support is reflected in *Staged*, which is, to all intents and purposes, the tool that the BBC offers its audience to understand the pandemic crisis. The value of this project emerges episode after episode when other actors are called to intervene through video calls and play themselves in the series. Judi Dench's appeal turns out to be a real call to arms to which the English actor world responds unitedly (even American actors, closely linked to Great Britain, would guest in the second season of the series).

The other celebrities participate in the story particularly in the second season, when the director is is asked to make an American version of *Staged*. Other actors begin to be auditioned for the roles of Tennant and Sheen. In the fiction of the series, if there had not been the pandemic, the two protagonists would have staged Pirandello's play *Six Characters in Search of an Author* (Pirandello, 1921). In this Italian play, the protagonists, i.e. the Characters, come to the conclusion that the group of Actors is unable to represent them and therefore decide to go on stage to play themselves. In the first season of *Staged*, Tennant and Sheen play themselves, but, just like the Characters, they have not yet become aware of their role as actors. In the second season, Tennant and Sheen, by interacting with their possible substitutes, make the same reflections and follow the same process of awareness that the Characters make by interacting with the Actors.

This is a kind of meta-theatre that takes the form of an adaptation. Tennant and Sheen bring the theatre to the stage (albeit in a TV series constructed with video calls), rehearsing *Six Characters in Search of an Author* online. Tennant and Sheen play themselves who play the Characters. The audience watch the 'making-of', that is the construction of the play (metatheatre). In the second season, as in Pirandello's play, the Characters become real: no longer in the theatrical fiction, but in the "serial reality" Tennant and Sheen have to face those who want to play their roles. Tennant and Sheen start to act exactly like the Characters, sabotaging the Actors because they do not accept to be replaced. If the numerous plans did not overlap and only the latter was taken into consideration, it could be said that the second season of *Staged* appears as an adaptation of Luigi Pirandello's play.

14.5   Conclusions

The BBC project was created to meet the citizens' need to enjoy theatre despite the closure of the theatres. But why do they need to enjoy theatre? Theatre is the medium which allows people to interpret reality; through theatre the audience can grasp, understand, and anticipate the changes that society is experiencing. In a period as difficult to understand as lockdown, the BBC considered it essential to provide its viewers with a key to interpreting reality.

As Ragone points out, "Literature and the other arts are evidence of mediamorphosis, and play it out in specific ways that can be identified, by taking advantage of their super-activities in interpreting the environment" (Ragone, 2014).

The contingent situation made it impossible to frequent theatres, resulting in the creation of a hybrid like *Staged*. What mainly differentiates *Staged* from a real play is the lack of a live performance before an audience. Yet, according to Auslander, this difference is becoming increasingly subtle and almost nonexistent today. "The ubiquity of reproductions of performances of all kinds in our culture has led to the depreciation of live presence, which can only be compensated for by making the perceptual experience of the live as much as possible like that of the mediatized, even in cases where the live event provides its own brand of proximity" (Auslander, 1999).

According to Auslander, there are two main phenomena that almost eliminate the differences existing between a live event and a mediated one. The first phenomenon is the mediatization of live events: the main live performances of any kind, from a play to a football match, are increasingly conceived to be filmed. Moreover, live events often incorporate mediated moments, such as the showing of a video during a theatre performance or the use of a VAR (Video Assistant Referee) during a football match, which the audience present at the live performance enjoy as if they were in front of any screen (Auslander, 2012). As Auslander explains, "live performance now often incorporates mediatization to the degree that the live event itself is a product of media technologies." (Auslander, 2008: 40)

Therefore, *Staged* is a form of remedial theatre that performs the function of interpreting reality but at the same time is in reality and modifies it. "Works of art act in culture dynamically, as media and consequently as mutant and hybrid subjectivities" (Ragone, 2014). *Staged* is an example of how a medium adapts to and lives in contemporaneity.

Bibliography

Auslander, P. (1999) *Liveness. Performance in mediatized culture*. London – NewYork: Routledge.

Auslander, P. (2008) Live and Technologically Mediated performance. In Davis, T. *The Cambridge Companion to Performance Studies*, Cambridge (UK): Cambridge University Press.

Auslander, P. (2012) Digital Liveness: A Historico Philosophical Perspective, *Journal of Performance and Art*, 34 (3): 3–11.

Bolter, J. D. and Grusin, R. A. (1999) *Remediation. Understanding New Media*, Cambridge (USA): MIT Press.

Del Gaudio, V. (2020) *Théatron. Verso una mediologia del teatro e della performance*, Milan: Meltemi.

McLuhan, M. (1962) *The Gutenberg Galaxy, the Making of Typographic Man*, Toronto: University of Toronto Press.

Pirandello, L. (1921) *Sei personaggi in cerca d'autore*, Florence: Bemporad & Figlio Editori.

Ragone, G. (2014) *Per una mediologia della letteratura. McLuhan e gli immaginari*, Between, vol. IV, n. 8: 1–38.

Williams, R. (1954) *Drama in Performance*, Maidenhead: Open University Press.

CHAPTER 15

Cultural Welfare

Theatre in the Limelight

Annalisa Cicerchia and Simona Staffieri

15.1   Introduction

The expression *Cultural Welfare* indicates a new integrated model for promoting the wellbeing and health of individuals and communities through practices based on visual and performing arts and cultural heritage.

Cultural Welfare is rooted in the recognition, also sanctioned by the World Health Organisation (2019), of the effectiveness of some specific cultural, artistic and creative activities as a factor of health promotion, subjective wellbeing and satisfaction with life, contrast to health inequalities and promotion of social cohesion, active ageing, inclusion and empowerment for people with disabilities and for marginalised or disadvantaged people, complement to traditional therapeutic treatment; support to the care and to the doctor-patient relationship, management of degenerative conditions, such as dementia and Parkinson's disease.

Although data in Europe are still scarce, official statistics in Italy allow some preliminary associations between cultural practices and levels of satisfaction with life.

Among the various cultural activities – intended as both cultural consumption and engagement in cultural and artistic practices – the benefits of theatre are recognised in several conditions and contexts, with impacts ranging from improved communication skills to increased empathy, trust, social engagement, collaboration, and transformative learning. Children in particular respond very well to theatre stimuli, which are playful and fun.

15.2   On the Notion of Cultural Welfare

The expression *Cultural Welfare* indicates a new integrated model for promoting the wellbeing and health of individuals and communities through practices involving visual and performing arts and cultural heritage.

Cultural Welfare draws its origins from the recognition, also sanctioned by the World Health Organisation (Fancourt and Finns 2019) based on a scoping review of over 3,000 studies in several European countries, of the effectiveness of some specific cultural, artistic and creative activities as a factor of:

1) Health promotion, also related to the acquisition of coping skills and development of life skills;
2) Subjective wellbeing and satisfaction with life;
3) Combating health inequalities and social cohesion by facilitating access to and development of individual and community social capital;
4) Active ageing, combating depression and psychophysical decline resulting from neglect and isolation;
5) Inclusion and empowerment for people with disabilities and for people in conditions of marginalisation or disadvantage;
6) Complement to traditional therapeutic treatment;
7) Support to the doctor-patient relationship, through medical humanities and the physical transformation of care places;
8) Support to the care relationship, also and especially for non-professional carers;
9) Management of some degenerative conditions, such as dementia and Parkinson's disease. (Fancourt and Finns 2019, Cicerchia, Rossi-Ghiglione and Seia 2020).

The WHO Report documents several specific and desirable impacts of theatre, both as an active practice (e.g. people who participate in laboratories, workshops, acting courses, etc.) and as a regular passive participation (going to the theatre and being a spectator of live acting performances).

15.3 Theatre, Wellbeing, and Health: Evidence and Experiences

A 2015 Report on the Arts on prescription practice in the UK presents the results of over one million observations, for tens of thousands of individuals in the UK, collected since August 2010. A regression analysis was performed to investigate if there were any links between the levels of happiness and relaxation an individual reported and their recorded activity. After controlling for a range of other factors that might affect wellbeing, all arts and culture activities were significantly associated with happiness and relaxation. Theatre, dance, and concert rank first, scoring 8.7 for happiness and 4.5 for relaxation (Hamilton et al., 2015).

On the level of health promotion and prevention, evidence collected by the WHO (Fancourt and Finn, 2019) shows that involvement in the theatre could foster greater social inclusion in "patients with dementia and their carers, children, and adults with and without disabilities, police and ex-offenders, and adults across different generations (Gjengedal, Lykkeslet, Sæther and Sørbø 2016; Fantozzi, Cicerchia, and Staffieri 2020). This all builds social and community capital within societies". Theatre has also shown its effectiveness in cases of conflict resolution through developing cognitive, emotional, and social skills for constructive engagement, supporting empathy, trust, social engagement, collaboration, and transformative learning (Madsen, 2018). Lifting social stigma is another important contribution of theatre: "Drama has been used to address mental health stigma, with theatre productions on bipolar disorder found to reduce stigma in the short term among health-care providers". Theatre performances are proved to be effective in conveying messages related to communicable diseases and broader health. Due to its playful nature and the fun it often implies, theatre-based programs are beneficial to child development, as they contribute to improving verbal communication in preschoolers and in children with verbal communication issues. Theatre interventions have helped improve social and behavioral functions of children with physical or developmental disabilities. Children's theatre has also been used for raising awareness about child sexual abuse among children and parents.

Another successful field of application of theatre is its contribution to the cognitive reserve, and the resulting contrast to cognitive decline among the elders. For them, being engaged in theatre also means improving memory and executive function, auditory evoked responses to sounds and visual processing. Regular attendance of theatre has been associated with a slower rate of cognitive decline and a lower risk of developing dementia. On the physical side, frailty is also reduced among the older people practicing theatre activities as they train movement, posture and flexibility and have been linked with better balance (Meeks, Vandenbroucke and Shryock 2020).

Theatre is also a powerful support to caregivers. The use of theatre formats, including interactive theatre and role play, can improve doctors' communication skills, listening skills and the ability to respond instinctively and spontaneously. "Theatre training/performances can improve case presentations from doctors to clinical teams, reduce the use of medical jargon when communicating with patients, and support clinicians in breaking bad news. Enhanced communication is critical, given that the very tone of voice used by clinicians has been associated with the likelihood of patients initiating malpractice litigation" (Fancourt and Finn, 2019). Among informal carers, theatre performances have also been found to improve awareness of their responsibilities and caring duties when looking after somebody with dementia. In cases of mild-moderate mental illness, theatre can enhance self-worth, provide a positive focus for rumination (repetitive thinking), help to change one's view of oneself, support the development of coping mechanisms and provide a support network. In cases of severe mental illness, theatre workshops may help reduce social anxiety (Corbett et al. 2017).

Among people with acute conditions, and especially inpatients, the provision of theatre performances by patients' bedsides has been found to reduce anxiety and pain and improve mood and compliance with medical procedures in children and adults alike. Among people with autism, theatre also reduces anxiety, through improving sociability and providing stability and self-soothing when experiencing new situations.

15.4 Theatregoers, Cultural Participation, and Life Satisfaction

Unfortunately, at the EU level, official data about theatre are scarce, if any. As is the case for many aspects of cultural life, theatre statistics for the EU are not collected by a single stand-alone survey, but come from different Eurostat data collections, and are subject to the diverse statistical capacity of the Member States.

On the supply side, one may find some EUROSTAT statistics on the number of theatres in an assorted collection of cities, but data are gathered on a voluntary basis, and the result is not homogenous, especially since the number and geographical coverage of cities vary from one country to another and from one year to another.[1]

As regards attendance, only a voluntary ad-hoc module in the Adult Education Survey (last wave in 2011) was included in the questionnaire interrogations about going to the theatre. Unfortunately, data from that survey are published together with concert attendances, which makes it impossible to distinguish the relative weights[2] of the two different forms of entertainment.

On a different level, the 2013 Eurobarometer no.399 on cultural access and participation[3] reported that the EU27 average rate of theatergoers (also in this case, those who reported having been to the theatre at least once in the previous 12 months) was 28%, with Italy scoring 24%, the Netherlands 53%, and Portugal 13%.

---

1 https://ec.europa.eu/eurostat/web/cities/data/database. https://ec.europa.eu/eurostat/statistics-explained/index.php?title=City_statistics_%E2%80%93_culture_and_recreation.
2 https://ec.europa.eu/eurostat/databrowser/view/cult_pcs_caa/default/table?lang=en.
3 https://data.europa.eu/data/datasets/s1115_79_2_399?locale=en.

No EU-level collection of data covers theatre-related behavior other than attendance. This is unfortunate, since, as the WHO report clearly indicates, it is a continued, engaging, and systematic practice which may produce significant impacts on people's wellbeing and health. At the present state of data coverage at the EU level, therefore, we can only infer the existence of a relationship of the public with the theatrical offer.

In Italy, the yearly multi-purpose sample survey *Aspects of Daily Life* of the Italian National Statistical Institute (ISTAT) does include *one* question (out of over 100) whereby the respondent is asked whether he or she has gone to the theatre at least once in the previous 12 months.

Figure 15.1 shows the percentage of theatregoers in Italy from 2010 to 2020. Even allowing for the sharp decline in 2020 due to the Covid-19 pandemic, the trend is constantly negative.

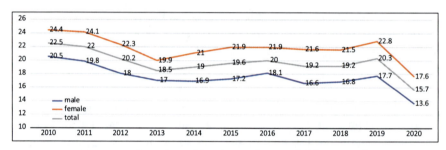

FIGURE 15.1 Percentage of people aged 6 and over who attended theatre performances at least once in the last 12 months by sex – 2010–2020

It is mostly the youngest who go to the theatre (21.6%). The lowest percentage is observed for those over 65 (9.9%) (see Figure 15.2). Cultural participation, and going to the theatre are associated with higher levels of wellbeing among people, especially older people in fragile conditions. Alas, data suggest that the elderly go to the theatre less than other age groups. Cultural welfare policies aimed at increasing cultural participation and addressed to senior citizens could be an important lever of personal wellbeing.

Information on theatre that is more detailed can be obtained from ISTAT's occasional sample survey of 2016, "Italian Citizens and Leisure Time".[4] In 2015, 17.9% of the respondents had been at least once to the theatre (of them, 80.4% 1 to 3 times, 12.2% 4 to 6 times). About 40% of the people with a university degree and 6.2% among people with only elementary education had attended

---

4 https://www.istat.it/it/archivio/232541.

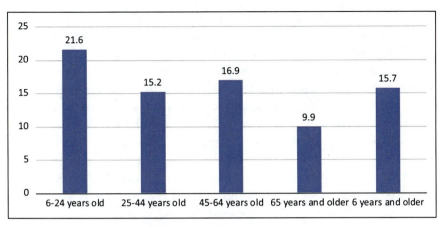

FIGURE 15.2 Percentage of people aged 6 and over who attended theatre performances at least once in the last 12 months by class age – 2020

the theatre at least once in a year. The age class with the highest quota of goers was 45–64 (20%). The largest quota, 35.5%, had chosen drama, 25.5% musical or operetta, about 20% each folk theatre and theatre for children. Those living in metropolitan centres preferred drama (50%), while 27% of the residents in areas with under 2,000 inhabitants favoured opera and folk theatre.

As for more active forms of participation and involvement, the 2016 survey shows that 4.8% attended theatre or dance associations, 2.8% attended theatre or dance festivals, 1.3% followed social networks, communities, forums, or blogs dedicated to theatre or dance, 6.2% were involved in puppet or marionette shows, 9.1% were involved in variety and magic shows, or cabaret; 1.1% were involved in burlesque or adult shows; and 11.7% were involved in travelling shows or street theatre. Respondents with higher educational levels expressed higher quotas of involvement for all the practices, while the age groups over 55 expressed quotas below the average.

The structure of the questionnaires used for surveys on everyday life allows us to investigate the association between theatre attendance and satisfaction with life. This, albeit in an indirect form, helps in assessing the significance in terms of wellbeing of the relatively low and declining levels of participation in theatres that the 2010–2020 data documented.

Our elaboration reveals a positive relationship between participation in theatre performances and satisfaction with life in general. In 2019, the share of the *very satisfied*, among those (14 years old and over) who had been to the theatre at least once in the 12 months preceding the interview was higher than among those who never went to the theatre (51% vs. 41.8%). This difference narrows for the younger age groups and rises to 11 percentage points for those aged 55–64.

For a comparison with a different cultural activity, and acknowledged as equally relevant for wellbeing, we have also calculated the association between satisfaction with life and museum attendance. Museumgoers present a corresponding picture, but with a somewhat limited impact. The relationship between museum attendance and satisfaction with life in general is in fact also always positive, but with slightly lower shares than theatre between the two groups (those who go to the museum vs. those who do not): 49.7% were very satisfied among those who went to the museum at least once vs. 40.9% of those who never went. Such a difference was wider among males, where 51% of museumgoers and only 42% of non-goers were very satisfied with life. The gap narrowed among younger people and widened among those over 65: 48.5% among participants vs. 36.7% of non-participants.

To understand the determinants of wellbeing and, more specifically, of satisfaction with life, we decided to include theatre in a more robust and inclusive indicator of the different cultural activities covered by the sample survey *Aspects of Daily Life*.

In the present elaboration, we have carried out logistic model estimates to test whether the descriptive evidence of cultural participation influences life satisfaction controlling individual and socioeconomic characteristics."Cultural participation" is an indicator drawn from the Italian National Statistical Institute project of wellbeing measures (BES, *Benessere Equo e Sostenibile*). It describes, by means of data collected in the yearly multipurpose sample survey *Aspetti della vita quotidiana* (Aspects of Daily Life), the people (6 years and over) who report taking part in a set of cultural practices in the 12 months before the interview. The activities included in the set are: having gone to the cinema at least four times, to the theatre, having visited at least once exhibitions and museums, archaeological sites, and/or monuments, having attended at least once concerts of classical music, opera, concerts of other kinds of music; having read newspapers at least three times a week, having read at least four books for purposes different from study or work.

The individual characteristics used in the model are demographic (gender), socioeconomic (educational qualification, employment status, judgment on economic resources, family typology), perceived state of health, cultural participation, social participation and territorial context variables.

To this end, we make use of a logit model to compute the effect of cultural participation dividing the reference population in two groups: people aged 24 and over in good health (understood as the absence of severe limitations) and people aged 24 with severe limitations.

We then analyse the average marginal effect (AME) of cultural participation – the mean change of the dependent variable as each independent variable included in the model specification changes, a parity of the others – using the data released by ISTAT (average value 2018–2019).

According to our strategy, we use, in the models, the following independent variables: Economic resources (reference mode: none or absolutely insufficient); Cultural participation (reference mode: none); Social participation (reference mode: none); Family type (reference mode: Sigle); self-declared occupational status (reference mode: Seeking for job); density areas (reference mode: until 2.000 inhabitants); Sex (reference mode: Male); Educational level (reference mode: none, primary and lower secondary education) and perceived state of health (reference mode: bad/very bad).

The dependent variable (y_i) is constructed based on the value of the scores expressed on life satisfaction (in range 1–10); if the score is in the range 8–10 then $y_i=1$, while if the score is equal to or less than 7 then $y_i=0$.

The estimated coefficients – statistically significant – (see Figure 15.3) confirm that, for both groups: a good perception of one's state of health has a positive effect on satisfaction; the territory/context of residence affects the assessments on general satisfaction with life: living in the central municipalities of the metropolitan area compared to a small municipality (up to 2,000 inhabitants) reduces the propensity to be satisfied; a satisfactory (excellent/adequate) economic situation has positive effects for both groups; being employed, retired or in other conditions compared to those seeking employment, has a positive effect, especially among the population without severe limitations; the family type (single reference group) has effects on satisfaction: living in a couple both without and with children has positive effects in both collectives considered compared to being single, living in another family type has a negative effect.

Cultural participation, our key variable, shows a positive effect, even if with less intensity, on life satisfaction on both collectives. The effect is greater for people with limitations.

A good perception of one's state of health greatly increases satisfaction. The territory/context of residence affects the assessments of general satisfaction with life: living in the central municipalities of the metropolitan area compared to a small municipality (up to 2,000 inhabitants) reduces the degree of satisfaction. A satisfactory (excellent/adequate) economic situation has positive effects for both groups. Being employed, retired or in other conditions compared to those seeking employment, has a positive effect, especially among the population without severe limitations. The family type (single reference group) has effects on satisfaction: living in a couple both without and with children has positive effects in both collectives considered compared to being single, living in another family type has a negative effect.

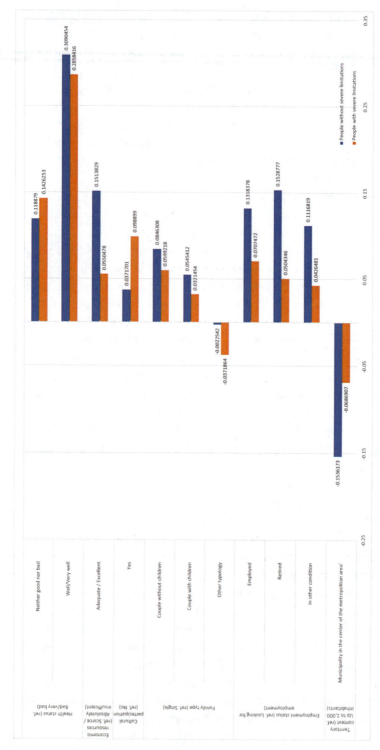

FIGURE 15.3 Logistic model estimates of coefficients (a) in model with life satisfaction as dependent variable

15.5 Looking Ahead: *Theatre Syrup*

Even though the lack of targeted data collection forces us to resort to a set of statistics that are not specifically collected for the purpose of describing cultural participation (and involvement with theatre), the statistics we accessed point to a robust association between a lively cultural activity and high levels of satisfaction with life.

During the Covid-19 pandemic, long periods of interruption of school attendance, together with the impossibility of enjoying sports, extracurricular and cultural activities, especially in the most fragile sectors of the population, have led to damage to the cognitive and learning spheres of children and adolescents and a lack of positive social and emotional experiences. The risk is that the phenomena of educational poverty and marginalization will increase further.

In response to this, the Italian Region of Emilia-Romagna has launched in December 2021, a special experimental program of "Arts on Prescription", focused on theatre. For children and families, the theatre is a place that arouses emotions, makes experiences to be shared, stimulates curiosity, and creates shared and playful educational experiences. A theatre is a place open to all where attention to the most fragile children and families in difficulty can and must be translated into actions aimed at supporting them.

The Region's Culture, Health and Welfare Departments, local authorities and territories, regional organizations, and scientific associations of pediatricians and pharmacies have started to collaborate. The basic idea is that, through the project, children will go to the theatre with *Theatre Syrup*, 'prescribed' by their pediatrician or purchased at the pharmacy. The way the project works is simple: pediatricians and pharmacies can provide children between the ages of 3 and 8 with Theatre Syrup: an "exceptional medicine to get excited about. A true wonder that cures the whole family".

The 'syrup' is a booklet, with a cover depicting a small bottle that looks just like any other cough syrup. The booklet also includes a leaflet, which contains instructions on how to administer and take this extraordinary medicine.

In the booklet, there are six 'prescriptions', each of which corresponds to a ticket, at the price of 2 Euro, for each child and each accompanying adult, who will thus be able to attend a season of 3 children's theatre shows in the theatres of the municipalities participating in the network. Over 150 pediatricians and 234 pharmacies take part in the program. Theatre Syrup comprises 71 shows.

Theatre Syrup represents one of the first cases of planned Cultural Welfare interventions in Italy, one with a careful and detailed cooperative institutional setting, where health and culture operators work together, each with their specific competencies and roles. A thorough monitoring and evaluation program will accompany the experiment. The results will be precious for redesigning future editions of the projects, as well as for gathering evidence on the impact of systematic involvement in theatrical activities on the well-being of children and their families.

Bibliography

Cicerchia, A., Seia, C. and Rossi Ghiglione, A. (2020) Welfare culturale. Atlante della cultura. Rome: Treccani. Available at: http://www.treccani.it/magazine/atlante/cultura/Welfare.html.

Corbett, B. A., Blain, S. D., Ioannou, S., Balser, M. (2017) Changes in anxiety following a randomized control trial of a theatre-based intervention for youth with autism spectrum disorder. *Autism.* 2017;21(3): pp. 333–43.

Fancourt, D, Finn S. (2019) What is the evidence on the role of the arts in improving health and wellbeing? A scoping review. Copenhagen: WHO Regional Office for Europe (Health Evidence Network (HEN) synthesis report 67).

Fantozzi, R., Cicerchia, A., Staffieri, S. (2020) *Cultural Services and Social Inclusion: Towards a New Idea of Welfare.* A.I.S.Re., Associazione Italiana di Scienze Regionali – XLI Conferenza Scientifica Annuale – Web Conference, 2–4 September 2020.

Gjengedal, E., Lykkeslet, E., Sæther, W. S., Sørbø, J. I. (2016) Theatre as an eye-opener: how theatre may contribute to knowledge about living close to persons with dementia. *Dementia.* 2016;17(4): 439–51.

Hamilton, K., Buchanan-Hughes, A., Lim, S. and Eddowes, L. (2015) The Value of Arts on Prescription Programmes for the Mental Health and Wellbeing of Individuals and Communities. Cambridge: Arts and Minds.

Madsen, W. (2018) Raising social consciousness through verbatim theatre: a realist evaluation. *Arts Health*;10(2):181–94. doi: 1080/17533015.2017.1354898.

Meeks, S., Vandenbroucke, R. J. & Shryock, S. K. (2020) Psychological benefits of attending the theatre associated with positive affect and wellbeing for subscribers over age 60. *Aging & Mental Health*, Vol. 24, Iss. 2: 333–340.

Sitography

ATER Fondazione, https://www.ater.emr.it/it/news/sciroppo-di-teatro.
DATA.EUROPA, https://data.europa.eu/data/datasets/s1115_79_2_399?locale=en.
EUROSTAT, https://ec.europa.eu/eurostat/web/cities/data/database.
EUROSTAT, https://ec.europa.eu/eurostat/databrowser/view/cult_pcs_caa/default/table?lang=en
ISTAT, https://www.istat.it/it/archivio/232541.

CHAPTER 16

Measuring Culture – How and Why?

Giulia Cavrini

> When you can measure what you are speaking about, and express it in numbers, you know something about it; but when you cannot measure it, when you cannot express it in numbers, your knowledge is of a meager and unsatisfactory kind; it may be the beginning of knowledge, but you have scarcely in your thoughts advanced to the state of Science, whatever the matter may be.
> LORD KELVIN, 1883

∴

16.1 Introduction

The scientific literature has identified the power of cultural enjoyment as an opportunity to educate individuals and 'cultivate' the psychological and social facets of the human soul. Statistics show a strong correlation between cultural enjoyment, education level, and people's socioeconomic status. The indirect influence of culture on longevity and life satisfaction is also undeniable.

Culture is a trendy concept. A search of the word 'culture' on Google reveals over seven hundred million results, more than twice as many as for the term 'politics', a little less than half as many as for the word 'war', and a similar number to the word 'environment'.

"You cannot eat culture!" – This unfortunate remark by an Italian Minister of Economy and Finance, Giulio Tremonti, has often been repeated in the classrooms and corridors of schools, universities and cultural institutions over the past decade. However, culture is an essential economic factor, and Italian households devote, on average, almost 7% of their total consumption expenditure to culture and leisure (ISTAT, 2019).

As Enzo Grossi and Pier Luigi Sacco, two of Italy's leading exponents of research in this area wrote:

> Hardly anyone would be willing to deny the impact of culture from a psychological, social and economic point of view, and thus the indirect influence it can exert on aspects such as longevity and life satisfaction levels. However, considering culture as one of the major determinants of physical and psychological health or well-being is a less incontrovertible point.
> GROSSI and SACCO, 2001–2018

This vast and complex subject encompasses multiple disciplines encompassing economics, cultural sciences, anthropology, medicine, psychology, and statistics. This chapter has a twofold objective. On the one hand, to analyse certain myths concerning the ability to measuring culture and, on the other hand, to explore the association between culture and education.

Two central figures in international research on the subject are psychologists Eunkook M. Suh in Korea and the American Ed Diener. Their book *Culture and Subjective Well-Being* (Diener & Suh, 2000) is still seen as a reference point on the subject and as a good introduction to the central studies and topics to be considered:

> There is a rich literature exploring the wellbeing implications of cultural socio-environmental traits, starting from the seminal work of Ed Diener and co-authors which has firmly marked the development of the discipline.
> GROSSI, SACCO, CERUTTI, & BLESSI, 2011: 388

Numerous sources report data on culture and well-being in Italy. The most important is undoubtedly the National Institute of Statistics (ISTAT), which collects data, conducts studies, and publishes reports on all phenomena related to life in Italy. One of the ISTAT's most important projects is 'The measurement of well-being (BES)', which was launched in 2010. It is aimed at measuring fair and sustainable well-being to assess the progress of society not only from an economic point of view but also from a social and environmental perspective. Together with representatives of social partners and civil society, ISTAT has identified 12 fundamental domains for measuring well-being in Italy which complement the information provided by indicators on economic activities. They are: health, education and training, work and reconciliation of lifetimes, economic well-being, social relations, politics and institutions, security, subjective well-being, landscape and cultural heritage, the environment, research and innovation, and the quality of services.

The analysis of these indicators, which has been published in an annual report since 2013, provides information for public debate on the subject. It not only makes citizens and political representatives more aware of Italy's strengths, but also highlights where the quality of life of Italians can be improved, influencing individual and public policy choices (ISTAT, 2019). This makes it an essential tool for a comprehensive territory view.

Most of the data used in constructing the BES indices comes from the Multipurpose Survey "Aspects of Daily Life". This social survey is carried out by ISTAT every year to learn about daily habits and the degree of satisfaction with certain aspects of everyday life. The different areas, such as school, work, family life, relationships, home and living area, leisure time, political and social participation, health, lifestyles and relationships with society, are investigated both from an 'objective' behavioural point of view and from the 'subjective' point of view of motivations, expectations and judgements. Information on the individual, such as behaviour, motivations, expectations, judgements and perceptions, are contextualised within the family dimension. As the family is the statistical unit, information is collected on all the individuals that make up the family, and the characteristics of the family members are analysed by relating and comparing them with each other. The final result is the construction and analysis of an overall picture of social reality, observing both individuals and their relationships (Bagatta, 2006).

16.2 Measuring Culture Is Possible!

Can we really measure culture? If so, how?
To invest in data to avoid short-sighted choices, including culture in policies and measuring it not as a process but as a result (Simmel, 1995).

The connection between cultural investment and social cohesion and inclusion is powerful. Culture can be a decisive contributor to achieving sustainable development. The challenging issue of metrics, proposed in the UNESCO report "Culture 2030 Indicators", was addressed by Valentina Montalto, the European Commission's Joint Research Centre (JRC) policy analyst. During a meeting, promoted by the Unipolis Foundation 2020, aimed at highlighting how investment and cultural production are relevant components in the achievement of the 17 Sustainable Development Goals (SDGs) and how now, more than ever, it is fundamental to have shared long-term planning, with a focus on sustainability. Montaldo said:

> We must try to change perspective: culture cannot be measured as a process but as a result (Simmel, 1995). It would already be an achievement if we could have comparative and accessible data on cultural participation.

A lot has been done since the 1980s on cultural indicators. It is true that even today, data are often non-existent and incomparable, but there is much data that is worth harmonising. One risks making short-sighted choices if one does not invest in the data, figuring out how to use it and for what purpose in the transition to decision making. How do we measure the contribution of culture to sustainable development? UNESCO has tried, considering culture as a guide for new paradigms of growth, as an enabler of change and as a pivotal point for creating new knowledge and new processes of social inclusion that guarantee diversity.

It is said that "culture is both result and process" (Simmel, 1995). Perhaps, culture cannot be measured as a process, but as a result, with data on cultural products and services, cultural infrastructures, or even cultural audiences. Such data will not provide a detailed view of the cultural phenomenon, but, like any learning process, having such data in a regular, harmonised and accessible way would already be an outstanding achievement.

It is frequently affirmed that we have no indicators for culture, and this recurrent myth to needs to be dispelled. After all the work that has been carried out on the subject – at all levels: local, regional, national, international – this myth risks undermining all the efforts made since the 1980s. Of course, the fact remains that there are no agreed indicators, and the predominant indicators are economic. However, this does not mean that they should not be used or, even worse, ignored. Results (economic or otherwise) are no more important than the process, but they are essential. Otherwise, the result can only be the paradoxical situation we find ourselves in today – despite the proliferation of economic indicators for culture, we are still unable to measure them with appropriate data.

In this regard, Federculture[1] publishes an annual report that tries to take stock of the cultural supply and production system in Italy, based, in particular, on ISTAT data. However, the report's structure is mainly addressed to the financial world. The data presented are always interpreted in terms of growth or decrease of cultural consumption focusing on economic factors. In 2018,

---

1 FEDERCULTURE "Federation of companies, societies, bodies whose activity is aimed at promoting, production and management in the field of culture, tourism, services, sport and leisure". Federculture is a unique reality in the national panorama, and started in June 1997 with 13 founding members. Today, the association represents the essential cultural companies in Italy, many of them natural excellences also at the European level, together with Regions, Provinces, Municipalities, and all public and private entities involved in the management of services related to culture, tourism, and leisure.

the cultural expenditure of Italian families on theatre, cinema, museums and concerts was worth a total of 31 billion euros, an increase of 3.1% compared to the previous year. However, the same cultural expenditure in the regions of northern Italy is on average more than 150 euros per month, while in the South it drops to around 90 euros. The opposite extremes are Trentino Alto Adige, at about 180 euros spent per month, and Sicily, at 64 euros.

Table 16.1 shows data on the average monthly expenditure on recreation, entertainment and culture of Italian households in 2019. In comparison to 2018, there is a general decline in all regions, which became an absolute collapse in 2020 due to the Covid-19 pandemic.

In Figure 16.1, household expenditure on culture is compared to total average household expenditure. Umbria, Emilia-Romagna, Friuli-Venezia giulia and Trentino Alto Adige are the regions with the highest household expenditure on cultural heritage. In contrast, Basilicata, Sicilia and Puglia are the worst performers.

Figure 16.2 shows the composition of Italian household expenditure on recreational and cultural activities. These data show that the share of expenditure reserved by families for cultural activities is minimal compared to other goods.

Comparing Italy's figures with those of the Eurozone, it emerges that spending on culture by Italian families is below the European average: 6.6% for Italy out of total general consumption compared to 8.5% in Europe, with Sweden standing out with a total of 11% (Eurostat National accounts). This comparison, added to the previous data, draws a rather depressing picture of the cultural expenditure of the inhabitants of a country with such an extensive cultural heritage.

Figure 16.2 reveals that apart from the item 'other expenditure', spending on books is the lowest compared to all other items.

It is well known that Italy is one of the countries in Europe that reads books the least. The data on the low frequency of reading by Italians emerges from a report published by Eurostat (the statistical office of the European Union) on the occasion of World Book Day sponsored by UNESCO in 2018. The report shows that Italians read for an average of 5 minutes a day: in this statistic – which examines 14 EU countries plus Norway, the United Kingdom and Serbia – only Austria, Romania and France have lower percentages. The research on the reading habits of Europeans provides a rather negative general picture. In the old continent, the average daily reading time ranges from 2 to 13 minutes. The best results were recorded in Eastern European countries (13 minutes in Estonia, 12 in Poland, 10 in Hungary) and in Finland (12 minutes). Italians who read on average about 5 minutes a day are in the penultimate place of the ranking with Austria and Romania. The French take the black jersey at 2 minutes per day.

TABLE 16.1 ISTAT: Average monthly household expenditure and monthly household expenditure on recreational activities, entertainment and culture by Region – Year 2019 (Euros)

Italian region	Average monthly expenditure (€)	Average monthly expenditure on recreational activities, entertainment and culture (€)	%
Puglia	1,996.04	63.85	3.20
Sicilia	2,017.99	67.97	3.37
Basilicata	2,003.06	73.78	3.68
Calabria	1,998.64	80.73	4.04
Molise	2,171.25	91.26	4.20
Campania	2,113.94	90.71	4.29
Abruzzo	2,193.32	95.51	4.35
Marche	2,402.69	109.80	4.57
Sardegna	2,216.17	101.76	4.59
Liguria	2,499.63	118.08	4.72
Valle d'Aosta	2,805.50	137.78	4.91
Lazio	2,779.50	138.45	4.98
Lombardia	2,965.10	156.97	5.29
Piemonte	2,583.22	136.82	5.30
Toscana	2,922.43	156.41	5.35
Veneto	2,680.91	147.59	5.51
Trentino-Alto Adige	2,991.73	173.01	5.78
Friuli-Venezia Giulia	2,611.06	151.04	5.78
Emilia-Romagna	2,906.75	170.86	5.88
Umbria	2,446.76	146.60	5.99
Italy	2,559.85	127.01	4.96

The Eurostat report also considers the percentage of habitual readers (Figure 16.3), i.e. those who include reading among their main daily activities. The result recorded in Italy is 8.5%. Finland (16.8%), Poland (16.4%) and

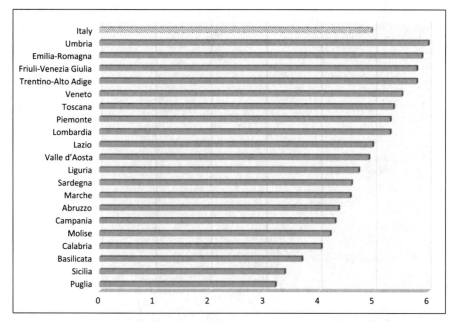

FIGURE 16.1 Percentage of monthly household expenditure on recreational activities, entertainment and culture out of average monthly household expenditure by Region – Year 2019
AUTHOR'S REWORKING OF ISTAT DATA

Estonia (15%) are also at the top of this statistic. In the last places, immediately below Italy, are Serbia (8.2%), Belgium (7.9%), Austria (7.2%), Romania (6.2%) and France (2.6%).

Another interesting fact concerns the composition of reader population. In all countries, most regular readers are women, however, men read for more time than women. On average, the daily reading time of regular readers ranges from 1 hour and 1 minute in France to 1 hour and 37 minutes in Hungary.

Figure 16.4 shows the percentage of Italians who did not read a single book in 2019, broken down by region. The national figure is alarming, with a percentage close to 60%. Moreover, even more, impressive is the great divide at a territorial level, with Trentino Alto Adige and Valle d'Aosta having the lowest percentages of non-readers (around 45–47%) and the southern regions (Sicily, Campania, Calabria and Apulia) topping the podium in this ranking, reaching and exceeding 70% of non-readers.

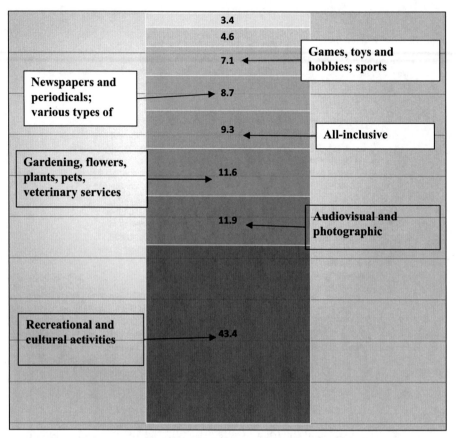

FIGURE 16.2   Percentage composition of Italian household expenditure on culture – Year 2017
SOURCE: "IMPRESA CULTURA, COMUNITÀ, TERRITORI, SVILUPPO"

16.3   How Should We Use Cultural Indicators? A Special Focus on Education

The indicators collected annually by ISTAT and other institutions can be appropriately used to highlight associations or, where possible, causal relationships with phenomena such as education, employment, economy and people's well-being.

Education and training affect the well-being of citizens, not only because they increase the level of skills but also because they open up pathways and opportunities. In Italy, the level of education and skills that young people in particular manage to achieve is unevenly distributed and strongly depends on social background, socio-economic context and the territory in which they live. In Italy, there is a wide territorial disparity between North and South and

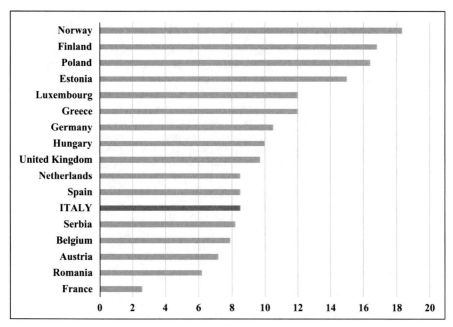

FIGURE 16.3   Percentage of regular readers in Europe, Eurostat survey conducted between 2008 and 2015

educational inequalities have become more pronounced since the Covid-19 pandemic. In the BES project, the indicators of the domain "education and training" follow the education pathway over the life span of individuals, i.e. from kindergarten to pre-school, from primary school to lower and upper secondary school, up to university and further education. Moreover, as regards further education, it is clear that cultural participation activities play a central role (ISTAT, 2021). There are 15 well-being indicators for the education and training domain. They concern the percentage of children enrolled in kindergarten, the participation of children in the school system, the percentage of high school and university graduates, and the participation in further education for various age groups. In addition, some more specific variables are taken into account, such as the university transition rate, i.e. the percentage of new graduates who enrolled at university for the first time in the same year as their secondary school diploma (cohort-specific rate), and the percentage of graduates in technical and scientific disciplines. The BES indicators also take into account phenomena that can be considered harmful, such as the percentage of students who leave the education system early, often with only a secondary school leaving certificate, and the level of NEET – the percentage of young people between 15 and 29 who are neither employed nor in education or training.

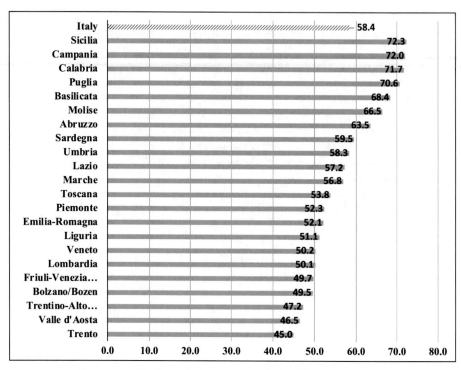

FIGURE 16.4   Percentage of Italians who have never read a book by region – Year 2019
AUTHOR'S ANALYSIS OF ISTAT DATA

Finally, student literacy, numeracy and digital competence are taken into account, as well as cultural participation outside the home, reading books and newspapers and library use (ISTAT, 2021).

One aspect that should not be overlooked is that culture has a significant influence on the success of education, which is decisively influenced by two factors: the individuals' socio-economic background and exposure to cultural activities from childhood. According to ISTAT data, the effect of the former can be seen as early as kindergarten because it is the children of higher-educated parents who attend kindergarten most often (ISTAT, 2021) and then continues throughout their school careers and beyond.

Figure 16.5 shows data on early exit from education and training by gender, geographical breakdown, citizenship, educational qualification and highest parental profession. As might be expected, being an immigrant is the most relevant aspect but, in second place, parental education qualification level profoundly conditions school success and permanence in the education and training system. The children of parents with a lower secondary school diploma as their highest qualification have a 24% drop-out rate from education and training, which decreases to 5.5% for the children of parents with an upper secondary school diploma and 1.9% for the children of parents with at least a university degree. Similarly, children with at least one parent employed in skilled and technical occupations drop out of school in 2.5% of cases compared to 24% for children of parents employed in unskilled occupations. Finally, as is well known, living in the South is also an essential disadvantage from this point of view. (ISTAT, 2021).

Therefore, it could be argued that education and cultural capital are passed down through generations. This phenomenon can be explained by Pierre Bourdieu' theory of cultural capital. For Bourdieu, cultural capital is the set of linguistic and cultural skills and broad knowledge of one's own culture that often belongs to the upper socioeconomic classes. This kind of knowledge is not taught in school but is transmitted by the family. Different socioeconomic classes possess different cultural capital, but the ruling class often dictates which cultural capital is transmitted or is important, and the accumulation

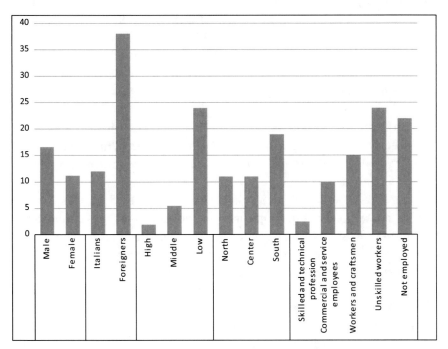

FIGURE 16.5   Early exit from education and training by gender, geographical breakdown, citizenship, educational qualification and highest occupation of parents – Year 2019
PERCENTAGE VALUES (ISTAT, 2021)

of that specific cultural capital is encouraged by institutions. Those with that kind of cultural capital often do better in school. Studies by Bourdieu, Di Maggio and Useem have shown that teachers tend to reward students with more cultural capital within the dominant classes. Students who have already accumulated cultural capital because they have been exposed to cultural activities from an early age feel more comfortable in school, communicate more efficiently with teachers, and do better.

On the other hand, students from lower socioeconomic classes do not possess sufficient cultural capital and often feel uncomfortable at school, partly because the cultural environment is very different from what they have known at home (Dumais, 2002). However, a student's academic success is not only influenced by the cultural capital he or she possesses but also by his or her habitus. According to Bourdieu, the habitus is the inner disposition of an individual that is determined by his or her place in the structure of society and influences their every action. Individuals learn their place in society from an early age, which determines how they see themselves and their potential. This ends up influencing their ambitions. For example, individuals born into a low socioeconomic class tend to think that they will remain in that class all their lives and do not aspire to social mobility. This belief in life is then expressed and externalised in actions that keep individuals within their class. In this way, the social structure is reproduced. The habitus has a significant influence on the academic success of individuals and especially on the decision whether or not to continue their studies:

> Students' decisions to invest in their education, study hard and go to college depend on students' place in the class system and their expectations of whether people from that class tend to be successful academically.
> DUMAIS, 2002

In 2019, 20.7 per cent of the population did not engage in any cultural activity, however occasional and straightforward, a figure that has remained completely stable over the last three years. From the age of 55, those who do not participate exceed the national average and increase markedly at later ages to 44.8 per cent of those over 75. Women are slightly less active in the cultural field than men. 22.8 per cent of women declare themselves inactive compared to 18.4 per cent of men; among the over 75s, the gap widens, and the percentages of inactivity reach 50.7 per cent of women compared to 35.9 per cent of men. The absence of cultural practice thus varies considerably by gender and age, but there are also differences concerning the type of cultural activity considered and the territory. In the regions of the South, the percentage of those who say they have not visited museums, exhibitions, archaeological sites or monuments, have not read a newspaper once a week or read a single book in a year, have not gone to the cinema, the theatre, a concert, a sports show or danced, is higher than in the other divisions and is 28.9 per cent (stable figure compared to 2018). Residents in the North-East regions, on the other hand, report the lowest non-participation: 14.3 per cent. Total non-participation is exceptionally high (24.1 per cent) among those residing in municipalities with fewer than two thousand inhabitants, also for obvious reasons of lower availability of cultural activities on offer.

In recent decades, various studies have explored the relationship between socio-economic background, cultural capital, and academic success, and many have focused on the impact that cultural participation can have on the latter. For example, the Dutch scholar De Graaf in 1986 examined the relationship between social background, cultural participation and academic achievement. De Graaf found a correlation between cultural participation and socio-economic class but also noted that this does not explain why students graduate or not. On the other hand, Stephen Lamb (Lamb, 1989) tries to answer this question, also taking into account the aspirations of students. However, although these studies have been constructive in showing that different social classes have different ambitions, they also tend to see the school system as an isolated entity, accessible to all with the same approach and values. This idea has since been rejected. Many researchers have shown that educational opportunities within the school system also depend on the socio-economic class of the students.

Whether or not to continue with an education depends on the students' family background and whether they manage to achieve adequate levels of competence in various areas, such as literacy, numeracy, and the digital world. Proficiency levels are influenced by gender, the students' foreign or non-foreign citizenship, and their families' socio-economic and cultural conditions. Lack of competence in one or more domains is perpetuated over the years and affects the choice of schooling, learning, and possibly leaving school (ISTAT, 2021: 65). On the other hand, some factors positively influence competence development, especially literacy and numeracy. Attending pre-school and speaking Italian at home rather than a foreign language helps, but what is surprising is that culture is again the decisive factor. As ISTAT has pointed out, access to the Internet and books contributes most to developing skills.

> In particular, having a large number of books in the home (more than 100), all other things being equal, is associated with a probability of achieving sufficient skills 2.5 times higher than having no books or less

> than 25 [...] Having a PC, and an Internet connection helps in the development of skills: 59% more likely than having no connection and a PC. Among children from disadvantaged families, it is interesting to note that using a PC and a network connection increases the probability of having adequate skills (69%).
>
> ISTAT, 2021

Moreover, having access to culture helps in the development of academic skills and the development of social skills, creativity, and self-esteem. There are even those who argue that cultural participation helps to decrease crime and promote behaviour geared towards helping others. For this to happen, however, it is crucial to have access to culture from an early age, and though school plays a crucial role, it is family background that has the most influence. In addition, many studies have shown that those who have access to culture in childhood are more likely to continue these activities into adulthood. For example, a study conducted by the Osaka et al. team in 2009 showed that children who participate in cultural activities of an artistic nature are more likely to do the same activities as adults, either continuously or after a break. Subsequent studies have shown that these adults are also more likely to engage in behaviours considered helpful to society, such as volunteering or giving money to charity (Garrod & Dowell, 2020).

16.4 Conclusions

Even the European Union has now realised how beneficial access to culture is for education, especially for those types of education outside the school environment acquired throughout life, i.e. lifelong learning. For the EU, access to culture is even a fundamental right, and it has therefore set up a platform to guarantee this. One of the pillars of this platform is the working group on education and training, which explores the benefits created by the interaction between education and culture and the role that cultural participation plays in different areas of education, not only within the school system but also in the acquisition of civic and social competences and during lifelong learning. In a paper, scientist Lidia Verbanova summarises these benefits. Introducing cultural activities into education has an impact on individuals and helps them to:

1) have greater self-esteem (which affects their whole life, their well-being and their happiness);
2) develop their creativity;
3) be more socially cohesive and thus solve social problems;

4) develop an interest in art, thus making them part of creative processes;
5) develop their curiosity and willingness to learn;
6) increase their ability to learn.

As a result of lifelong learning, individuals acquire skills that positively influence their well-being and financial situation and benefit them and the whole community in which they live. Communities also benefit from lifelong learning because it helps members of marginalised communities become more involved in creative processes, helps immigrants integrate and increase cultural sensitivity, raises educational levels, makes culture more inclusive, and facilitates the social and economic participation of members. Finally, this also benefits cultural organisations, thus finding a new audience of supporters (Varbanova, 2012).

Furthermore, even if the magnitude of the impact that culture has on education and training is still a matter of debate, it is now clear that a solid and positive relationship exists and therefore when talking about training, one should always talk about culture as well.

Bibliography

Bagatta, G. (2006). *Il sistema di indagini sociali multiscopo. Contenuti e metodologie delle indagini*. Roma: ISTAT, Vol. 31.

Diener, E., and Suh, E. M. (2000) *Culture and Subjective Well-Being*. Cambridge & Londra, Massachusetts & Inghilterra. The MIT Press.

Dumais, S. A. (2002, January) Cultural Capital, Gender, and School Success: The Role of Habitus. *Sociology of Education, I*(75): 44–68.

Garrod, B., & Dowell, D. (2020). The Role of Childhood Participation in Cultural Activities in the Promotion of Pro-Social Behaviours in Later Life. Sustainability, Vol. 12(14): 1–16.

Grossi, E., and Sacco, P. L. (2001–2018) *Cultura e Benessere Soggettivo Individuale: un ruolo centrale*. Christianini, G. (a cura di). Available (consulted October 1st 2020) at: https://www.geragogia.net/editoriali/cultura-benessere.html.

Grossi, E., Sacco, P. L., Cerutti, R., and Blessi, G. T. (2011, 12) The Impact of Culture on the Individual Subjective Well-Being of the Italian Population: An Exploratory Study. (T. I.-o.-L. Studies, A cura di) *Applied Research in Quality of Life, VI*(4):387–410.

ISTAT. (2019) 10 Cultura e tempo libero. In ISTAT, *Annuario Statistico Italiano 2019*.

ISTAT. (2021) 2 Istruzione e formazione. In ISTAT, *BES 2020. Il benessere equo e sostenibile in Italia*.

Lamb, S. (1989). Cultural Consumption and the Educational Plans of Australian Secondary School. *Sociology of Education, II*(62): 95–108.

Kelvin, W., T. Lord (1883). Electrical Units of Measurement in *Popular lectures and Addresses* (1889), Vol. 1: 80–81
Simmel, G. (1995) *Die beiden Formen des Individualismus* in Aufsätze und Abhandlungen 1901–1908. Bd. 1. Gesamtausgabe 7. Frankfurt am Main, S. 49–56.
Varbanova, L. (2012, 28th September). Cultural participation in education and lifelong learning: a catatalyst for personal advancement, community development, social change and economic growth. Available (consulted April 25th 2021) at: Lidia Varbanova https://lidiavarbanova.ca/cultural-participation-education-lifelong-learning.

Index

Accademia degli Artefatti 165n.1, 167, 168
Actor's flagranza 72
Anagoor 165n.1
Anderson, Laurie 57
André, Carl 51
Argan, Giulio Carlo 64
Aristotle 110, 111
Artaud, Antonin 33, 32–38
Ateliersi 165n.1, 169
Audience v, x, xii, 4, 12, 20, 24, 30, 32, 33, 46, 47, 49, 55, 58, 59, 68, 72, 74–81 84, 89–92, 101–103, 110–112, 117–118, 130, 140, 142, 143, 145, 146, 150–152, 154, 155, 158, 162–164, 168–170, 180, 181, 183–185, 200, 211
  attendance 103
  development 46, 47
  engagement 46, 47
  reception 102
aura 168, 169, 174

Babilonia Teatri 165n.1
Badiou, Alain 32, 38
Bakhtin, Mikhail 2–3
Barba, Eugenio 12, 35, 36
Barry, Robert 61–62
Bartolucci, Giuseppe 66
Bassetti, Nicolò 67
Baudrillard, Jean 18, 19
Beckett, Samuel 21
Berlin, Isaiah 31–32
bes indicators 205
bes indices 199
Beuys, Josef x, 53, 54, 56
Bogomolov, Konstantin 3
Bourdieu v, viii, xi, xx, 1, 2, 5, 7, 14, 15, 22, 26, 38, 103, 103n.13, 104, 106, 108, 207, 208
Brecht, Bertolt 1, 110–112, 114, 139
Brook, Peter 12, 36, 150, 152
Brus, Günter x, 58
Byars, James Lee 60

Calderoni, Silvia 173
Careri, Francesco 67
Castorf, Frank 3, 4, 5

Childs, Lucinda 9, 10
Collettivo Cinetico 165n.1, 173
Collective practices 16, 18–19, 76
Community 18, 22, 23–24, 26, 35, 41–44, 46, 65, 74, 81, 90, 94, 96, 97, 144, 146, 171, 172, 182, 187, 188, 211
Community theatre 8
concept art 53, 55, 57, 61
contemporary theatre field 165
Coordinamento dei Festival Italiani del Contemporaneo 165
Covid-19 8, 13, 41, 162, 165, 175, 177–179, 181, 182, 190, 195, 201, 205
Crisafulli, Fabrizio 68
CrowdTangle xv, 165, 165n.2, 170f.13.1
Cruciani, Fabrizio 65, 150
Cultural abilities 43
cultural indicators 200, 204
cultural participation 199, 205, 209, 210
Cultural welfare vi, xii, 43–47, 186–187, 190, 195

D'Agostin, Marco 173
Debord, Guy 2, 15, 36, 37, 64
Documenta 5, 51, 56
DOM 67–68
Dramaturgical sociology 96
Duchamp, Marcel 56
Durkheim Émile 23–24, 92
Duvignaud, Jean viii, x, 1, 2, 15, 24, 25, 27, 35, 37, 38, 81, 82, 83, 96, 97, 98n.8, 100, 101, 101n.11, 102, 106, 107

Ecology x, 68–69
Educational method vi, 122, 124, 131
educational opportunities 209
Emotional engagement 111–114
Emotional field 116–117
Environment v, viii, x, 8, 47, 51, 56, 61, 64, 65, 68–69, 78, 123–124, 126, 152, 154, 164, 184, 197–198, 208, 210
Ephemeral 65–66
ephemeral turn 162
Epic Theatre 110–112
Eva Geatti/Cosmesi 165n.1

Experience   viii, xi, 2, 7, 8, 16, 18–19, 22–24, 26, 31–33, 36, 41, 50, 52, 54, 58–59, 64–65, 67–69, 71, 73, 76–79, 81, 85, 87, 90–92, 110–117, 123–124, 127, 131, 133, 136, 139–141, 143–148, 151, 153–154, 156–159, 165, 177, 180, 182–184, 187, 195

Facebook   162, 165, 167, 169, 172
Fanny e Alexander   165n.1
Fava, Federica   64
Ferrarotti, Franco   22
First Love   173
Fluxus   49, 50, 64
Freud, Sigmund   113–118
Frosini/Timpano   165n.1, 169, 172
Future community   81

Game of uncertainty   79
Genetic structuralism   99, 101
Gerz, Jochen   59
Gilbert & George   57
Glass, Philip   9
Globalization   12
Goffman, Erving   25, 35, 37, 38, 96, 107
Grotowski   35, 36, 37, 38
Gruppo Nanou   165n.1
Guarino, Raimondo   64–65
Gurvitch, Georges   viii, x, 1, 2, 24, 35, 37, 94–102, 105

Habitus   5–7, 10–12, 26, 54, 168, 208
Happening   49, 51–52, 57, 64, 79, 111, 131, 144, 180–181
hic et nunc   57
Historical reenactment   122, 123, 124, 125, 127, 128, 129, 130, 134, 136
Historical reconstruction   125, 128, 129, 131
History of theatre   101, 105
household expenditure on culture   201
Huebler, Douglas   53

Identification   35, 110–112, 114, 115
   introjective and projective   115–117
Instagram   175
Institutional approaches   100, 103
institutions   vii, viii, ix, xi, 4, 17, 20, 22, 29, 30, 33, 42, 46, 47, 49, 50, 55, 57, 61, 65, 67, 100, 122, 125, 128, 197, 198, 204, 208
Interdisciplinary   3, 10, 48

intermedial performance   163, 166
Interpretive approaches   100
Intersubjectivity   115–118
Ionesco, Eugène   21
Italian contemporary theatre   162, 164, 165n.1, 169

Judd, Donald   51

Kinkaleri   165n.1, 168
Klein, Melanie   114–115

La Monte, Young T.   51
Landscape   60, 61
Lefebvre, Henry   65
Lepage, Robert   12
Lepsius, Reiner Maria   28–31
live tweeting   162
Lockdown   177, 180, 182, 183, 184
Long, Richard   57

Marenzi, Samantha   67
Markers   5, 6
Masque Teatro   165n.1
Measuring culture   197, 199
Mediamorphosis   184
Meldolesi   33, 34, 35, 37, 39, 95n.4, 101, 102, 107
Menoventi   165n.1, 166
Merleau-Ponty, Maurice   22
Meyerhold, Vsevolod   4
Mitchell, Katie   4
Mnouchkine, Ariane   12
Modern drama   98
Motus   165n.1, 166, 167, 172
Mutual attunement   78

Nietzsche, Friedrich   21, 27
Neoliberalism   12
Nicolini, Renato   64
Nield, Sophie   68
Ninagawa, Yukio   12

Object   47, 50–55
Oscar Cassiani, Mara   165n.1
Ostermeier, Thomas   4

Palma, Mattia   68
Pane, Gina   58

INDEX

Participation ix, xi, 24–25, 42, 44–47, 65, 68, 80–81, 128, 130, 131, 187, 189–193, 195, 199, 205–206, 209–211
Pearson, Mike 68
Performance 18, 19, 25, 26, 29, 31, 32, 33, 34, 35, 36
Personal development 126
Philosophy of the actor 98
Piscator, Erwin 4
Plato 110
Politics 32, 62, 63, 70, 108
    Political action 31
Practice 4, 5, 6, 11, 12, 16, 18, 19, 21, 24, 26, 27, 31, 32, 34, 35
Presence 55, 56
promotional logic 168, 174
Public Space 33, 70
Public Sphere 32, 162, 163, 172, 175
Purini, Franco 65–66

Questorio, Stefano 165n.1

Rau, Milo 12, 13
Readymade 56
relational work 164
Remediation 178, 179
Rimini Protokoll 68
Rosi, Gianfranco 67
Royal Shakespeare Company 163
Russian education 122, 123, 125
Ryman, Robert 51

Schipper, Imanuel 68
Schutz, Alfred 22
Self-actualization 127, 129, 136
Self-reflexivity 117–118
Sellars, Peter 14
Semiotics 11
Sennett, Richard 65
Settlement 66–69
Sieni, Virgilio 68
Signs 3, 11
Simmel, Georg 18, 27
Sini, Carlo 22, 23
Site-specific 65–69
Social context 105
Socialization 13
Social context
Social criticism 21

Social group 17, 27
Social resistance vii–ix, 20–21, 34, 36
Social sphere 20, 118
Society as theatre 96
Sociology of knowledge 99
Sotterraneo 165n.1, 168
Staged 177, 178, 179, 180, 181, 182, 183, 184, 185
Stalker 67–68
Strehler, Giorgio 5, 6

Tafuri, Manfredo 65
Teatro delle Albe 166
Teatro Stabile of Bolzano
    TSB xiv
Theatre
    in society 37, 96n, 97, 98, 100, 103, 105
    and society 26, 35, 105
theatre paratexts 163, 166, 172
Theatre studies vii, 2, 104–106
Theatrical performance 122, 123, 124, 126, 129, 130, 126
Theatrical space x, 71, 111, 156, 159
theatrical trailers 164
Time x–xi, 1, 3–5, 8–9, 14, 20–24, 32–34, 36, 44, 46–47, 49– 55, 57, 59, 61, 64–65, 71–73, 76–82, 84–85, 87–89, 91, 94–95, 98–99, 110, 113, 115, 117, 124, 127–128, 131, 133–136, 139, 141, 143–144, 147, 151–156, 163, 165–166, 190, 199, 201
TV series 177, 178, 184
TTV (Performing Arts on screen) 166
Twitter 162

Unconscious 111–119
Urban environment v, 64–69
Urban history 64–65

Video call 177, 178, 179, 180, 183, 184
Viennese Actionism 58

Weber, Max 20, 22, 84–85, 94, 99
Wilson, Robert 8, 9, 10

Xiaonan, Guo 12
YouTube 163

Zombitudine 172
Zorzi, Ludovico 65